"Suzanne Roberts sets off on a remarkable Sierra journey that will test the limits of physical endurance, of friendship, and of faith in self. . . . This is not the usual wilderness story of independence, competition, and violence. Here, thankfully, is the more urgent story of intimacy, community, and compassion. A loving, and lovely, ode to life."

—JOHN T. PRICE, author of *All Is Leaf: Essays and Transformations*

"In *Almost Somewhere* we get to travel both the physical John Muir Trail—its history, its flowers and trees and shadowy peaks—and the gritty emotional landscape of the three women who make the journey. Where are we in the world, anyway? Suzanne Roberts helps us know that the only place we can be is here, giving it all we have, day by day."

—FLEDA BROWN, author of *Driving with Dvořák*

"This is not a backpacking primer, but rather one on young women in search of themselves as they prepare for life after college. We read about insecurities, jealousy, lust, self-esteem, tears, bingeing, self-realization, learning to appreciate oneself for oneself, and interpersonal relationships. And come away with the author's realization that mountains in general, and the John Muir Trail specifically, provide a spectacular backdrop to work through these issues and absorb the associated lessons."

—KURT REPANSHEK, *National Parks Traveler*

"[*Almost Somewhere*] will appeal to readers of travel and nature books, as well as those who enjoy reading about social interactions and group dynamics."

—*Kirkus Reviews*

"Readers who have walked sections of the John Muir Trail will appreciate Roberts's accurate descriptions of lakes and passes, of trail-worn feet, and of the fleeting moments when you seem to float down the trail."

—BRADLEY JOHN MONSMA, *ISLE: Interdisciplinary Studies of Literature and Environment*

"This book is one I didn't want to end. I felt as if I were hiking with Roberts. When she finished, I would be finished, and like her, I would be sad to be done."

—EVE QUESNEL, *Moonshine Ink*

T0310966

"*Almost Somewhere* will not disappoint. It is a wonderful read for outdoor lovers and inspirational for anyone experiencing self-doubt. The message that resonates is, as Roberts says, 'It's not just in the having done but in the doing . . . being almost somewhere.'"

—GLORIA SINIBALDI, *North Lake Tahoe Bonanza*

Praise for *Bad Tourist: Misadventures in Love and Travel*

Gold Medal Winner for Best Travel Book from the Independent Publisher Book Awards

Gold Medal in Travel for the Next Generation Indie Book Award

Bronze Prize Winner for Best Travel Book from the North American Travel Journalists Association

Bronze Medal in Travel for the Foreword INDIES Excellence Awards

Finalist for the Gilda Award, Story Circle's Women's Book Award for Humor

"In this collection of essays, Roberts recounts her adventures while traveling mostly solo to fifteen countries. Along the way she navigates mishaps both large and small, from a dangerous mudslide in Peru to a tricky romantic entanglement in Greece. Each experience offers a chance to probe her inner 'bad tourist,' as she wrestles with issues of privilege, cultural blind spots, and her own insecurities on a journey to self-discovery."

—*National Geographic*

"I love travel, armchair and otherwise, so I knew it would be a pleasure letting Suzanne Roberts take me around the world on a shoestring, from India's Grand Elephant Festival, to the steppes of Mongolia on the trail of Genghis Khan, to the cool tiles of another one-star bathroom, wondering if this would be the time she'd puke herself to death. Even more satisfying are her honesty, courage, and eventual clarity as she tackles her own understories—family dysfunction and alcoholism, internalized misogyny, and what the climate catastrophe means for the travel-addicted among us—combining these essays into a thoroughly relatable journey of the heart."

—PAM HOUSTON, author of *Deep Creek: Finding Hope in the High Country*

"If Michel de Montaigne and Chelsea Handler could get together in a bar in some far-flung part of the world and get good and drunk, they might dream up a book like this. This is not your parents' travel writing! If you're thirsting for a literary triple shot of sex, booze, and misadventures, *Bad Tourist* is your passport to a trip you won't want to come home from."

—MICHAEL P. BRANCH, author of *On the Trail of the Jackalope: How a Legend Captured the World's Imagination and Helped Us Cure Cancer*

"I'm breathless after this trip around the globe with Suzanne Roberts. *Bad Tourist* makes beautiful the absurdity and heartbreak accompanying us whenever we leave home. Roberts's intimate, fiercely honest narrative voice imbues these realities with grace and demonstrates just how much is to be gained by living a life in the present tense."

—KATHRYN MILES, author of *Trailed: One Woman's Quest to Solve the Shenandoah Murders*

"Suzanne Roberts's journey—both inward and outward—is illuminated by eloquent portraits of countries, cultures, and compassionate insights into human nature. I love this book."

—ANN MARIE BROWN, author of *150 Nature Hot Spots in California: The Best Parks, Conservation Areas, and Wild Places*

"These thoughtful, hilarious, lusty essays will either have you renewing your passport or blowtorching it for good. Suzanne Roberts may be a bad tourist, but she's one hell of a great writer."

—GAYLE BRANDEIS, author of *Drawing Breath: Essays on Writing, the Body, and Loss*

"In an age where cultures, people, and places are so easily objectified, reduced to abstractions, commodities, or statistics, *Bad Tourist* is a collection that returns us, thankfully, to Earth. Across India and Mongolia to Mexico and California, Suzanne Roberts shares the view at ground level, the brutality and grace and sometimes transcendence in the lives of everyday people. She reminds us that travel can be an act of remembrance. This is an important and moving work."

—DAVID MILLER, travel writer and documentary filmmaker

"Replete with harrowing and laugh-out-loud accounts of misadventures at home and abroad, Suzanne Roberts's *Bad Tourist* collects entertaining stories from around the world. . . . Authentic, surprising, and irresistible, *Bad Tourist* is a travel text worth getting lost in."

—MICHELLE ANNE SCHINGLER, *Foreword Reviews*

"Roberts has spent decades circling the globe, chasing experience, understanding, and identity. This book is the culmination of her young adulthood on the move."

—COURTNEY EATHORNE, *Booklist*

"A fast-paced, smart, and very enjoyable book."

—MELISSA OLIVEIRA, *Hippocampus Magazine*

Praise for *Animal Bodies*

Longlisted for the 2023 PEN/Diamonstein-Spielvogel Award for the Art of the Essay

2022 Memoir Prize for Books from *Memoir Magazine*, second place overall

"Suzanne Roberts's essays are eloquent and vibrantly imaginative. They are lyrical in the best sense: the language is rhythmic, pulsing on the page, but never poeticized, flowery, or vague. Roberts's wisdom and humor are evident throughout. I so welcome a collection of her essays, all in one place."

—CAROLYN FORCHÉ, author of *What You Have Heard Is True*

"I have been thinking about one particular Suzanne Roberts essay, 'Breaking the Codes,' since I first read it. Sometimes I open a closet door and my stomach drops, remembering one painful scene in her essay. Sometimes I see a group of teenagers and I wonder, and worry, about all of them. Roberts's writing rearranges me in some fundamental and necessary ways. A book like this, a book by her, is a book I desperately need."

—CAMILLE T. DUNGY, author of *Soil: The History of a Black Mother's Garden*

"No one travels the depths of place and experience more phenomenally than Suzanne Roberts. In these essays that explore being, beauty, desire, death, and our collective animal journeys on the planet, *Animal Bodies* gathers our questions about life and brings them to the only place where meaning might emerge: adaptation. This book is a triumph that transcends humans and gives us a chance to re-story ourselves into the larger world."

—LIDIA YUKNAVITCH, author of *The Chronology of Water*

"In *Animal Bodies*, Suzanne Roberts offers surprising insight, both intimate and universal, into death, desire, and how we all move through this difficult world. Her essays are ruthless, beautiful, graceful, and endlessly fascinating. A wonderful book."

—DINTY W. MOORE, author of *Between Panic and Desire*

"*Animal Bodies* is a marvel, a heartbreaking road map of living, loving, and grieving. Roberts bravely recalls the deaths of her alcoholic father, her dear friend, and her mother, a complex force in her life. Here, we read about rape, escape, affairs, and repair. There is wilderness and then, somehow, the clearing—both in her world travels and the dying around her. Thinking about death clarifies life, and Roberts knows the thin line between grief and joy, the importance of living fully and fighting for freedom without apology. This is hard-earned wisdom and liberation. I can't stop thinking about it."

—LEE HERRICK, California Poet Laureate and author of *Scar and Flower*

"Grief pervades the essays, but *Animal Bodies* is not actually a bleak ride. Roberts always finds a way to make you laugh. And her observations about the natural world can stun with their beauty."

—JENNIFER LEVIN, *Santa Fe New Mexican*

"Here, we travel with Roberts to beaches in Florida, to hospital rooms for chemotherapy, to Nashville honky-tonks, and to the Amazon rainforest. She carries to each of the locations her acute insight and her courageous and uncompromising desire to witness and record the world."

—DIDI JACKSON, author of *Moon Jar*

"Roberts's language and reflections are also startling in their honesty and perceptions. Some of her sentences stop the reader cold. Roberts's writing and this book are gifts to the reader."

—MORGAN BAKER, *Hippocampus Magazine*

"Poetic sensibilities permeate the book. Some essays take surprising formal shifts or embody the shapes of their subject matter. The result is prose that folds back on itself, intertwining memory and story. 'Bone and Skin' is a particularly affecting piece, told in just five short paragraphs. Its series of memories takes place in Roberts's first person, as most of the essays do, and addresses a second person, who we understand to be an unnamed lover. It builds to a gorgeous meditation on the body, the system of bones beneath skin, and what it holds and knows."

—EMMA DALEY, *Cleveland Review*

"Beautifully observed and realized, heartfelt and informed, self-deprecating and often wryly witty. These essays explore how the bodies we inhabit bring pleasure and shame; how the planet which hosts us is beautiful and terrible [and] how sometimes we cherish it, and sometimes we treat it as carelessly as we would a disdainful ex; [and] how grief is the residue of love."

—ELIZABETH BALES FRANK, *Brevity*

"For readers who have experienced grief—and that's all of us—*Animal Bodies* by Suzanne Roberts will resonate. Readers will not have had all of the same experiences as the author, but we certainly have felt the same sorts of confusion and pain, and this connection, this bond between reader and writer can make us all feel less alone in our own grief."

—PAM ANDERSON, *Portland Review*

ALMOST

OUTDOOR LIVES SERIES ☀

SOMEWHERE

*Twenty-Eight Days
on the John Muir Trail*

New Edition

SUZANNE ROBERTS

University of Nebraska Press | Lincoln

The University of Nebraska Press is part of a land-
grant institution with campuses and programs on
the past, present, and future homelands of the
Pawnee, Ponca, Otoe-Missouria, Omaha, Dakota,
Lakota, Kaw, Cheyenne, and Arapaho Peoples, as
well as those of the relocated Ho-Chunk, Sac and
Fox, and Iowa Peoples.

First new edition printing: 2023

Library of Congress Control Number: 2023931088

Set in Chaparral Pro by Kim Essman.
Designed by A. Shahan.

For Dionne and Erika,
both strong women, each in her own way

And for women hiking everywhere

PREFACE

After college I set off on a hike that I imagined would be a diversion from thinking about my future. The year was 1993, the United States was in a recession, and most college graduates were finding it difficult to secure jobs. Many of my friends moved back in with their parents while they figured out what to do. When I'd left for college at seventeen, I knew I would never move back home. My friend Erika suggested we hike California's John Muir Trail, and the 211-mile path seemed like a fine adventure, a good distraction from what I considered to be "real life." I couldn't imagine a twenty-eight-day hike would change my life.

We ended up picking up another girlfriend, Dionne, making it an all-women's hiking trip, but at the last minute a fourth decided to tag along, a guy we picked up in Mammoth Lakes before the trip. He didn't last for long, and if this weren't a memoir, I might have written him out completely. But I think he shows how even though I claimed to be committed to the "girl power" of an all-women's trip, I really wasn't. Not at the beginning, anyway. To some degree all of us had internalized the stereotype that we were "just girls." The need to prove ourselves within a largely male world put us in competition with each other until we finally realized what we needed was connection.

When we lost our token man and the hike became an all-women's trip, we encountered both men and women who could not believe that three twenty-two-year-old "girls" were wandering around out in the woods for weeks, miles away from paved roads, before cell phones and GPS systems, "alone."

No records exist of the number of people hiking the John Muir Trail, but the Pacific Crest Trail does keep track. In 1993, 13 percent of the people completing the PCT were women, and many of them, I imagine, hiked with male companions. Today there are more women hiking, and many more hiking with other women or solo, but still, only 26 percent of the people who completed the PCT in 2011 were women. While the PCT is much more monumental in scale than the JMT, the records do offer some information regarding the number of women backpacking versus the number of men. Anecdotally, I can say that I see many more women on the trails now, and when I hike alone, people don't react with the shock or dismay of twenty years ago.

Although I have hiked the John Muir Trail several times in the thirty years since this trip took place, that initial journey, my own first summer in the Sierra, ended up altering my view of myself and my notions of the natural world. I had always felt a connection to nature, been bookish, and looked for a way to combine the two. The nature writers we read back when I was a girl and young woman were all men: Charles Darwin, Henry David Thoreau, Edward Abbey, and of course, the father of preservation himself, John Muir. Although I had, and still have, great respect for these writers, I could not relate to the way they viewed nature and their relationship to the natural landscape. While these male writers sought autonomy, I craved community. Where they were out to conquer oceans and deserts, woods and mountains, I wanted only to connect.

John Muir says when we go out into the woods, we are really going in. I wanted to see the Sierra Nevada in all the glory that Muir did, but when I got there, I still couldn't adopt his vision, at least not wholly. Over time I realized I needed a uniquely feminine way of being in nature, of "going in," one that included fears and failings (and even crying) but also intimacy and community. On the trail I wrote in a tiny journal every day, in search of my voice. I didn't know I would write a book at the time. I first needed to find Isabella Bird, Mary Austin, Annie Dillard, Linda Hogan, Mary Oliver, and the other women nature writers who would help me navigate the way. Since then, I have found a whole community of women writing about the natural world, and this memoir is my attempt to enter the conversation, a conversation that has finally begun to include women of color as well.

Certainly, there are now women writing guidebooks and natural histories of the Sierra Nevada, which was not the case thirty years ago. When I started writing this book, I did not find many women who had yet written personal narratives about the Sierra Nevada. Mary Austin writes about the high desert in *Land of Little Rain*, and Isabella Bird provides a short excerpt of Lake Tahoe in *A Lady's Life in the Rocky Mountains*. When I searched "women and the Sierra" online, the book that came up explored the early prostitutes of the West. A fine book, I am sure, but not exactly what I was looking for. Because of various fears of being in the outdoors alone, many women write from their own backyards. After twenty-eight days on the John Muir Trail, I moved to the Rockies and then finally settled in South Lake Tahoe, where I now write from my own backyard. That hike in 1993, my own first summer in the Sierra, led to a lifelong love of the mountains, of the place I now call home.

The twenty-two-year-old girl who set off for the mountains in 1993 is me and not-me in the way that we all carry our younger selves with us. That young self knew she needed something; she just wasn't sure what. Luckily, she hiked into the Sierra to find out.

ACKNOWLEDGMENTS

First of all, I would like to acknowledge John Muir, who writes about the Sierra Nevada with beauty and grace and whose reverence for the land led not only to the creation of the John Muir Trail and the Sierra Club but to the United States National Parks system. Also, without Thomas Winnett's *Guide to the John Muir Trail* we might still be wandering around out there, lost. I would also like to acknowledge Laird R. Blackwell's wildflower guides, which helped me to key out the various flowers along the trail, as well as Dr. Sue Kloss, who taught me how to identify trees. Many thanks also to Mark McLaughlin, the "storm king" for information regarding the 1992–93 snow levels. I am grateful to Centrum for a residency, where I completed the first draft of this book.

I would also like to acknowledge that before John Muir and other early immigrant explorers came to California, it was home to hundreds of Indigenous tribes. The land the current-day John Muir Trail traverses is the ancestral homelands of the Sierra Miwok, Nüümu (Northern Paiute), Western Mono Waksachi (Monache), Kawaiisu, Tübatulabal, and Yokuts peoples, among many others. The route on which the John Muir Trail was built was the path used by Native Americans for thousands of years before European settlers colonized the region. The original name for this footpath is Nüümü

Poyo, meaning "The People's Road." The history of humans living in and traversing across the beautiful landscape of California's Sierra Nevada goes back much further than two hundred years.

I would also like to thank the University of Nebraska Press, especially Robert J. Taylor and Sara Springsteen. Also, many thanks to Elizabeth Gratch for both encouragement and her terrific editing.

I would also like to acknowledge my husband, Thomas Greene, for his love, support, and understanding through draft after draft of this book.

And finally, many thanks to Dionne and Erika, who not only allowed me to use their real names but also let me tell their stories along with my own.

Although this memoir adheres to the truth of my fallible memory, some of the names of minor characters have been changed.

ALMOST SOMEW

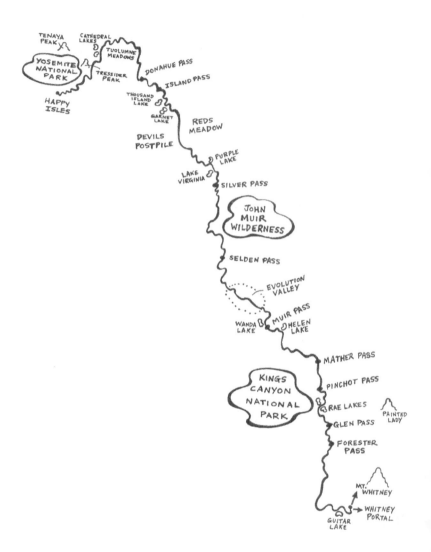

The John Muir Trail.

I only went out for a walk and finally concluded
to stay out till sundown, for going out, I found
was really going in. / JOHN MUIR

Day 1

Summer's 3 Percent

Whitney Portal (8,360) to Outpost Camp (10,080)   3.8 MILES

Going on twenty-three, I fancied myself a naturalist, thought I knew about the wilderness, about wildness, because I had been an avid reader of John Muir and Henry David Thoreau. I enjoyed reading about Muir's exciting climb into a giant Douglas spruce during a torrential windstorm. I liked to imagine a young bearded Muir scrambling into the treetops, wind whipped like a kite.

Once on the trail, however, I had my doubts.

Bent under the weight of my backpack, hiking through rain, I began to see that Muir's windstorm appealed to me in the figurative sense. Now the rain was more than metaphor. I splashed through puddles, and a stinging rain pelted my face. Soaked chaparral and spicy sagebrush layered with damp earth, with pine. A plastic poncho hid my head, and a garbage bag covered my pack. I wanted to revel in the outdoors, feel, like Muir had, a part of the wilderness; instead, I thought, *Mile 2. What have I gotten myself into this time?* We followed the trail through swaying Jeffrey pine and red fir. Our guidebook claimed that only 3 percent of the year's precipitation would fall during the summer, yet gray sheets of rain drenched the forest. I tried to forget the weather then realized if I was going to make it, I had better do my best to accept all of it—the wind and the rain, summer's 3 percent. Lightning cut white branches through a cloud-ribboned sky. I waited for the rumble of thunder, counting the seconds between claps to determine the distance of the storm, as I had as a child. One–one thousand, two–one thousand. Thunder seemed to shake the pewter sky. Trees wavered like indecision.

We had bragged to our friends in the bar, told them how we'd be hiking for a month, following the 211-mile John Muir Trail from Mt. Whitney to Yosemite. Completed in 1938 as a memorial to the nineteenth-century preservationist and writer, the John Muir Trail, or JMT for short, is California's most scenic trail. The JMT follows roughly 211 miles of the Pacific Crest Trail along the spine of the Sierra Nevada, through one of the most stunning mountainscapes in the world. We imagined swimming in high alpine lakes, sunning on granite rocks, walking out into the wide blue sky. "A diet with a view," I'd told all my friends.

I can't remember how we initially came up with the idea to hike the trail, and certainly, it had been proposed by Erika, but once we settled on it, I believed it as fine a plan as any. It was the summer of 1993, and I had just graduated from college with a degree in biology and carried no aspirations aside from chasing boys and complaining in my journal about how they didn't like me back. In college I could concentrate on those things, staving off the seriousness of adulthood. Though some of my friends moved back home after college, I knew I couldn't. The night of my college graduation I went out to dinner with my parents, and my father, as usual, drank rye for dinner. My mother, in her typical manner, ignored it. After dinner we went for a walk along the cliffs on Shell Beach, and I told my father I didn't want to see him anymore if he didn't stop drinking. I stared out at the sea, refusing to look at him, making him feel all the more a failure. Did I think my words were cruel then? Or was I merely acting out of self-protection? Certainly, I was thinking only of myself and my need to escape. At the time I didn't know that my father was undergoing chemotherapy for leukemia. I didn't have any idea that within the next year he would be dead.

So, I adopted John Muir as a sort of father figure, a ghost I could manipulate into a benevolent man who loved flowers and gray squirrels, windstorms and water ouzels. With a copy of Muir's *My First Summer in the Sierra* in my ridiculously heavy backpack, I set off to hike the John Muir Trail.

Backpacking seemed like it would come naturally to me, at least in theory. Even though I grew up in the suburbs of Los Angeles, I had always enjoyed playing in the dirt, collecting insects, planting gardens. I joined our college wilderness club and liked to describe myself as "outdoorsy." I thought, like some of the male nature writers I had read, that Mother Nature was a kind grandmotherly woman who smelled like oatmeal cookies and would hug me to her soft bosom and make everything okay. With the idea of both Grandmother Nature and Papa Muir on my side, it's no wonder I embraced the idea of hiking the John Muir Trail. People had asked me what I planned to do upon graduation, and I now had an answer: why, I was hiking the John Muir Trail. The trip became my postcollege plan, a vacation from considering grown-up concerns.

While Erika and I were sitting at Pismo Beach, figuring out the food drops and our daily mileage, the trip seemed romantic—like riding off into the sunset with a gorgeous cowboy without ever having to pick up dirty socks or touch a toilet seat. The numbers—the nine mountain passes over eleven thousand feet, the forty-eight thousand feet of net elevation gain—seemed like minor details, unreal and hazy like the plot of a dream. So, to prepare for the trip, I read Muir's effusive prose, certain that I could follow in his footsteps, learn to see the Sierra as he did, a glorious range of light.

The original plan was that after graduation Erika and I would set off on our own to hike the John Muir Trail. Erika and I, the two most unlikely picks for our sorority—neither of us had a clue which fork to use first at a dinner party—gravitated toward each other on pledge welcome night and became fast friends. We both had an affinity for long-haired boys, the Grateful Dead, skiing, and the outdoors in general. That's where the similarities stopped. She was, and still is, a mystery to me. The fastest, strongest, most athletic woman I have ever met, Erika sometimes seemed more machine than girl, whereas I could usually be found bumbling around in circles, certainly daydreaming, most often lost. Erika's world, however, didn't include the nonsense of daydreams; she was practical to the extreme, and for her the world presented no more mystery than a solvable algebra equation. She didn't see obstacles, only challenges. And I admired her. She represented what I wanted in myself—the ability to let go of the uncertainties that made my head spin and see the world as a controlled system, one that I could navigate, if only I tried harder.

Erika, built like a deer, seemed equipped to spend the summer in the Sierra, her legs long and lanky, her body hard and angular. With her long blonde braids, she looked like a Viking woman warrior. I took two clumsy steps to her deliberate one and felt hungry hours before she started to think about lunch. Erika had been backpacking since she could walk and planned a whole list of long-distance trips—the Tahoe-Yosemite Trail, the Pacific Crest Trail, the Appalachian Trail, El Camino de Santiago. The John Muir Trail, she said, was just the beginning.

Erika wanted to complete the trail for a sense of accomplishment, for bragging rights. She also thought it might get her in with a mountain man, which at the time didn't seem wholly unreasonable to me. She had joined our college logging team, her specialty the axe throw, for the same reasons—to boast and meet men. On the trail Erika wanted to hike at least twelve miles a day. In her mind she had arrived to Yosemite before setting one boot on dirt at Whitney Portal. From the beginning she talked about the trip as if it were in the past tense. When we applied for our permits, she told the ranger, "We'll be in Yosemite by the end of the month." At the trailhead, she told fellow hikers, "We are just beginning the 240 miles we plan to hike. We're hiking out for our food, so we are going to have hiked 240 miles, not 211." Erika had the ability to enjoy the romantic notions of a long-distance hike without ever dwelling on the discomfort of the present moment.

I knew that hiking for a month alone in the wilderness with Erika would most likely kill me. In part that's why I agreed to invite Dionne, who didn't know the first thing about hiking or camping, but that fact hid among the secrets I intended to keep from Erika. With short blonde hair, close-set blue eyes, and a ninety-eight-pound frame, Dionne resembled a pixie. Although she lacked experience in the outdoors, Dionne was all grace. Her heels tapped the earth like a bird's, the toes following, always pointing outward. A trained ballerina, she had danced her entire life. Aside from my not wanting to be alone with Erika, I invited Dionne because her boyfriend, Geoff, had begged me to bring her along. We had been college housemates, and he thought this trip might function as a cure.

"If she goes on the trip," he had said, "maybe it will help her get better."

"Maybe," I answered, "but no way. She's not coming."

Geoff sat on my bed and started to cry.

I told myself it was a good cause and at the same time—the selfish truth of altruism—a way to make myself feel better because I could be so helpful; more than that, however, I couldn't stand to see a man cry. I had seen my father cry only once. And he was drunk, making both the drinking and the crying frightening. I couldn't do anything to stop my father from crying, but I could do something to stop Geoff. So I said yes.

Geoff whisked Dionne off to the sporting goods store, outfitted her with gear, and handed her over like a kitten we'd adopted from the pound. She had never been backpacking, or even hiking, in her life. And there she was, on the first day of our month-long trip. Rather than dwell on the true gravity of the situation, I thought about myself—what a good Samaritan I was—and about my reward: I would no longer have to hike alone with Erika.

Erika and Dionne hardly knew each other before the trip, so I decided it best that Erika didn't know about Dionne's lack of experience. Or her illness. Erika had looked a little suspicious when

Dionne pulled out all her shiny gear, so I quickly said, "Dionne got all new gear for this trip," as if old, well-worn hiking boots and backpacks were squirreled away in her closet at home. I saw Dionne as an ally, so I acted out of selfishness. I didn't think about how dangerous the hike could have been for her. I didn't think about how the trip that Erika had so carefully organized could have been jeopardized.

And once Dionne joined our group, the three of us bragged about "girl power" and how it would be us three women, out in the wilderness "alone."

That didn't last long.

We didn't really know Jesse—we picked him up in a bar three weeks before the hike. We were in Mammoth Lakes, planning our trip, and met him through our friend Jason's stepbrother Neil. Erika, Neil, Jesse, and I ended up skiing together at Mammoth Mountain on closing day, the Fourth of July. Jesse was a twenty-five-year-old snowboarder, one of those guys who always said things like "It's cool" and "No worries." Being a friend of a friend's stepbrother, he was technically a stranger. At the bar after skiing, I told Jesse about our plan to hike the John Muir Trail, and after a few beers he decided to join us. And I encouraged him. "We've planned it all," I said. "All you have to do is show up. It's going to be a blast." Maybe Erika didn't want to spend a month alone with me and Dionne either, because she agreed to it.

In my twenty-two-year-old hormone-addled mind, a man's value was directly proportional to his relative attractiveness, but with Jesse's lanky body, pimple-scarred face, and swoopy, sun-bleached snowboarder hair, try as I might, I didn't find him attractive. So this once it wasn't the fling factor. I thought having a man around in the wilderness might come in handy, proving I hadn't been quite as committed to girl power as I had let on. I liked the idea of an all-women's trip, yet still, something in me felt relieved when Jesse decided to join us. Even then, I hated myself for feeling it.

Also, because of the secrets about Dionne I held from Erika, I hoped Jesse would function as a diversion. Jesse, however, imagined a little hiking, some fishing—fun and relaxation. He clearly had no idea what he'd gotten himself into.

Our Day 1 Plan, making it the six miles to Trail Camp, proved ambitious, considering our late start, the elevation gain, the rain, and our heavy packs. I had already nicknamed my pack "Big Fucking Heinous Load," "Big Heiny" for short, because I couldn't even get her on without either sitting on a rock to do it or else having someone else help me.

Mile 1 rated wet but novel. I enjoyed the sagey smell of earth, the sounds of water filtering through the canopy above. The trail twined through a mixed pine and fir forest, into the cool, misty air. I tried to remember the names of trees, looked around for wildflowers, watched the rivulets of water stream down our trail. I felt self-sufficient, smug even, carrying everything I would need on my very own back. I didn't feel like quitting.

Not until mile 2.

That's when raindrops snapped at my face like rubber bands. My wet bangs hung into my eyes, making me feel like a soggy sheepdog. That's when I had that feeling of panic, rising like acid from my stomach: *What was I doing out there?* Water puddled on the trail, soaking into my cotton socks. I tried to keep from feeling sorry for myself by imagining conversations with John Muir. He would have said something about the "glorious" rainfall or the "noble" roar of the wind. I tried to see it that way.

"Isn't this so great?" Erika turned around and asked. "The perfect start." With her poncho draped over her large external-frame pack, she looked like a giant turtle. She claimed that the old-fashioned external frames were superior to the new internal frame packs. No sweat on my back, she had said, and I can find everything right away. I had only worn a backpack like that once, when I first went backpacking a few years earlier and had rented one; I felt like I was carrying a refrigerator down the trail, so I quickly went out

7

and bought an internal-frame pack. The salesman called it "sleek," though on the trail I would not describe anything about myself as sleek.

The pines creaked to the wind's rhythm. Muir says he "never saw a discontented tree. They grip the ground as though they liked it, and though fast rooted they travel about as far as we do." At my pace the trees seemed to be traveling faster than I did. By mile 3 I wished I no longer had Muir's prose in my head. Day 1, and I wanted nothing more to do with Papa Muir's positive attitude. The gray mist turned to true rain, and I wiped water from my eyes. I gave up trying to avoid the puddles on the trail. I knew it rained in the mountains, yet somehow that detail had never made it into my picture of hiking the trail.

The trail followed Lone Pine Creek, and I watched as the raindrops vanished into the tumbling water. "I'm a little hungover," Dionne said to me. Her face glistened. I nodded, not because I felt hungover but because I imagined her face shined wet with tears, not rain—something I could relate to.

The night before, we had gone out to the natural hot springs with Jesse and his roommates. After only one wine cooler Dionne laughed and swayed about like a dinghy in wind. We toasted our upcoming trip. Erika and Dionne went into the springs naked. I wore my bathing suit and consequently ranked the least interesting. In truth I was probably the most likely to engage in a little last-minute fling before our foray into the forest, but I had already learned that nice girls weren't supposed to do those types of things, so whenever possible, I feigned modesty.

Like many young women, I wanted more than anything to attract men. I tried to fill the space inside of me with flirtations and flings and, truth be told, fucking. I felt sure that if I persuaded a man to love me, I would feel complete, worthy. Of course, like many young women do, I equated sex with love, yet the second I slept with someone, he inevitably lost interest. And like many young women, this never stopped failing to surprise me. At the time I didn't have any idea what a cliché I was. All I knew was that the way I went about relationships left me feeling empty, like an abandoned suitcase left in the attic.

After a while I tried, not always successfully, to change tactics. Though I failed to question the impulse behind my desire, I finally figured out that men would be more interested if they couldn't see it all up front. Why give away the entire shop, as my mother would say, in the storefront?

I had studied biology and tried to make sense of the human dating world through the animal world—something like the opposite of anthropocentrism. I told myself, the male peacock and mallard were adorned with the fancy plumage; the male lion and buck endowed with the ostentatious mane and horns. In biology the females aren't flashy, and the males are quick to fight over them. By the end of my college career I had created my own dating-by-Darwin theory. So that night I soaked in the hot sulfur water, sipping a bottle of Zima, watching steam rise while the sun sank into the folds of the mountains. I hoped someone would notice me, but to no one's surprise save my own, no one did—not even the guy I had briefly dated.

Meanwhile, Erika and Dionne posed for photographs, black silhouettes against the Owens River Valley and brindled sky, all feathers and flash. The guy I had briefly dated seemed to be flirting with Erika. I told myself he spelled t-r-o-u-b-l-e anyway, and Erika knew that. I can't remember if I felt smug or jealous. Probably a mixture of both. Either way, my relationship with Erika had always been complicated. Too often we ended up competing for the attention of a man who didn't really want either one of us. Rather than displaying a true sort of girl power, we turned on each other. I was passive-aggressive to her aggressive. Because of the various jealousies in our friendship, a former boyfriend had once told me he thought Erika liked me, that maybe she was a lesbian. I told him that, unfortunately, it wasn't that simple.

At Outpost Camp Jesse asked, "Should we stop here?" Rain washed over the trail, through the creek, and into a waterfall. We could hardly hear him. The rumble of water echoed like a passing train.

"Here. Stop. For tonight. Now," he yelled. We were supposed to make it to Trail Camp the first night according to the Day 1 Plan. We were only at Outpost Camp, just 3.8 miles in.

Yes, yes, yes. It seemed too cold for rain yet somehow wasn't. We huddled under a canopy of lodgepole pine and red fir. I felt sure more than 3 percent of the year's precipitation had already soaked into my skin. I wanted to stop too, but I didn't dare say a word. I knew all about the Day 1 Plan. Six miles on day 1. That was that. I stood still, shouldering Big Heiny, listening to the wind and rain, waiting to see what would happen.

"We have to stick to our agenda," Erika said. "We need to stay on track." Dionne's face glowed red like a radish. Jesse crossed his arms over his raincoat, making it evident he wouldn't be moving anytime soon. Would Erika make us hike on without him?

It wasn't in Erika's nature, like it was mine, to swerve from a plan. The main reason I had agreed to hike the John Muir Trail with her was that with Erika I knew it would happen. Even my mother had said, "Without Erika, you and Dionne would be wandering around the wilderness in circles."

"Well, you do what you want. I'm stopping here," Jesse said. He let his pack drop to the wet earth. Dionne and I waited there like two aspens connected by a single root, until Erika finally agreed. Jesse had already come in handy.

I dropped Big Heiny with a thud, and I felt light, as if I were floating. I had used that cliché about a load being lifted from my shoulders, but I don't think I ever really appreciated exactly what that felt like. Psychological burdens may weigh on us, yet in reality they are forgotten once we are faced with actual physical ones. Maybe that's why we choose to carry the physical burdens—they take our minds off the intangible, the real troubles in life.

"Dionne and I will sleep in my tent. You and Jesse sleep in yours," Erika said. I pulled out the tent poles and stopped for a minute to watch Jesse unpack. I tried to find him attractive. A fling could take my mind off all the walking. A little excitement, and I might not care so much about the rain, the switchbacks, or Big Heiny. We set up the tents, ate granola bars, and got into our sleeping bags. Before I could talk myself into Jesse, he fell asleep.

Wet chaparral and pine filled the evening air. The metronome of rain and Jesse's snoring created a weird trancelike song. I listened for a while, feeling a yearning I couldn't name, unable to sleep. Then the panic began rising again like floodwaters. Determined to push it back, I turned on my headlamp and pulled out my paperback anthology of Muir's writings and my journal. Muir says, "The weather of spring and summer in the middle region of the Sierra is usually well flecked with rains and light dustings of snow, most of which are far too obviously joyful and life-giving to be regarded as storms." I tried to imagine the rain and wind as joyful and life-giving. I turned onto my side to write in my journal: "August 2, 1993: The joyous rain welcomed us today into the forest." I sketched a tiny picture of our camp by looking out the mesh window: Jeffrey pine, granite, manzanita, water, red fir, sky. Even though I couldn't see it, I added a moon because I knew it was full. Day 1 and already lying in my journal.

Day 2

Hiking to Tent City in Men's Underwear

Outpost Camp (10,080) to Trail Camp (12,000)   2.5 MILES

An old mountaineer once told me it's tradition that the guide in a backcountry expedition wears a white cap. The white cap has to be given to the guide by someone in the group. Erika wore a white cap. She bought it for herself. She said it kept the sun off her head and that white goes with anything, but I knew she had designated herself the guide of our ragged crew.

Before even the birds started, Erika tromped about camp and sang, "Wake up, wake up. It's time to go." I had always seen getting up early as a moral act; still, I hated it. We had already fallen behind schedule, so I knew Erika was right—we had to get up. Erika wanted to summit Whitney from Outpost Camp, yet with the way things had started, I had my doubts again.

Dionne had already climbed out of Erika's tent. She wore a green fleece sweatshirt and men's underwear—not boxers but tighty-whiteys, the kind with the peephole in front. I figured that she was still wearing her pajamas and would change before we set off on our hike.

Jesse pulled on a tie-dyed T-shirt and shorts, stuffed his sleeping bag in its stuff sack, and headed for the food. Before Erika noticed, he had fetched the food from the tree—a preventative measure used against the bears in the days before the now-required bear canister—and was eating oatmeal. Erika carefully measured out exactly two and a half tablespoons of oatmeal per person per day. Jesse filled his plastic bowl to the top, added the boiling water that Erika had heated, and inhaled his breakfast. I waited for Erika to scold him for eating too much, yet she didn't say a word. That was fine by me because I was hungry.

Like most women, I had been on enough diets to know how many calories were in things. Although this skill was mostly a waste of brain space, I could rattle off the caloric content of common food items: an apple, 80 calories; a slice of cheesecake, 350; a Big Mac with cheese, 700; a family-sized bag of Doritos, 2,150; two and a half tablespoons of oatmeal, 110 calories. Our oatmeal breakfast wasn't even enough energy for a twenty-minute Jane Fonda workout, much less hiking up the tallest mountain in the Lower 48.

Chubby from childhood, I thought the hike would be a good way to lose a little weight, but as usual, I wasn't willing to be uncomfortable. When my mother, a former British beauty queen, took me to a modeling agency when I was twelve, the talent scout laughed us out of his office. "Maybe if she loses twenty pounds," he had said, "or more." Chubby apparently rated "cute," but it didn't meet the qualifications for the runway. My mother was more upset than I was, and to make me feel better, my father took me out for ice cream. After I finished my first cone, my father had said, "How about another one? Do you want to try the mint chip?" My mother volleyed me her look, so I said, "No thanks, Daddy. One cone is enough."

"Are you going to eat?" I asked Dionne.

"I already ate." Dionne ran her fingers through her short blonde hair, attempted a smile.

"What did you eat?"

"A granola bar I had in the tent." Erika overheard this and marched over, and we got a twenty-minute lecture about hanging all of our food, plus lotion, toothpaste, and lip balm. We all have to do our part, Erika said, to protect the bears. Dionne and I both knew there had been no granola bar in that tent, but Dionne would rather be chastised by Erika than admit she hadn't eaten.

"Well, I'm hungry," I said. Dionne wouldn't look at me. I poured oatmeal into my bowl—more than the ration yet certainly not as much as Jesse had.

"Two and a half tablespoons," Erika said. "You definitely have too much there."

"You can have my part," Dionne said.

"But you might want it later," Erika told her.

"Fine." I poured the oatmeal back into the plastic bag and carefully measured two and a half tablespoons. It didn't even cover the bottom of my stainless steel bowl.

After eating, which didn't take long, we broke down the tents and packed up our things. "Time for camp check," Erika called. "We should make it look better than when we arrived." I had already checked my area, but I walked around in circles looking at the ground in order to satisfy Erika. Jesse sat on his backpack, arms crossed, waiting.

"Okay. Looks good," Erika said.

"Good. Let's go," Jesse said.

Erika sported her white cap, and Dionne still wore her men's underwear. When Dionne passed oncoming hikers, they would look straight at the peephole in her underwear and roll their eyes or shake their heads, especially the women. For the most part we found women supportive on the trail but not always—and there was something about the underwear that really got to them. They gave her a "how dare she" look, and to this day I'm not sure if they were mad because the underwear implied some sort of conformation to gender roles or a rebuttal against them. Or perhaps they saw the underwear as just plain embarrassing, unseemly.

But Dionne wasn't trying to make a statement with the underwear. They were a matter of practicality. Dionne had intended to wear the underwear to bed and the tight jean cutoffs to hike in—that is, until she wore the denim shorts in the rain. Anyone who has attempted tight denim for a hike in the rain, or even in the sun, knows exactly why Dionne chose the underwear the next day. Yet I didn't want to expose Dionne's inexperience and poor clothing options, so I kept my mouth shut. And who was I to talk? I wore flower-print men's boxers to hike in, so I figured I would bring that point up if Erika mentioned Dionne's choice in hiking attire.

The weather cleared, and the early sky shined purple. We forded Lone Pine Creek and followed the switchbacks past Sierra chinquapin and patches of Indian paintbrush. Bright pink fireweed lined the rocky trail. After a footbridge and more switchbacks, we reached Mirror Lake, a greenish lake, reflecting the surrounding mountains, pocketed in a granite valley. Thor Peak towered above.

We climbed a granite stairway, passed broken and weathered whitebark pine and a few willows. Two hikers approached us. They were shirtless, and both glowed neon pink with sunburns. They had come from Death Valley and were going to "bag" Whitney that afternoon. "We will have been to the lowest and the highest elevation in the United States in one day," they said with German accents. I told them that Whitney was the highest mountain in the Lower 48, but fifteen stood taller in Alaska. I asked them why they wanted to do all of it in one day. They just said good-bye and jogged up the trail, likely thinking I was a know-it-all, which I have to admit is still one of my unfortunate tendencies.

Often people say they hike mountains because they are there. Even though some women have taken on this attitude, it seems to me that it is an internalization of man's view of nature. For Erika the idea of the conquest made sense, but for me it didn't—and still doesn't—fit, yet I had no better way of looking at things, though in part maybe that's one of the reasons I was there: I was in search of my own view of wildness, my own connection to the natural landscape.

The previous summer I had hiked Mt. Elbert, the highest mountain in Colorado, with Jack, a man I had dated for a few months. I had never questioned whether or not we would reach the top, and it wasn't all that important to me. Jack insisted on getting up early because the weather service had called for thunderstorms. I agreed, and I didn't think about breakfast or water or anything else. As we started to hike, small cumulus clouds began to form. I knew these clouds could grow into huge anvil-shaped thunderheads in under an hour in the high country.

"Hey, don't those look like thunderclouds?" I asked.

"Those little things? Naw. We're fine."

I knew Jack was worried, though, because he picked up the pace. He had worked for the Forest Service building trail all summer, so he was fast and strong. I worked as a waitress at a Mexican restaurant, eating chips and drinking margaritas. Still, I tried to keep up with him, thinking if I could, he would be impressed. I also kept a close eye on the clouds, spiraling up like stairs into the sky.

We had reached timberline, usually about eleven thousand feet in Colorado, when my stomach started to sour and my head filled with cotton. The windswept trail unfolded in front of us, up a grassy slope, and then through a field of uneven granite, a landscape that always reminded me of the cratered moon.

"The clouds are getting bigger."

"We're okay," Jack said. "We just have to hurry."

"I thought we were hurrying." The clouds climbed the sky above us, and the wind gained strength. The air dampened, and I knew the conditions were just right for an electrical storm.

"I don't feel so good."

"Eat a PowerBar."

"I'm not hungry."

But Jack had hiked too far ahead to hear me. We climbed quickly over the granite, and I felt sicker and sicker. I began to dry heave and suddenly figured it out.

"Down. I'm going down," I shouted.

"What? You're not stopping, are you? We're almost there. We can't go down now," Jack called from above. He then turned to continue climbing. I knew at that point I had the beginning signs of altitude sickness. Thunder rumbled through the valley below us. I began running down the mountain. I had finished with chasing

Jack up the peak. It had become obvious that impressing him with my hiking prowess wasn't going to happen. Who cared if we made it to the top? Jack cared, that's who, so he kept going. I descended at least a thousand feet before I began to feel better. I drank a lot of water, ate, and continued down. With each step I began to feel normal again.

Jack caught up to me on his way back down. "I really wanted to have lunch up there, but I didn't know where you went."

"I was getting altitude sickness, Jack. You know you can die from that, right?"

"That's impossible."

"Right." It wasn't worth arguing over. He had reached the peak, and the important thing was that I hadn't been stupid enough to follow him the whole way up. We hiked down through the forest in the rain; the gray sky quivered with thunder. In truth most of my wilderness experiences had been defined for me by the men I dated or hoped to date. They chose the route, the goal, characterizing the way we would see the wilderness. Sometimes I kept up, but most times I didn't. John Muir says, "In every walk with nature one receives far more than he seeks." That hike up Mt. Elbert helped me envision a future without trying to impress Jack with skills I didn't possess, so I did receive more than I was seeking. That may not be exactly what Muir meant, yet I wanted to believe Muir's ideas could include the likes of me.

"Look. There it is." Erika pointed to Mt. Whitney rising up over Pinnacle Ridge, the smoky granite towers like carved totems, ancient faces with white beards, looking down on us. I tried to imagine myself on top of the rock needle. I could focus only on the landscape between the peak and me, the largeness of it, which gave me vertigo. The contours no longer brown lines on a topographic map, faint like a long-ago memory. Instead, the earth pressed into a steep granite ridge, and beyond, the jagged snow-patched peaks poked at the sky's blue dome like spires.

From Trail Camp a small lake in the basin reflected Wotans

Throne and its snowy skirt. A granite and talus-covered world, except the multicolored tents dotting primary colors across the white, gray, and brown landscape.

Jesse threw down his pack. "I'm not hiking Whitney today," he said. "That's another five miles to the top, and then we have to get down the other side." Erika consulted her map, read about the frequency of afternoon thunderstorms on top of Whitney, checked the cloud-patched sky, and finally agreed that we should wait until the next day. Two days of hiking, and we had only covered 6.3 miles. At this rate our trip would take us two months.

I dropped my pack, grabbed my journal and a bottle of Gatorade, and climbed the rocks above the scattering of tents. I tried to follow the hundred or so switchbacks that we would climb the next day but couldn't see them between the barren rocks and snow. Even though I couldn't make them out, I knew that concrete steps had been poured by trail crews to help with our ascent, and I wondered what Muir would have thought about all of these improvements on the trail. Since then, wire hand cables have been erected for added safety.

I counted twenty-nine tents below. A middle-aged couple argued about how to start their camp stove. I imagined Muir sitting on this spot, looking at Mt. Whitney. What would he think of all these people? He once said, "Thousands of tired, nerve-shaken, over-civilized people are beginning to find out that going to the mountains is going home; that wildness is necessity; that mountain parks and reservations are useful not only as fountains of timber and irrigating rivers, but as fountains of life." The nerve-shaken people had found out, and Trail Camp itself was now a metropolis of rip-stop nylon and reinforced canvas. Toward the later part of his life Muir agreed that the parks needed to be accessible to the people to foster an appreciation of wildness, but he could not have foreseen this. Even in the "backcountry," the world finally was too much with us.

A fat marmot scampered across the rocks and looked me in the eye. "Lots of people, huh?" I asked him. The marmot scurried even closer in, looking for food. He reared back on his hind legs and chirped. He stood so close I could see his yellow buckteeth. I went back to writing in my journal but was interrupted by the sound of plastic against rock. For a moment I sat astonished, then I yelled, "Hey, marmot! Give me back that water bottle!" I chased after him. He dropped the bottle and waddled along, across the rocks. Even though marmots sleep nine months of the year—one of the only animals to go into a true hibernation—this one had managed, in just three months, to get fat off the food and Gatorade from the overcivilized visitors at Trail Camp.

I sat back down, opened my journal, and, still thinking about Muir, wrote, "Even the animals here are tame. What wildness is left? How do we fit in? How do I fit?" I had no language of my own for the landscape, no way to define myself within it. The unanswerable questions hovered like the buzzing of an insect at night, and every time you turn on the lights, you can't find the source. The low din of wings resumes only in the dark.

I sighed and turned to drawing, a way to try to capture what I saw without overthinking it. I sketched Whitney. From my studies in college I knew that all of this had been under the sea eighty million years ago, another idea impossible to fathom. It was hard enough to imagine the glaciers of two million years ago, carving canyons, scraping out lake basins, making mountains.

A little boy, no older than seven or eight, walked down to the lake with a pot and a bottle of Dawn dish soap and began washing his dishes in the water. I looked around. Although I knew only the basics of backcountry travel, I certainly understood that soap should not be used in alpine lakes, or any lakes for that matter. Shouldn't somebody do something? Bubbles formed in the water, and without any other way to respond, I began to dislike the small boy. A man came over, and I listened. I felt confident that this man would reprimand his son.

"Good job," the man said and patted the boy on the shoulder. My disgust moved to the father. How could the boy know that soap pollutes mountain lakes when his father either doesn't know or knows but doesn't care? Didn't they pay attention to the ranger's talk about keeping soap out of lakes and streams? Maybe they had, yet being responsible in the backcountry is inconvenient. It was much easier to wash dishes in the lake than to scrub pots and pans with sand. Rarely do we set out to pollute or destroy a landscape; rather, it's a consequence of carelessness.

I hoped this boy and his father were not going to the bathroom too close to the water; luckily, at the time a solar toilet had been provided at Trail Camp for solid waste. Because people also used the toilet for their garbage, the toilet has since been removed, and now campers are given a bag when they get their permits, and they are instructed to carry out their waste, which I would think deters people from camping at Trail Camp, especially thru-hikers. Carrying toilet paper and tampons seems trivial in comparison to carrying out one's own waste. I'm glad we weren't confronted with the choice of holding it or carrying it all the way to Lake Edison.

Erika, Dionne, and I made a pact to carry out all toilet paper, tampons, and other personal hygiene items. We each carried a zip-lock bag for the purpose. When I was dating Jack, he couldn't even stand the sight of a tampon in the wrapper, so I would hide the pink-and-blue boxes behind the toilet paper under my bathroom sink. Now I would be carrying around a baggie full of used tampons. We knew that a month in the wilderness necessarily meant at least one period for each of us, something men don't have to consider when planning a long hike, another reason men can forget about their physical bodies in a way women never can, because even if we try, our baggies of feminine products remind us.

We didn't discuss this matter or any other bathroom issue with Jesse, aside from Erika handing him a bag and saying, "Here is your personal baggie." He frowned at her and stuffed the bag into his pack. He also backed away when he saw us putting our toilet paper baggies into the bear bags with the food.

The boy and his father walked back to their camp, passing Erika on her way over to me. "There you are. We need water. Your turn." Erika tossed me six water bottles and the filter.

I was careful to avoid the area where the boy had just washed his dishes, as if it made any difference. This water was somewhat polluted, which was why we filtered, boiled, or added iodine to it before we drank it. I felt ashamed because I had just sat there while that little boy poured soap into the lake. I didn't feel like I had the experience or the authority to say anything. Erika would have said something to that father and son, and maybe they would have listened to her. I pumped the water and justified my silence: *What do the rocks care?*

I filtered the six quarts of water and then returned to my sketch. I worked quickly to finish because the sun had dipped behind the granite backdrop, and with it dropped the temperature. The alpenglow slid from the mountain like a yellow scarf off a woman's shoulder. The rock I sat on sent a shiver, like a cold fish, swimming up my back. I looked at my drawing. My mountain scene could very well be under the ocean: the mountains shot up like coral, and rocks floated in sand. On the back of my picture I wrote, "Day 2, August something. Mt. Whitney, eighty million years ago as seen from present-day Tent City."

Day 3

Caught

......

*Trail Camp (12,000), Mt. Whitney (14,496),
and Crabtree Meadows (10,640)*   12.2 MILES

......

"Look, look. Get up." Erika shook the tent. I unzipped the rain fly
and pulled the nylon back. She flashed her headlamp in my face
and said, "Look."

"I would look, but I can't see anything with that stupid light."

"What the fuck?" Jesse said and buried his head in his sleeping
bag.

Erika snapped off the light and pointed, "Just look." The round
tip of the sun peeked like a voyeur over Owens Valley. Altocumu-
lus clouds stretched across the glowing horizon, shimmering like
the silver and pink scales of a fish. I remembered my father saying,
"Mackerel sky, mackerel sky, not long wet and not long dry." I knew
that if his rhyme proved correct, we needed to get going because
we'd be sure to encounter more rain—yet I couldn't pull myself from
the sunrise. The clouds marched across the bridge of the sky, becoming ephemeral characters, some playing cricket, others the animals
and aerialists of a three-ringed circus. Finally, yellow faded to blue.
I tried not to look directly at the sun, the orchestrating pink orb;

instead, I focused on the clouds, dancing like painted circus elephants.

I ate a granola bar in order to avoid the oatmeal wars, Dionne and I helped each other with our packs, and we all got going. I tried to mentally prepare myself for the hundred switchbacks. We wouldn't pick up a food drop for two weeks, so Big Heiny weighed nearly sixty pounds, about fifteen pounds more than she should. I had not heard of Ray Jardine and his go-light campaign, so I carried a heft that would be unheard of today with lighter packs and better equipment. It also didn't help that I had brought along a library of books, including an anthology of John Muir's nature writing, a wildflower guide, a journal, and of course our trail bible, Thomas Winnett's *Guide to the John Muir Trail*. Years later I would read books about thru-hiking trips, and in all of them people ditched stuff along the way. For some reason that never occurred to me. I just saw Big Heiny as a burden I was destined to carry.

Even though Erika was far skinnier than me, she was also five inches taller and weighed more, but somehow "we" had decided she and I should carry the same amount. Jesse's pack weighed a few pounds more than ours, and Dionne carried just thirty pounds because she was so small. Big Heiny looked the biggest of them all, though, because I had strapped so many things to the outside. Organization had never been my strong suit. When people passed me, they'd say, "Oh my, look at that big pack" and "Why are you carrying so much more than the rest of your group?" I knew I looked ridiculous. Still, I liked these people, and I hoped my hiking partners heard them.

Despite spending all night and morning worrying about the switchbacks, they turned out to be easier than I had imagined, and we made good time. Often the dread proves worse than the actuality of a thing. But in the case of the hike, my trepidation encouraged me to train beforehand; in addition to reading Muir in pre-trip preparation, I agreed to compete in a triathlon with Erika to get into shape. I should say Erika competed, and I participated. Erika told our friends, "All I want to do is beat Suzanne." And beat me she did—by at least an hour.

I have never held illusions regarding my athletic prowess. In high school I ran track and was ironically nicknamed "Speed Demon." My teammates would be at home, showered, watching *The Love Boat* reruns and eating popcorn before I finished the long-distance runs. And because of a serious lack of hand-eye coordination, I don't play sports with a ball—no tennis, no soccer, no volleyball, no Ping-Pong. In grade school I played softball, and I stood way out in the outfield—they called it "backup outfield"—either praying the ball would not come my way or else daydreaming. So either way, I would drop the ball, and everyone would shout at me, or the ball would roll right past me without my notice, and everyone would shout at me.

Trying to go fast in a triathlon would have just depressed me. So I cheered on the blue-haired ladies who passed me and chatted with the volunteers at the water stations. When I finally reached the finish line, I wasn't even that tired. Even my own mother, who would never consider running around the block, said, "Well, that sure took you a *long* time."

Erika, on the other hand, looked like she had just outrun the bulls in Pamplona. She asked me my time, and I told her I didn't know. I didn't ask her about her time, but she told me anyway. We both got the same medal and certificate of completion.

I always knew an undercurrent of competition existed between Erika and me. I also understood that I couldn't outright rival her on any athletic level, yet I did compete with her for men. And I relied on one of my least attractive qualities: passive aggression. Erika was the prettier one, the blonde with the enviable figure—like hiking Barbie without the giant boobs. But her dating life lacked subtlety. As soon as any guy showed interest in her, she suggested rock climbing, mountain biking, or skiing and then proceeded to outperform him. I knew that approach wasn't going to work for me, and I used that knowledge as leverage in the dating world. I now see how unfortunate it was that men didn't, and maybe still don't, appreciate a strong woman.

I once went along on a first date with Erika. We had been at a bar in Telluride, and a guy she met named John asked her to go mountain biking with him. She agreed and had fast plans to ditch me; however, when John found out that we were traveling together, he insisted I come along. I would have been far happier left behind at the café, drinking coffee, eating angel food cake, and reading one of the Brontës, but when Erika saw that there was no chance the date was happening without me, she insisted I tag along. John let Erika choose the ride, and she picked Lizard Head Canyon, the scariest, dirtiest, steepest trail in Telluride, which wasn't technically a mountain biking trail at all; in fact, the trail weaved through a wilderness area, and bikes were not allowed—all part of the danger and fun.

Though Erika typically abided most wilderness regulations, she didn't agree with the rule about mountain bikes in wilderness areas, especially because horses were allowed, so the ban on mountain biking was a rule she had no problem ignoring. I suppose we all pick and choose which rules suit us and which don't. I wanted to follow the rules, but more than that, I wasn't much of a mountain biker, and I looked at the map and saw what I was in for, so I asked about a ride in Black Bear Canyon, thinking that it might satisfy Erika because it rated "most difficult," with a trio of black diamonds. Erika shook her head—too easy, so we rode off into the wilderness.

We pedaled over log bridges, through streams, over a section known as the rock garden, and along sheer cliffs. I should say they pedaled; I carried my bicycle over or through most of these obstacles. This was in the days before bicycles came with suspension systems, so technical terrain meant butt-bumping, bone-shaking, teeth-chattering riding. I seriously began to think I might be giving myself a heart attack at the age of twenty-one. I couldn't get enough air in my lungs, no matter how quickly I gulped at it, and my limbs began to shake. I started to appreciate falling off my bike because I could rest in the dirt for a minute, looking up at the yellow aspen leaves and blue sky. Erika stayed in the lead, and John traveled back and forth between us, coming back to make sure I hadn't killed myself. By the time we had finished, pine sap, mud, grease, aspen leaves, and blood coated my body like a second skin. Scratches and scrapes crisscrossed every exposed patch. Erika, however, looked as neat and tidy as when she started. She could have stepped out of a Nike commercial; with my torn clothes, muddy face, bloody body, and twigs in my hair, I was the "Just Do It" motto gone terribly awry.

To Erika's great dismay, that night at the bar, John didn't brag about Erika's technical mountain biking skills or her Supergirl stamina; instead, he told everyone what a "sport" and "trooper" I had been. He laughed and said, "Suzanne doesn't just get back to nature; she wears it." He bought all my drinks. Erika frowned, quietly drinking the beer she had bought herself, because clearly, she had outperformed me. In fact, she had outperformed John as well. All the while I tried to act as demure as possible, sipping my free drinks, glad that clumsy sometimes had its rewards, even if it came in the form of draft beer, without ever considering that John should have gained a healthy respect for Erika, should have been pleased that not all women were wimps, that some women were just as proficient in the outdoors as men, or more, and that should be something to celebrate. None of us, it seemed, had enough sense, or maybe self-confidence, to go there. I know that at the time I hadn't even considered the implications. I wanted to be an expert at the game; I never considered that, instead, I should have been questioning the rules.

From the ridge of Trail Crest, Sequoia National Park and the Great Western Divide unfolded before us. Half-frozen lakes scattered below the Whitney Crest. One path continued two more miles to Whitney's peak, and the other marked the official start of the John Muir Trail. We had only just arrived at the beginning. The JMT switch-backed down the rock face toward the cluster of speckled gray and black alpine lakes. Erika, Jesse, and I sat on our packs and waited for Dionne.

We cheered for Dionne when she finished the switchbacks. She looked up at us, her face bright pink and puffed out like a blowfish in danger.

"Are you okay?" I asked.

"Dizzy and nauseous," she cried and shook her head. Her swollen face made her eyes look like slits, commas on their sides.

"You can't go any higher, Dionne," Erika said.

"She's right." I recognized Dionne's symptoms.

"You stay here," Erika said. She and Jesse then turned and started up the trail before anyone could say another word. I realized this time reaching the top was important to me too. I knew someone should stay with Dionne, hike down the other side toward Guitar Lake with her. I knew that the only someone left was me. I realized for the first time that letting her come with us might have been a terrible mistake.

"Look, you have to eat. And you have to drink water."

"I'm not hungry." She bent at the waist.

"I know. I know how you're feeling. It's either the altitude, or you're dehydrated, or both. Either way, you have to drink something." Dionne drank the rest of the water in her bottle, and I gave her my Gatorade.

"I feel better," she said. "Go ahead. I'll wait here."

"Okay, but don't try to climb any higher. Or start down the other side and wait for us below."

I left her and began to climb the rocky trail to the top of Whitney. After a few minutes I scolded myself for leaving her, yet I knew that if I stayed with her, I would have resented her. I told myself it was different from when Jack left me on the side of Mt. Elbert, yet I couldn't explain why. I also knew altitude sickness could turn into edema, that it really could be life threatening. Although I knew what I was doing was wrong, I couldn't seem to stop myself. I felt bad for Dionne but not bad enough to sacrifice what I wanted. I told myself she was just dehydrated, yet I knew even then I had acted selfishly. I was mad at Geoff for asking me to bring her.

I stepped out of the way for a man, spindly with age, to pass.

"Uphill hiker has the right of way," he said. "But I'll take it because I'm eighty today." He raised his hiking stick and said, "Twenty-third time up Whitney, and I'm coming back next year." I watched him pick his way down the trail and hoped that I would be able to climb mountains at eighty. A friend's grandmother used to say, "If I could do it yesterday, I can do it today. And if I can do it today, I'll be able to do it tomorrow." At eighty-nine she still played golf and practiced yoga.

I felt a little woozy, light-headed, counted ten steps, rest, ten steps, rest. The trail clung to the ribcage of the mountain. The rocky edge dropped off thousands of feet. Gray clouds lurched over the distant horizon. I continued on, watching the placement of each step until I realized I had reached the top. People gathered next to a stone hut, took pictures of each other, smiling with the pride of accomplishment, the relief of finally being there. A squeal escaped my mouth, surprising me. The general feel of elation entered my body then guilt because of Dionne. The mountain tumbled thousands of feet down into the Owens Valley, and snow-splotched mountains, white and jagged like shark's teeth, formed in rows at the mouth of the desert on the eastern horizon.

I found Erika and Jesse eating brownies with some new friends, Dan and Phil from Fresno. We took turns photographing one another.

"Why do we climb mountains?" I asked.

"What are you talking about?" Erika said. Jesse just shook his head and walked away.

Phil said, "Because it's a goal I set for myself."

Dan said, "I almost didn't come. My wife has lupus, and I massage her back every night because she's in pain. But she wanted me to come, so I'm here for both of us. She's my soul mate."

Phil and I both nodded. Erika walked over to find Jesse and take more pictures.

I thought about Dan massaging his wife, and I didn't know if it was the story or exhaustion or the very idea of soul mates, but my throat tightened, and my vision went blurry. I immediately felt silly, so I walked away to find Jesse and Erika. When I found them, Jesse whispered, "Those guys were sort of weird." I nodded, even though I didn't agree; it was just easier to pretend.

We walked over to sign the ledger and check out the stone hut. "Built in 1909," a dark-haired man next to me said, "and you aren't supposed to sleep here, but I have. I'm Jim. Where you from?"

When I realized he was looking at me, waiting for an answer, I said, "Southern California originally. Now I live in San Luis Obispo mostly. And Vail."

"How can you live in two places?" he asked. He wore short cutoff army pants, a white tank top, and Teva sandals. He also looked sort of slumped over, even without his pack.

"I have spent the last few winters in Colorado ski bumming; the rest of the year I've gone to college at Cal Poly."

He nodded.

"We're hiking the whole John Muir Trail," Erika said, when she realized she held a captive audience.

"Me too. Solo," Jim said. Erika was evidently impressed by this, and she invited him to hike with us. I whispered to Erika that he had a scary look in his eye, and she said loudly enough for everyone to hear, "You're always so paranoid."

"I would like to sleep up here someday," Erika said.

Erika, Jesse, Jim, and I started down, and who should be summiting but Dionne in her tighty-whiteys? We stared for a minute in disbelief, and then Erika began to cheer. Jesse and I soon joined in, and so did Jim. Dan and Phil with the brownies cheered too.

Jim said, "It's Charlie's Angels." I realized he was referring to two blondes, Dionne and Erika, with a brunette, me. Just like when I was little, the blonde girls always played the glamorous Cheryl Ladd and sexy Farrah Fawcett, and I got stuck being the least interesting character, Kate Jackson. At least since I was the only brunette there, I could be Jaclyn Smith, who I always thought was pretty fabulous. Because of this, I decided to be flattered by Jim's comment. As little girls growing up in the 1970s, we had idolized the Angels not just because they were tough but because they were beautiful. They could take out the bad guys because they could trick them by posing as fashion models or roller derby girls. Their insidious beauty made them sneaky, made them bad in a good way. They won shoot-outs without displacing their feathered hair or breaking a polished nail. We wanted to be them. Yet we ignored the fact that they were directed and essentially owned by the illusive Charlie, the patriarchal voice to which they kowtowed, foreheads to the ground.

Dionne signed in on the ledger, and then she said, "I'm so glad I made it. What an incredible view. Ha-ha, I'm sitting on top of the world. Now I know why people do this." Erika looked at me, eyebrows raised. I hoped Erika thought Dionne meant climbing Whitney, not just hiking in general.

"I know," I said, hoping to throw off Erika. "This is an incredible view." The hills, brown and crumpled like a taffeta dress that had been unfastened, left to drop from the sky, draped into the distant horizon. I had never seen Dionne so happy. She also ate a brownie on top, so I convinced myself that maybe Geoff had been right; maybe she could be cured. But mostly, by making it to the top, she assuaged my guilt for having left her. I knew things could have turned out badly, yet now that she had made it, I didn't have to think about it. For the moment everything seemed right with the world, everything remarkable, the liquid sunlight filling our eyes. And like a moth's flight toward flame, the wings flicker most beautifully right before the darkness.

The skies went a steely gray.

"We made it just in time," Jesse said, and thunder coughed in the distance. We struggled against the wind to pull our packs on.

"Weather changes quick around here," Erika said. Wisps of blonde hair escaped her braids and blew around her pink face.

"No kidding. Let's get down off this fucker," Jim said and laughed. The rest of us looked at each other because we weren't sure what was so funny. We helped each other stretch our rain ponchos over our packs and hurried down the trail. Hail ricocheted off our packs, and the dirt filled with Styrofoam-looking balls. Lightning laddered across the sky. I counted again, trying to remember the formula. Light traveled 186,000 miles per second, and sound traveled one-fifth of a mile per second. If lightning occurred a mile away, it would be five seconds before we heard the thunder. Lightning exploded across the sky. I counted. One second—less than a quarter of a mile away.

"We need to get off of this mountain," I yelled over the bouncing hail, the sound like popcorn in hot oil. I hiked in front of Dionne but behind Erika, Jesse, and Jim, and for the first time I thought they were hiking much too slowly. I came up right behind Jesse and said, "Don't you think we should pick up the pace?" Another flash and then a zipper of light, as if the lightning had ripped open the cloud-pleated air. I was often afraid of the wrong things, yet at that moment I felt my fear justified. Lightning, on average, struck at least one person a year on top of Whitney. Just as I considered this, a blinding flash and a crashing boom happened all at once like the blast of a bomb. I screamed and dropped to the ground, my face against the wet earth, the mineral smell of decomposed granite. The ice gathered like white marbles. By the time I looked up, Erika and Jesse were already running down the trail. Dionne ran toward me. Jim hovered over me with the lopsided grin of a Halloween jack-o'-lantern. I stood up and began running, practically side checking Jesse as I passed him. I tripped down the mountain—carrying nearly two hundred pounds with the weight of my pack.

"I've never seen Suzanne move that fast," Erika laughed.

"Just a bit o' fire. That's all," Jim said and sauntered down the trail like he was enjoying an afternoon stroll. The rest of us ran. Finally, hail turned to rain, and I realized we had escaped the danger. We hiked, our wet clothes suctioned onto our bodies, down to Timberline Lake. I began to feel a twinge in my right knee, almost a tickle, a little not-so-right feeling.

Soon after we arrived at the lake, the wind netted the clouds and dragged them off toward the distant horizon. I peeled off my wet clothes and arranged them over the rocks to dry.

Jesse, Jim, and Erika decided to catch our dinner. I dug my journal out of my pack and sat near the lake. I wrote, "Today we hiked Whitney. A day of changes—lightning, hail, rain, sunshine. Anticipation then guilt; tired then elated. Rock, sky, trees, lake. Dionne,

Erika, Jesse, and Jim. The days stretch long, but tonight we'll eat fish."

Jim walked over and asked, "Is the author ready to do some fishing?"

"What?"

"You're scribbling away in that tiny book. What are you writing?"

"Just recording where we are and all that. And drawing some pictures."

"Can I see it?"

"Well. Here's our first campsite." I showed him the picture of the waterfall at Outpost Camp. Before I could protest, he snatched my journal, and I immediately wished I hadn't shown him anything. He started reading aloud: "The joyous rain welcomed us today into the forest. A departing sun, a full moon rising beneath a tent of gray clouds into the remembering sky. *That* doesn't sound like it's just a record. Who knew we had a girl poet here, a real poetess." I felt exposed, naked. Caught.

He held the journal above my head, waving it in the air, and I remembered when I was a girl, and two older girls from my preschool had taken a picture I had drawn, wouldn't let me have it, and then ripped it up. The bones remember the language of shame. My insides hurt. I reached for the journal. Jim held it away from me and laughed. I got that stone in the throat, pressure behind the eyes, cry-feeling yet knew I couldn't do it. Crying would have just made Jim's teasing worse.

"Can I please have my journal back, Jim?" My voice stuttered out, high-pitched like a balloon losing air.

He started flipping through my journal and said, "This picture looks like the ocean. Or weird stalagmites in a cave. What's up with that?"

"Well, I'm not much of an artist," I managed. "Now can I have my book back?"

Dionne passed us, her sandals flip-flopping on her way to filter water, and she called, "Hey guys."

"Hey right back at you," Jim said, his eyes following Dionne. He tossed my journal at me and laughed. "Here you go, poetess."

I caught my journal and felt glad I didn't go into full cry. I hated the words *scribbling* and *poetess*, and I hated Jim. I wanted to tell Erika we would have to ditch him as soon as possible.

"I'll come filter with you," I told Dionne. "It's easier with two people."

After pumping water, Dionne and I sat on the grass, watching Jesse, Jim, and Erika catch fish. Jim and Jesse shared one of Jesse's fishing poles and caught twenty-two fish between them. I thought about what Muir had told Theodore Roosevelt, that fishing and hunting are "boyish." I agreed. Something about a man holding a fishing pole made him look like a little boy. Like Huckleberry Finn. I tried to imagine Jesse's lanky body in overalls, and it made me laugh. Erika used Jesse's other pole but snared just one fish, and a small one at that. Even though I knew she wanted to keep it, she was a stickler for rules, and that fish wasn't a keeper, so back it went, hook through the eye and all.

"You guys want to try?" Jesse asked.

"They don't have fishing licenses," Erika said.

Jesse looked around and said, "And who's going to know?"

"I'm okay," I said. Muir writes, "Catching trout with a bit of bent wire is a rather trivial business, but fortunately people fish better than they know. In most cases it is the man who is caught." But I didn't want to catch fish—I had a hard enough time watching. The trout's scales glimmered a rainbowed iridescence in the water. Then the fish were pulled from the lake, and they became a dull brown. They flopped, gills gasping, eyes wide in what I imagined as terror. Suffocating. Erika said you have to stick your fingers down the throat to break their necks. Jesse and Jim made feeble attempts, and their plastic fish bag quivered with the movement of dying trout. I could hardly look. Erika said I was too sensitive.

"If you are going to eat them," Erika said, "you should be able to kill them." She was right, of course, but most people eat meat and never give a second thought to where it comes from. Most of us encounter meat after it has been cut up and tidied into plastic packaging. Many children who grow up in cities, like I did, haven't a clue about the connection between the animal and the Happy Meal, but I learned young on account of my mother trying to get me into kindergarten early because, like all mothers, mine was sure she had a child genius on her hands. To get in, I had to take an entrance exam to make sure I was ready. I missed two questions. A lady with big rose-colored glasses had asked, "Can you cross the street alone?" My mother answered this question for me with a definite no. In fact, I don't think I was allowed to cross the street alone until high school.

Then my examiner peered at me through her glasses and asked, "Where does meat come from?"

I answered, "The grocery store, of course." I thought I was pretty smart too.

"No, honey. Before that." The lady knew she had me.

"We get our meat at the grocery store," I insisted. Even as a four-year-old, I was stubborn. The lady proceeded to tell me the truth about meat. I don't know if she was a vegetarian working on a conversion, or she simply thought that a kindergartner ought to know the truth—that chickens and *even baby cows* are killed, and we eat their muscles. At this point she tugged on her bicep to make sure I understood.

I understood all right, so I was allowed to go to kindergarten early, and my mother had to disguise any meat she fed me for the next ten years. At fourteen I began eating fish again because I could rationalize it. The fish, I told myself, lived happy lives up until the very moment they were pulled from the water. My father had taken me clamming on Fire Island when I was a girl, and after a little digging, the clams went in the bucket. I was certainly smart enough to know fish and clams might react differently to being taken from water, but I hadn't really been forced to think about it until I sat on the bank of that lake watching them fish. So, in a way I too had been caught.

Though I was quite sure I didn't want to be any closer to the action than I already was, Dionne wanted to give fishing a try. Jesse showed her how to put the bait on, cast the line, and reel the fish in. Because Dionne didn't have a license, Erika shook her head in disdain for this blatant rule breaking. I tried to tell myself that if I allowed myself to eat fish, I had to deal with the realities of it. I turned back to my drawing of Whitney mirrored in Timberline Lake. The ripples from the fishing lines distorted the reflection.

"I got one. I got one. I got one," Dionne yelled.

"Reel it in, reel it in," Jesse and Jim shouted back. Dionne just kept screaming, so Jesse ran over and reeled it in for her. The fish, bigger than any of the others, struggled with iridescent energy, the bend from tail to nose, the silver shudder.

"Grab hold of it," Jesse told Dionne. She did and started squealing.

"Break its neck," called Erika. Dionne held the trout with both hands and looked into its eyes. I sat close enough that my suspicions about fish and terror were confirmed.

"We have enough fish," Dionne said and carefully pulled the hook out of its lip. She placed the fish back in the water and watched it swim away. "Besides, isn't it always the big one that gets away?"

I smiled at Dionne and said, "You've been caught." She smiled back.

Camping was prohibited at the lake, so Erika insisted that we pack up to find a place to spend the night. Jesse tied the still-quivering plastic bag to his pack. The afternoon turned quickly to dusk, so we knew we had to hurry. We passed the Crabtree ranger station, and the ranger, a gray-haired man with a ruddy face and a white moustache, asked for our fishing permits. Erika and Jesse showed him theirs.

"And you two are the only ones fishing?" the ranger asked.

"Yes sir," Jesse said. Erika's face turned splotchy red like a turnip.

"Okay, great. Have a good time. Where you headed?"

"Yosemite," Erika answered. "We're hiking the whole John Muir Trail."

"I mean tonight," the ranger said with a chuckle.

"Around here, somewhere," I offered.

After looking at our camping permits, the ranger said, "Well, there's some decent spots on the north side of Whitney Creek. Toward Crabtree Meadows. Just a little ways."

We followed the ranger's advice, making it a twelve-mile day, our first respectable hiking day in terms of mileage. While we set up camp, the sky faded from a dusky blue to a twilight purple. Erika got to work preparing the fish. Jim unpacked his bag and let all his food tumble onto a tarp he'd set on the ground—twenty freeze-dried dinners, beef jerky, a few cans of beans, and oatmeal. No wonder he had been so happy to catch fish. Compared to him, we were going gourmet with our macaroni and cheese, tortellini and pesto, burrito fixings, and tabbouleh.

Jim's plan was to hike the John Muir Trail solo, but so far there had been nothing solo about his trip. I sat down on a rock next to Erika and whispered, "How long do you think he'll hike with us?"

"I don't know. Why?" Erika fiddled with her camp stove.

"He's weird. I don't like him."

"You're just paranoid."

"No really. There's something about him."

"What?" Erika asked. Her stove lit with a poof.

"He took my journal."

"Did he give it back?"

"Well, yes. But he made fun of it."

"Whatever." Erika rolled her eyes.

I tried again. "He has beady eyes and walks sort of slumped over. He also says weird things."

"Like what?" Erika put one fish in the frying pan and pulled another out of the plastic bag.

"I don't know. Weird things." I couldn't think of anything specific, yet I knew he seemed strange. I made a mental note to remember the odd things he said so I could prove it to Erika.

"Weird things, but you can't say what? You're paranoid. I think he's nice." Erika cut the head off a trout.

"Not paranoid," I said, "intuitive."

"Same difference."

After we hung the bear rope and filtered water, we all sat around the camp stoves, eating fish. Erika had fried them up with cornmeal, oil, and lemon pepper, and Jim complimented her cooking. The fish tasted god-awful, and each one had about a thousand bones, but I didn't dare say anything because I hadn't done any of the work involved.

"Who's that?" I whispered. I heard something, or someone, rustling in the bushes. "Someone is over there, in the bushes."

"Scaredy-cat," Erika laughed. "You are just like a little kid."

"No, Listen," Jesse said. "I hear something too." We all pointed our headlamps toward the creek, and our lights reflected silverish red off four eyes—two bears, a mama and a cub. The mama stood up on her hind legs, her nose in the air. They had smelled our fish.

"What do we do?" Dionne whispered.

"Go away, bear. Get out of here," Erika yelled.

"Don't scare them," Jesse said. "I want a picture." I knew California black bears were usually harmless. I also knew that mama bears could get aggressive if they were with cubs, so I banged two pots together and shouted. Jim formed his hand into the shape of a gun and made the sounds "pshoot, pshoot." He then leaned back in his camp chair, laughing hysterically. I made a mental note of his behavior, hoping to later bring it to Erika's attention. Jesse grabbed his camera and started flashing away, but the bears had already wandered off.

"I've never seen a bear before. Except for at the zoo," Dionne said. Jim reenacted his gun noises again and laughed so hard he fell backward out of his camp chair. I looked at Erika, trying to catch her eye, but she kept busy, scraping the last bits of fish off her plate. She always ate slowly and deliberately, cleaning up every last crumb. She even sometimes licked the plate like a dog would. And it wasn't because we were camping. She ate that way all the time. I tried to imagine her out on a date, licking her plate by candlelight.

Jesse, Jim, and Erika decided to sleep outside because they didn't want to mess with pitching the tent in the dark. Dionne and I agreed that we didn't want to be anywhere near Jim so we would pitch my tent and sleep together.

"I ate too much," Dionne whispered right after we got into our sleeping bags.

"Too much fish? How could you eat too much fish? They were all bones."

"Too much," Dionne said with an unhappiness that bordered on despair. She wriggled out of her sleeping bag and started unzipping the tent.

I sat up and asked, "Where are you going?"

"To the bathroom."

"You just went."

"I have to go again." I wanted to stop her. I thought with a wild conviction, *Maybe this trip can cure her. Maybe I can help her.* I couldn't force her to stay in the tent. She was almost out the mesh door, and I said, "You better be really quiet, or you'll attract that mean mama bear."

"You think she's still out there?" Dionne asked.

"I'm sure she is."

Dionne got back in her sleeping bag and mumbled, "Fine." She knew I knew about her disorder, though we had never talked about it. "This is really hard for me," Dionne said after a few minutes.

"I know. It'll get easier." I thought that because I had tricked her into staying in the tent, because she hadn't gone out to vomit at that very moment, she was getting better. Like Geoff, I began to assume that hiking would fix it, that bulimia was no more than a little habit Dionne could kick if she just put her mind to it. If only that were true.

"You promise?" she asked me. "You promise it will get easier?"

I didn't know if it would or not, yet I knew enough to admit I couldn't make her those sorts of promises; the "I-don't-know" truth would have been too hard, too much, so I pretended I was already asleep.

Day 4

How Would You Die?

Crabtree Meadows (10,640) to the Unnamed Lakes (11,160)   10 MILES

We woke to an arching blue sky and began hiking early in the dewy
light. The trail spiraled up a sandy slope through foxtail pines. The
ancient trees grew twisted and warped, the upshot of years of storm.
Everything seemed different, easier with the sun out. "Here's the
Pacific Crest Trail," Erika said. "That's the next trip for me."

We traversed through a glacial moraine, a trail of rock left by
migrating fields of ice. The mountains of the Kings-Kern Divide
and the Sierra Crest drew a jagged line across the horizon. Erika
stopped ahead, talking to two hikers, both men, probably in their
late twenties. They told us their "trail names," Doc and Stony. Ice
axes and crampons hung from their enormous packs. Their clothes
were torn and dirty; shaggy beards covered their faces; weary eyes
reflected miles of trail. They smelled of layered, spicy sweat. They
were on their way to Canada from Mexico, a 2,650-mile odyssey. This
was the first year the Pacific Crest Trail, or PCT, had been officially
completed, though people had been thru-hiking it since 1970. Av-
eraging twenty-five miles a day, they hoped to make it to Canada
before winter, but it was already August, and they hadn't even hit

the halfway mark. Their trip made our trek look like an afternoon stroll. We wished them luck.

"You still want to do the PCT?" I asked Erika.

"Yeah. Why not?"

"Didn't you see how terrible those guys looked?" I took long strides to keep up with her.

"But think about how happy they'll be when they've finished."

"A month out here is long enough for me." Only day 4, and already I was thinking about the hot showers over a hundred miles away at Lake Edison. "What do you think about trail names?" I asked. "Shouldn't we have them too?"

"I think you have to do something longer than the JMT," Erika said, "to deserve a trail name."

"I like Zsa Zsa."

"Do the PCT then," Erika said. "Besides, someone else has to give you your trail name. You can't name yourself."

"Why not?"

"I don't know. You just can't."

The trail followed boulders up to Bighorn Plateau. The lupine bloomed purple across the large, open meadow. I wanted to take off my shoes and run through the grass, Zsa Zsa in the meadow, but I knew we had a schedule to keep. I also knew about the fragility of meadow ecosystems, and trampling across flowers and grass was a bad idea, not to mention strictly prohibited by Erika. No cutting trail, she had said. Still, I couldn't help picturing myself, without Big Heiny of course, running barefoot. I wanted to frolic in the morning sun like a mountain nymph, perhaps sing to a shepherd. Instead, we all stood there, having our own secret fantasies, I suppose. I caught Jim staring at me, but I wouldn't look at him. Still, I could feel his eyes on me.

We took turns being in pictures and then ate trail mix, except Erika, who had her own private stash of beef jerky. She shared it with Jim, and they both tore into the dried meat like animals enjoying a kill.

We carried on and reached Tyndall Creek, which looked more like a river, and the trail ended at the edge of the gushing white water.

"Maybe there's a log or something farther down," I said.

"Thomas says we ford the river here," Erika said. Even though our trail guide was out-of-date, we had been using the 1978 first edition of Winnett's *Guide to the John Muir Trail* to plot out every step. We had started to call the author by his first name. He was Winnett for the first few days then Thomas.

"Here?" The creek looked more like a river to me.

"He calls the ford formidable," Erika read from the guidebook.

"That's a lot of alliteration," Dionne said. She had been an English major. "But looking at this river, *formidable* is the right word."

"What's *that* mean?" Jim asked.

"It means that the water is fast and deep," Dionne said.

"So *forma-dibble* means scary?" Jim laughed his wild laugh. I took note of this strange behavior so I could add it to the list of examples for Erika, but I could already hear her saying, "He laughed? What's so weird about that?"

"Formidable." I couldn't help myself.

"Must be here then," Jesse said and sat down to take off his boots. We all did the same, except Jim, who already hiked in his Teva sandals. We unbuckled our packs, decreasing our chances of being pinned facedown in the water should we lose our footing. As I crossed, I felt unsteady. The fast-moving water sloshed against my thighs, numbing my legs. The water came directly from the melting snow on the peaks above. I held my arms out, trying to steady myself over the tumbling rocks on the bottom. The icy water reached my shorts, swallowed my hips. As the current shoved me sideways, I pushed each sandaled foot forward. I passed through the deepest section, and the water started to shallow. I was thankful I made it and that for a few minutes I couldn't feel the ache in my knee. My knee had been swollen and stiff when I woke up, and as I hiked, it had worsened.

When Jim reached the other side, he said, "Forma-dibble," and laughed his vaudeville laugh. This time Erika laughed too. I couldn't figure out if she was laughing with him or at him. I hoped the latter. I looked at Dionne. She was busy lacing her boots.

We began the ascent to a junction with the Lake South America Trail. Within no time Dionne and I fell behind. "My knee hurts," I told her.

"Mine does too."

"It must have been that hike down Whitney?"

"You mean the run down Whitney?" Dionne and I limped along. Erika came back twice to tell us we were hiking too slowly. I tried not to think about my knee, but I was afraid of making it worse, ruining future hiking and skiing endeavors because Erika had us on a schedule. Dionne and I took four aspirin each and managed to pick up the pace.

"You go ahead," Dionne said. I felt better than she did, so I hiked ahead.

When I caught up to Jim, he said, "I'm tired today too," and he let me pass him; then he hiked right behind me, breathing heavily like Darth Vader. He asked, "You want to play twenty questions?"

"Like where you think of something, and I guess what it is?"

"No, not that game. You ask me twenty questions. Then I ask you," he said. "It's like a get-to-know-you game."

"Do they have to be yes or no?"

"It doesn't matter."

"Okay." I asked my twenty questions and found out Jim was originally from Michigan, had finished some community college, had a brother named Rich, whom he didn't like, and in fact he didn't really get along with the rest of his family; he had served in the army as a machine gunner, and he wanted to be a police officer. He also didn't have a girlfriend, which was a question that I wished I hadn't asked the second it came out of my mouth. He also said he had a pet snake named Viper, and he liked video games, hockey, and movies. He didn't like drawing, reading, or cooking. He also liked Snoop Doggy Dogg but not Sheryl Crow or Madonna, whom he called a whore.

"My turn," he said.

"Okay. Shoot."

"How old are you?"

"Twenty-two. Twenty-three in October."

"Do you have any pets?"

"One dog."

"What kind?"

"A husky-wolf mix named Dylan."

"That was my next question."

"What was?"

"His name."

"Okay then. Count that as two." The game took my mind off the ache in my knee.

"He's a bad dog, though," I told Jim. "I'm on a first-name basis with all the dog catchers in town. Once Dylan escaped by gnawing down the aspen tree he had been chained to, ran across the highway, caused a six-car pileup, and killed twelve blue-winged show ducks. I had to pay for the show ducks, along with a dog-at-large fine."

"Why do you keep him?"

"He's my friend. When I'm sad, we sit on the couch together and share a pizza, and he cheers me up. He also makes me feel safe. It's hard to explain."

"I guess. If I had a dog like that, I'd shoot him. Did you go to college?" Jim asked, continuing our game.

"Uh-huh. This is our graduation trip." I tried to ignore the bit about shooting my dog, especially because Erika, Jesse, and Dionne were nowhere in sight.

"What was your major?"

"Biology."

"Why?"

"Because it seems most real to me. I like literature, and my father's a writer, but studying biology felt more real to me. That's the only way I can explain it. What could be more real than the study of life?" Jim didn't answer me.

In truth I didn't make a very competent scientist. I spent time reading books that were not part of my curriculum, everything from Muir and Thoreau (which I could justify because they seemed related, at least tangentially, to science) to Sylvia Plath and Edgar Allan Poe, so I didn't have time to read the textbooks for my classes. The only required science book I enjoyed was Darwin's *On the Origin of Species* because it read more like a story. I also broke the college record for the largest lab bill in chemistry because I had shattered so many beakers and test tubes. The only reason I passed is that I promised the professor I would never take another chemistry class again, thereby protecting their equipment from my clumsy ways. I enjoyed learning about plants and animals, but I was too sensitive for the dissections, especially the ones involving live animals. I claimed it was against my religion and was allowed to write a paper to get out of pithing both frogs and turtles, which is the scientific term for scrambling the brain while the animal is still alive.

My freshman year we had to do an experiment to test whether a hairless mouse would respirate faster in extreme cold than a furry mouse. You don't need an experiment to figure that one out. After watching both mice shiver in the glass cage, I finished my lab report and snuck the mice out in my backpack. I named them Harry and Sunshine, and they lived out the rest of their lives in the dorms with me in an old popcorn tin. I am not sure their lives were much improved. Sunshine seemed to be having a good time, humping poor Harry every chance he got. Harry just hid in the corner, shivering.

"I thought you must've been studying to be a writer or something because all you do when we get to camp is read books or scribble in that little diary."

"It isn't a diary. It's a journal."

"Same difference."

"No, it isn't. And you don't have to study to be a writer. You just have to read and write. A writer writes." I sounded defensive, which surprised me. More than anything, I did want to be a writer, and I had no clue how to go about it. My father wrote plays and then later daytime soaps, but all of this somehow seemed unrelated to my own obsession with stories and poems. And perhaps I pursued biology as a way to detach from him. The possibility of majoring in English as an undergraduate never even crossed my mind, and I had not yet heard that you could get a master's degree in reading books and writing poems and stories.

"Yeah, college is bullshit."

"That's not what I meant."

"Whatever. So, why are you here?"

"What do you mean 'here'?" I asked.

"Here. On the trail. Why are you hiking the JMT?"

"I love to hike," I said. The truth seemed too complicated. And before the trip I had believed I loved to hike, though I wasn't so sure anymore. Everything seemed mixed-up.

After a few minutes Jim asked, "Do you have a boyfriend?"

I should have known this was coming because I started it by asking him. *Stupid, stupid girl*, I thought. "No," I said, though I thought maybe I should have said yes, but then Erika would inevitably reveal the truth, and Jim would know I had lied to him.

"Are you looking?"

"No." Most of my teenage and young adult life had been devoted to that very pursuit, but at that moment I was not looking for a boyfriend.

We hiked on in silence for a while longer, and I wondered if Jim had gotten tired of playing. We followed a trail of small stones and crossed into a field of bigger rocks and boulders. I enjoyed the sound of my boots on the pebbles, the wind washing across the desolate landscape. After a few minutes he asked, "Have you ever thought about killing someone?"

"What? No. What do you mean?" Maybe it had been obvious that Erika was driving me crazy. By *killing* he surely meant in the figurative sense?

"How many questions is that? I have fourteen."

Erika and Jesse hiked way ahead, and Dionne, still way behind. I squinted and still couldn't see any of them.

"No, this is eleven. Have you ever thought someone wanted to kill you?"

"No."

"Never?"

"That counts as another question."

"Then answer it."

"Maybe once," I said, though in truth this was the second time. I didn't elaborate because he had eight more questions. Plus, I had seen enough movies to know that if I acted scared, I'd be doomed for sure. Everyone who has seen a horror film knows that killers love to see their victims grovel.

"When?"

"Once in Colorado. A man who picked me up hitchhiking. He wouldn't let me out of his car."

"What happened?"

"Well, I was trying to get a ride from our trailer park in Edwards up to Beaver Creek. I didn't think I would find a ride to the resort because it was the middle of the day, and I had all my ski stuff with me," I said.

"Go on." Jim continued to breathe like Darth Vader.

"So, this old jalopy pulled up, and I was so happy for a ride, I didn't even look at the driver. Usually, I look at the driver to make sure he isn't a, you know, weirdo. I'm a pretty good judge of character."

"And?"

"Well, I put my skis inside the car because he didn't have a ski rack, and I got in. When we drove onto the highway, I finally looked at him, and I realized what a terrible mistake I had made."

"Why?"

"Well, I had gotten in the car with this strange guy from the trailer park. Everyone called him Psycho-Mike. He worked as a cashier at a cafeteria in Vail with my roommate Andrea, and he had this big crush on her, but she didn't give him the time of day. So, one day he gave her a love letter written on a roll of toilet paper. Can you believe that? Anyway, Andrea threw it away right in front of him without even unrolling it to read it. So Psycho-Mike went crazy. He knocked a bunch of sodas off the shelves and then grabbed a bottle of wine and guzzled it. They had to lock Andrea in the broom closet to protect her. Then he yelled, 'I'm a man, I'm a man,' and pounded on his chest like this." I pounded my own fists across my chest to show Jim.

"Like King Kong?" Jim asked.

"Yeah, or Tarzan."

"But what about the hitchhiking?"

"Oh. So anyway, I realized it was him, and I started to ask him questions about where he was going, and at first he said work."

"So?"

"So? He had been fired for the Tarzan episode. Everyone knew he no longer had a job."

"Then what?"

"He said he was going skiing, but he had already told me he didn't ski. Then he turned from the road, looked right at me, like this." I whipped around and looked at Jim, screwing my face up in as fierce a grin as I could. "And he told me he knew I was Andrea's roommate, and I knew I was in trouble. I told him I didn't care for Andrea, that we weren't even friends, so he would think I was on his side."

"And?"

"And he told me he knew we were friends. He even knew we shared a bedroom, which gave me the creeps. I mean, was he a Peeping Tom?"

"I don't know."

"Well, of course he was."

"So what happened? In the car?"

"He drove right past my stop. I started telling him what a good driver he was, you know, so he would like me and forgive me for lying, but he just ignored me. I thought I was going to have to leave my skis behind and leap out of the car into a snowbank."

"Did you?"

"No. We came to an intersection, and I rolled down my window and started screaming. I told him about a million times he was so very nice to pick me up but that he had inadvertently missed my stop. People were crossing at the intersection and in cars next to us who could hear me screaming my head off, so he pulled over right away."

"Do you still hitchhike?"

"Sometimes, but don't tell my mother." I laughed and turned around to look at Jim, but he didn't laugh this time. Here I was, telling a crazy person my method of dealing with crazy people. I was starting to feel like the craziest of them all.

I didn't realize how haphazardly I had regarded my own safety until years later. Once I took a ride back from the bars in Vail by a man who spent the twenty-minute car ride to my trailer in Edwards scolding me for getting into his car. He kept saying, "What if I were a rapist?" I told him I didn't think a rapist would ask that. He was middle-aged, and I thought he probably worried about what his own daughter might be up to. For someone who liked to read Emerson and Thoreau, I often failed to think.

I turned back and continued up the trail. "How many questions is that?" I asked.

"I have two more. If you had to pick the way you wanted to die, what would it be?"

"What? What do you mean?"

He repeated the question without a hint of irony.

"I'm thinking." I knew he couldn't get away with killing me that very moment, yet what was he scheming? I had no real experience with the psychology of killers, but I reasoned that if I accused him of saying strange things, he would definitely want to kill me. I couldn't say I wanted to die in my sleep, which was probably the truth, because he would be camping with us again. I could have told him I would have liked to be thrown from a skyscraper, but couldn't he substitute the edge of a mountain? He could arrange almost anything—fire, poison, death by water. I could say that I didn't want to die, but then he might get mad at me for not following the rules of his game.

Finally, I answered him: "Run over by a train. I would definitely choose a train."

"A train?"

"Sure. It would be a fast way to go, don't you think?"

I felt pleased with my answer, so for the moment I forgot about how very odd his questions seemed until he asked, "What about if someone killed you? Then how would you want to die?"

"That's your last question, right?" The path clung to the side of a sloping hill. The pebbles on the trail had worn to sand and crunched beneath my booths. A few mountain hemlocks grew in clumps between the rocks. Twisted foxtail pines reached for the canvas of sky. I squinted up and down the trail but couldn't make out the hiking forms of Dionne, Erika, or Jesse. A chipmunk crossed the trail in front of me, finally ducking beneath a rock.

"Yes. Unless you want to play again."

"I would want someone to run me over with a big car in a big city. A Lincoln Town Car. In New York City. Or London. Or Prague."

"A Lincoln what? But what if you weren't in New York? What then?"

"That was your last question."

"Do you want to play again?"

"No, I don't think so." I decided to write down our conversation in my journal, so I could show Erika, even though I knew she still might tell me I was being paranoid. After all, when I had told her about Psycho-Mike, she said, "Well maybe he has a hearing problem. Maybe that's why he didn't stop until you started screaming." It was true that at times I let my imagination swell; however, when I told Andrea about getting into the car with Psycho-Mike, she had said, "You dummy. I can't believe you got into a car with that whack job. He could have killed you."

I turned around and finally saw Dionne struggling up the trail in the distance. I told Jim I wanted to wait for her.

"Okay." Jim continued to move up the trail with his slumped walk, his large army pack clunking from side to side.

Dionne's face was tear streaked. "My knee," she said.

"I forgot all about mine. That Jim is crazy," I whispered, even though Jim had already disappeared up the trail.

"Why, what did he say?"

"He asked me how I would want someone to kill me."

"What?"

"I told you. He's crazy."

"Let's stick together from now on," Dionne said, and I agreed. My father had always said there was safety in numbers, that I should use the buddy system. In the past I had often ignored his advice.

The trail cut past stunted whitebark pine and passed a couple of rockbound lakes. It seemed that we had walked back up to the top of the world. Jim, Jesse, and Erika were setting up camp by a lone, lightning-topped tree.

I took out my journal to record my conversation with Jim. I figured that if nothing else, someone would find my journal and know who had murdered me.

"Let's see where the Murderer sets up his tent and camp far away," I whispered to Dionne. She nodded.

Jim dropped his stuff by a snag, and Erika plopped her pack down right next to his. They told us they wanted to sleep under the stars.

"Why don't you sleep over here by us?" I asked Jesse.

"Afraid of the bears?" Erika asked.

"Yes," Dionne and I both answered. Jesse laughed at us but brought his sleeping bag over anyway. He could laugh all he wanted. Every woman who has ever been out camping alone knows that bears are nothing to fear compared to predatory men. Whether real or imagined, that fear is always there in the wilderness, riding on our backs like a heavy pack. I have known women, myself included, who ignore that fear or eliminate it by bringing a big dog with them; still, the fear is something to get past, an obstacle that is a nonissue for most men. Women don't enter the wilderness in the same way men do; we constantly return to our physical bodies and the ways in which they could be threatened, not by bears or bugs but by men. Our bodies become a filter between us and the landscape, preventing us from enjoying both.

"Make yourselves useful," Erika said and tossed us the water filter. Dionne and I gathered up the water bottles and headed down to the lake. Dusk's web began to stich across the landscape, and the first stars glittered like mirrors in the sapphire sky. "Maybe we'll see Cassiopeia," I told her.

"Who?"

"The constellation, the W. Cassiopeia, that wild, wacky woman—that's how I remember."

"I like that. I'll look for her tonight—the wild, wacky woman," Dionne said. "Cassiopeia would be an awesome trail name."

When we reached the small lake, we found hundreds of frogs by the water's edge. We set down the filter to chase frogs. We caught them, giggling as they jumped off the palms of our hands and plopped into the water. I didn't know that these were the endangered yellow-legged mountain frogs. I did know we should leave the local wildlife alone, yet chasing and catching them made me feel like a girl again. I reasoned that perhaps these happy frogs enjoyed our game as much as we did. I could justify almost anything.

"What's taking so long?" Erika called. I was sure she would scold us. To my surprise she joined us. She probably didn't know the frogs were endangered either, or else she would have told us to leave them alone. Yet the reason for their tenuous status was because of the nonnative trout—the very fish Erika wanted so badly to catch and eat. But at the time I was having too much fun to consider the complexities of ecology. The tiny frogs hopped into the lake, plop, plop, plop, and created small, rippling waves. We laughed and laughed and finally caught our breath.

We filtered our water and turned back toward the campsite. Three mule deer grazed on the hillside, and Forester Pass hovered above us, reflecting the late-afternoon sun. A giddiness, a lightness of being, filled my body, giving me goose bumps, those small buttons of anticipation, of mystery and joy. I looked up to the pass, tried to imagine the me of tomorrow sitting up there, on the crest, looking down on this nameless lake, the frogs and deer, listening for the echo of three women laughing.

Fear not, therefore, to try the mountain-passes.
They will kill care, save you from deadly apathy,
set you free, and call forth every faculty into
vigorous, enthusiastic action. Even the sick
should try these so-called dangerous passes,
because for every unfortunate they kill, they
cure a thousand. / JOHN MUIR

Day 5

The Commander Cuddles Up to the Murderer?

Forester Divide (13,200)   9 MILES

We huddled together, eating breakfast in the early-morning light. Frost clung to our sleeping bags. Ice chunks floated in our water bottles.

"It was colder last night than I thought it would be," Dionne said.

"No kidding," I said.

"I wasn't cold at all," Erika said. She had a lopsided grin, and so did Jim. She wore huge gold hoop earrings, a big floppy hemp hat with a sunflower stitched to the front, and bright blue leggings. This outfit was her attempt to look cute. Instead, it made her look like a rag doll from the Island of Misfit Toys. I couldn't prove it, but I felt at the time certain she had been cuddling up to the Murderer.

We packed up and started up the pass. My knee felt stiff, and it was all I could think about, which may have been an improvement, considering the things I had been thinking about: how Jim was going to kill me. Or worse, rape me. Or how Erika was being mean to me. Or how I hoped Dionne would be cured before Erika found anything out, thereby saving me from getting caught in a lie. Thinking about my knee was a definite improvement, though at the time I would have taken back my various neuroses in trade for the physical pain.

Dionne and I took four aspirin each and plodded up the rocky face. My rain gear flapped on the outside of my pack, along with the usual sundries, because Thomas said to be prepared to wear wind garments. He also said the switchbacks on the other side could be covered with snow. The aspirin began to take effect, so I could alternate between worrying about the pain in my knee with my anxiety concerning the snow on the north side of Forester Pass. The thing about hiking is that you can't avoid the present tense for very long, a gift that escaped me at the time.

I looked up to the top of the divide, a wrinkled sheet of granite against the cloudless sky. Erika waved to me from the edge of the trail, and I waved back. Just a few more switchbacks. I tried to imagine Muir and other early explorers climbing this rugged mountain without a dynamite-blasted trail—impossible to fathom. Something about hiking without a trail has been alluring to every man I have ever known. No trail means getting scratched up, however, and for me, getting lost. Once, Jack and I set off into the canyons outside of Moab, evidently didn't pay enough attention, and were lost for eighteen hours. The weather turned from hot and dry to cold and rainy in a matter of hours, and I wandered around through the rainy night in a bikini top and shorts. By the time we found the truck, even Dylan, the tireless wonderdog, was exhausted. I started to realize that maybe I had been the one at fault for following men wherever it is they wanted to go, without so much as a second thought. This always drove my father crazy. If he had been drinking, which was most of the time, he would shout at me: "You are always driving who knows where, all over the goddamned place to see a boy." And my mother, who had the memory of an elephant, would add in her British accent, "Yes, you drove all the way up into those mountains that Thanksgiving to see that TJ." Whenever she talked about one of my boyfriends, she used the word *that*: that Roger, that Jack, that TJ. Then she asked, even though she knew the answer to the question, "Didn't he break up with you right after that trip?"

"Not right after," I answered. "I drove up to Big Bear to see him in November, and we didn't break up until March. That's not right after."

"Close enough," she'd said.

I reached the crest of Forester Pass, and I breathed a sigh of relief. Until I saw the snow on the other side.

The snow gleamed in the sunlight, and pine forests cut green swaths through Kings Canyon National Park to the north, and behind us the immense, snow-scattered Whitney now seemed impossibly far away. A man, who came to the top from the north side, started talking on his giant cell phone: "Hey, honey. I'm on top of Forester, 13,200 feet. Can you hear me? Are you there? Yes, Forester. Yes, 13,200 feet. Can you believe I can call you from here? Amazing." In 1993 cell phones were large, cumbersome things, weighing more than a pound and costing nearly a thousand dollars. We called them "car phones" because anyone who could afford one usually kept it in the car. And cell coverage was spotty at best, just on the tops of ridges and mountains, the places that should be most technology free, places with views that deserve one's full attention. We thought having a phone on the trail was cheating. So, when the man chatted up his wife, complete with shouting, "Hello? Are you there? I think I lost you. Hello?" every few seconds, we felt annoyed. Cheater, we thought.

After Car Phone Man finished his conversation with his wife, he asked us to take a picture of him. Then we all posed in front of the Forester Pass sign, and he took one of us. We made quite the picture—Erika with gold hoop earrings and floppy hat, Dionne wearing tighty-whiteys and a sports bra with the straps pulled low on her shoulders so she wouldn't get suntan lines, Jesse in his tie-dye, a shirtless Jim with his cutoff army pants, and me wearing flowery boxers and an ACE bandage wound around my knee. My raingear flapped behind me from the straps of Big Heiny.

We took off our packs and ate trail mix, tortillas, and cheese. Jim helped himself to our food, and Erika didn't say a word. It was only day 5, and I began to worry we would run out. We had sent ourselves food at Lake Edison, yet that was still over a hundred miles away, or ten more days, according to the plan, which we hadn't exactly been following. I waffled between wanting to mention this to Erika and not wanting to say anything because it could mean that my food would be further rationed. I wasn't sure if Erika thought that Jim would begin to share his freeze-dried gourmet selections with us, but as it was, she rationed Dionne and my food, which I think Dionne probably appreciated but I didn't, and she ignored how much Jim and Jesse had eaten from our supplies.

Two twenty-something women hiked up the trail. They asked us where we were going, where we had been—the usual trail talk.

"We're hiking to Yosemite," Erika said.

"That's where we came from," one of the women replied. They were hiking the John Muir Trail too. "Watch for bears," the other said. "We had our food stolen."

"We're counterbalancing," Erika said. "We've already seen bears."

"So were we. The bears in Yosemite are smart. They send their cubs up and have them leap onto the food bags. We had to hike out to get more food."

"Thanks for the information. We'll be careful." I could tell Erika thought that these women didn't know how to hang their food properly. I felt jealous of them because they weren't hiking with men, the way we were originally supposed to be hiking. That, and they were almost finished. Car Phone Man seemed impressed too.

"See you" and "Bye," the women said and started down the trail. Most people hiked from Yosemite to Whitney or north to south, getting in shape for the difficult passes in the south, but Erika decided it would be better to get the hard part over with first. I would be glad later, yet right then I wasn't so sure about our plan. I wanted to follow those two women back to Whitney Portal. They were free of the Jims and Jesses of the trail, making them smarter than us.

I watched the women hike south and then looked out over the sweeping views to the north. Snow patches held on to the rocks, melting into small alpine lakes. The trail switchbacked down past the lakes and disappeared into the forest. Pines and fir carpeted the valley below. I expected to feel something, but I didn't feel anything aside from the ache in my knee and anxiety in my chest. Muir says mountain passes will cure what ails you, set you free, but I didn't feel cured or free; instead, I thought about the hike down the snowy northern side, Big Heiny, dry food, our dreadful hiking partners, and the next three weeks out there. My cares didn't drop off like autumn leaves. They gathered like piles of dead ones. I had hoped that the mountains would give me joy, yet at the moment I couldn't see how they would.

I set Big Heiny on a rock and leaned into her to strap her on. We started down, and my knee ached with every step, and the uneven snow made it worse. The winter of 1992–93 came to be known as a "drought-busting" year. At 150 percent of average snowpack and with one of the wettest springs on record, the High Sierra stayed white with snow all summer. I had not thought much about that when we were skiing in Mammoth in July, so I never considered bringing an ice axe or crampons. I didn't even have hiking poles. With every step I became sure I would fall and have no way to self-arrest. I imagined myself crumpled into a pile on the rocks below.

I tried not to cry but couldn't help myself. What a baby I am, I thought, which only made the tears fall faster. I wondered if I really would make it—this time not in the rhetorical sense. This time I really believed the answer could very well be a resounding no. I stopped for a minute in an attempt to pull myself together. I didn't have the proper equipment for snow. I had no choice but to hike, so I navigated the snowy landscape as best I could.

"You okay?" Dionne said.

"No, but what am I going to do?" I asked.

"Every step is one step closer."

Jim and Erika had already reached the bottom of the steep section. Jesse said he felt like he was getting a cold, so he waited for Dionne and me. I was glad that I had stopped crying. I didn't want him to think of me as the stereotypical weak girl, even though that's how I felt.

Jesse told us Erika was driving him crazy. "Why does she think she's the boss?" he asked.

"We call her 'the Commander,'" Dionne told him.

We finally arrived at Bubbs Creek, supposedly a popular camping spot, but we were the only ones there. Erika and Jim had already set up her tent. Jesse and I went to filter water. Jesse said, "If Erika tells me how much to eat one more time, I'm going to go off."

"I know. Erika's bossy, but we won't get to our next food drop until day 15 or 16, and it isn't looking like we're going to make it, especially if we keep feeding Jim." As the words fell out of my mouth, I couldn't believe I was siding with Erika. Dionne, Erika, and I had done all the shopping, and we figured Jesse would eat the same amount as us, maybe a little more. We figured wrong. He ate double and had not yet paid us for his portion. He had it good compared to Dionne and me, but I didn't figure it would help to tell him that. And somehow the very virtue of his being male entitled him to more food. It wasn't fair, yet I didn't have the strength to stand up to him. Instead I asked, "Don't you think Jim shouldn't be eating our food?"

"He totally shouldn't. I haven't seen him eat one of those bags of freeze-dried crap yet."

I was glad he agreed with me, at least about that.

"I thought it would be fun to hang out, go fishing. It's totally not what I expected."

We finished with the water, and Erika and Jim were already busy making dinner—macaroni and cheese with hamburger helper, one of our more gourmet dishes. "What are you having for dinner, Jim?" I asked, and not in the way you ask when you are at a restaurant together, making chitchat. My question was pointed, an arrow headed right for his stomach.

"He's eating with us. We have enough," Erika said. Jim got up and walked over to his pack in his slumped-over way.

"Erika, I'm starving. We hiked nearly ten miles today. We don't have enough," I whispered. I turned to Jesse and asked, "Jesse, what do you think?"

"Whatever," Jesse said. Jim walked back over, and I didn't want to say anything in front of him. Erika dished out our rations. She looked at me like she was about to say something but then didn't.

I walked over to Jesse and said, "Why didn't you say anything about the food?"

"It's my birthday."

"What?"

"My birthday. It's today, and this isn't very much fun." He sounded like a little boy who had gotten a vanilla birthday cake when he wanted chocolate.

"Okay" is all I could manage. I took my dinner down to the lake. I couldn't believe Jesse didn't say anything to agree with me. Then I felt badly because of his birthday. Mostly, I was sorry for myself because I wasn't having much fun either. After a while Dionne came over and hugged me.

"It's just harder than I thought," I told her. She sat down next to me, and we looked out over the lake. The last light of day reflected off the Kearsarge Pinnacles.

"You okay, sweetie?" Dionne asked.

"Yeah. Thanks. We have another big day tomorrow—fifteen miles and Glen Pass. Then four more days of passes over eleven thousand feet. I'm not sure I'll make it." I cried again, which embarrassed me, made me cry more. I couldn't imagine John Muir sitting by this lake crying in his macaroni. I wanted to be more stoic, like Muir or even like Erika, yet that didn't feel right either. I wanted access to my feelings without them flowing over me like a turbulent creek, drowning everything else.

"None of it can be worse than today," Dionne said.

"How long do you think the Murderer is staying with us?"

"Maybe we can ditch him. And the Commander." We both laughed. I wondered what their trail names were for us. Erika had already called me "the Scaredy-Cat" and "the Worrywart," and she referred to Dionne and me as "the Turtles" because we were so slow.

I suspected they had other trail names for us as well, and they surely weren't the ones we had picked out for ourselves.

Dionne and I went back to join the others. Erika and Jim started singing "Happy Birthday" to Jesse, and Dionne and I joined in.

"Look what I brought?" Erika asked, and a ziplock baggie full of chocolate chip cookies appeared. Apparently, Erika hadn't forgotten Jesse was having a birthday on the trail, another example of Erika's strength and self-discipline. If I had cookies hiding in Big Heiny, I can tell you they would not have made it to day 5, birthday or no birthday.

"Here's to Jesse," Jim said. We all got a cookie, and eating it somehow made me feel worse than before.

Another glorious Sierra day in which one seems
to be dissolved and absorbed and sent pulsing
onward we know not where. / JOHN MUIR

Day 6

Symbiosis

Glen Pass (11,978) to Woods Creek (8,492)   15 MILES

The truth was that whenever something bad happened to me, something that would make others feel sorry for me, part of me, no
matter how bad the bad thing was, liked getting the attention. Not
pretty but true. Yet having an injured knee made me feel bad, and
even though it was swollen, no one could see how awful, how painful, it really was, so it was a bad thing that didn't even have the
attention-getting upside.

According to Thomas, our trail would climb to fiercely attack the
rock wall, but I had no energy for the military metaphors. My knee
hurt, and exhaustion gnawed at my bones. We passed an unnamed
lake just as lovely as the ones with names, and I wondered what it
took to name a lake. Maybe you had to die there, which at the moment I felt like doing. Unnamed lake could become Suzanne Lake or,
better yet, Zsa Zsa Lake. But enough of the complaining; it wasn't
like I hadn't chosen to be there. Here I was, in the developed world,
creating problems for myself because my life, in reality, was too easy.
Thousands of years ago our ancestors had to survive by roaming
around in the wild, looking for food. Yet that was before the idea
of the wilderness existed without a fabricated delineation between

humans and the rest of the natural world. Now we've demarcated "the wild," as a place we "go out into," and we call it recreation. Thoreau says, "In wildness is the preservation of the world," but the line is often misquoted as "In wilderness is the preservation of the world," which isn't what he meant at all. Wildness can exist both outside and inside of us, whereas the very definition of wilderness seems to be the absence of humans, further separating us from our wild places and our very own wild natures.

We reached a meadow, blooming with a prism of colorful wildflowers. A creek looped through the emerald green grass, and the yellow and purple flowers buzzed with bees. Even in my misery I couldn't help noticing the beauty. The others had noticed too and had stopped there for lunch.

"Where are we?" I asked.

"Vidette Meadow," Erika said.

"There are so many flowers," Dionne said. Because of the extra weight, I had debated about whether or not I should bring along my wildflower guide, but as it turned out, the book proved to be worth the extra weight. Identifying the wildflowers gave me something to do aside from feeling sorry for myself. I pointed out the purple monkshood, yellow arrowleaf senecio, white corn lily, and I realized how important it was to me to be able to call each thing by its right name.

Even though he had been acting like a big baby, I still felt badly about forgetting Jesse's birthday, so I picked him a small bouquet of wildflowers. I walked over to him, handed him the flowers, and began singing "Happy Birthday." Before I had gotten through the first verse, Erika stomped over, looking at me in horror, and I got the "leave only footsteps, take only pictures" lecture. Plus, Jesse said, "Oh, thanks," and looked at the wildflowers like they were a bunch of dead weeds, which really they were. They certainly weren't chocolate chip cookies.

Then the mosquitoes descended upon us, followed by the black flies. The sparkling meadow began to feel like an anti-pastoral nightmare. We quickly packed up our stuff and started hiking again. Jesse walked alongside me and said, "That was nice. Really. Thanks."

"Sure," I said. "Happy birthday. Sorry this isn't what you expected." I knew that I had helped form the image of fun that night in the bar. When I told him about the trip, I hadn't mentioned the food rations or the day-by-day plan, and I certainly hadn't told him about the group dynamic. Rather, I made us out to be a trio of carefree gals, traipsing out into nature for some hippie-dippie fun. In truth that was the pre-trip picture I had held in my own head, proving how easily I could ignore reality.

We passed a turn off to Charlotte Lake, and I wished that was our destination. I remembered a college trip to Charlotte Lake. I had done some backpacking before, but my trips had always featured a three-day base camp, where I'd relax, read books, and work on a suntan—the type of trip Jesse had imagined when he signed up to hike the JMT with us.

Erika had stopped for some beef jerky and water, so I caught up to her and asked, "Where's the pass? All I see is that granite wall."

"Yep. That's it." She smiled, her mouth full of jerky. Another challenge. Dionne may have been wrong when she had said that nothing could be as difficult as yesterday. Steep switchback cut into the naked rock like a zigzag of scars on a bald man's head.

"According to the map," Erika said, "we go straight up this for a while, then there's a few switchbacks, an unnamed lake, another few switchbacks, and we're there."

"That's it, huh?"

"Yep." She smiled, pulled her pack on, and started walking again. I waited for Dionne because my knee throbbed. Less than a week, and we had already depleted our aspirin supply. Muir says the body vanishes and the soul is freed in the wilderness. My body ached all over, and my knee felt like a knife was jabbing into it with each step. After a few minutes Dionne caught up. She was limping too.

"It hurts," she said, "but I know it will be worse on the way down."

"Let's concentrate on getting up first." She nodded, and we started hiking again. "Do you want to play 'Fuck, Marry, or Kill'?" I asked.

"What's that?"

"It's where I give you three names, and you decide who you would fuck, who you would marry, and who you would kill." Dionne agreed, so we played the game, both killing Jim or Jesse whenever the opportunity arose. The game took our minds off the hike, so I was about to introduce the game "Would You Rather?" when we saw Erika waiting for us up ahead. Behind us the water licked the granite like a tongue over the river's teeth. We turned back to the trail ahead of us, faced the rock wall.

"Where's the pass?" Dionne asked. "I still can't see it."

"There." Erika pointed with her long finger. Dionne and I both squinted, trying to find the trail, but could only make out a granite fortress.

"That?"

"Yup." Erika pulled the straps of her giant backpack over her shoulders and started back up the trail. We weaved through the craggy rocks, junipers, whitebark pine, passed another unnamed azure lake, bluer than the last, and I started to make out the trail, a narrow ledge cut like a mouth, in the cliff's face. I tried to spot Jesse or Jim, but they had dissolved into the landscape. Soon Erika vanished too.

A Clark's nutcracker landed on one of the whitebark pines. "See that bird over there." I pointed to the nutcracker. "They depend on the seeds of that tree, the whitebark pine, so they crack them out of the cones, hide them all over, and then remember where they put them. The birds help the trees reproduce."

"What do you mean?"

"Well, the birds spread the seeds around."

"I thought you said the bird finds the seeds and eats them."

"Well, not all of them." I thought this was how it worked, but I wasn't exactly sure. I added, "In science it's called symbiosis—when the tree and the bird benefit from each other. Cool, huh?"

"Sort of like us?"

"Sort of. Watch them. They're neat." The gray birds flitted among the pines, the tips of their wings, black-and-white triangles, flashing quickly like passing thoughts. We followed the short, steep switch-backs, and a marmot chirped at us from a rock.

"It's amazing," Dionne said, "that all these things live way up here."

"And under twenty feet of snow in the winter. Or this last winter, forty. I have another game."

"I don't think so," Dionne said, and then a minute later: "I don't think I can finish. I can't do it."

"Today?"

"No, the hike. I can't do it."

"Yes, you can," I said, but the truth was I wanted to hike out too.

We hiked on for a while, and then I said, "Well, maybe we should hike out and hitchhike to Mammoth."

"Then what?"

"We'll call someone to pick us up. Geoff can come early."

"Yeah. Maybe," Dionne said. Then she started to cry. "I can't call him. He'll be disappointed in me. Not after he bought all this camp-ing stuff for me. It hasn't even been a week. What was I thinking?"

"He'll understand." I wasn't sure what either of us had been thinking, but it was true: Geoff might have been sorry that he spent all that money on her gear, and she wasn't cured yet. She had been eating the same as me, and to my knowledge she hadn't thrown up, yet we lived like anorexics out there, so it was hard to tell if there was any change. I could tell I had already lost some weight, which would usually make me happy, but I felt too tired and sore to care.

We kept up our slow pace; my knee ached like something had broken inside, and I knew I wouldn't be able to finish the trail ei-ther. My knee had become swollen, and I knew I should elevate it, not walk miles and miles carrying a heavy pack. The switchbacks as-cended so quickly I couldn't even see the ones above of us. I was so preoccupied by the pain in my knee that I almost didn't notice the colors of the rock wall—the pink granite, white strips of feldspar, quartz crystals, black diorite. I tried to study the colors of the rock to take my mind off my knee. I had been missing out on so much of the beauty because I was too focused on myself. What I needed was to drop out of the self-pity parade and pull myself together. There were people in the world, after all, with real problems. I tried to pick up the pace, and when I reached the top, I found Jesse sitting there eating M&M's.

"Hey." I threw off Big Heiny, letting her land with a thud on the rocks.

"You shouldn't throw your pack like that. M&M?" Jesse asked with his mouth full of candy.

"No thanks." Normally, I wouldn't turn down chocolate, but I was too tired to eat.

The view north opened into a patchwork of azure lakes with Rae Lakes beyond. The aim was to get all the way to Woods Creek, but I wasn't sure I could do it. And if we didn't get there, we would have a hard time getting over Pinchot Pass the next day; every hike set us up for the pass the following day. We had made a pact that we would get up as early as possible in order to avoid afternoon thunderstorms on the passes.

Two middle-aged men came up to the pass from the other way. One had on glacier glasses; the other wore curly hair.

"What's wrong?" they asked.

"My knee." I pointed to my ACE bandage.

"Where you headed?"

Now I was Erika, telling them, "Yosemite Valley." They looked at me like I had left my brain back at Mt. Whitney.

"With a hurt knee?" Glacier Glasses asked, and then Curly Hair added, "That's a long way off. Do you need anything?"

"Aspirin."

They both dug into their packs and found me Advil, at least twenty tablets. I felt like I had been saved.

"If you're injured, though," Curly Hair advised, "you should hike out because if it gets much worse, you won't be able to. You're going to be in some pretty desolate country for the next fifty miles or so."

Then Jesse told me, "Yeah. You'll never make it. Dionne either." Even though Dionne and I had thought about bailing out, I felt betrayed by Jesse's suggestion. And now, for no other reason than to prove him wrong, I wanted to finish the trail. Glacier Glasses and Curly Hair wished us luck and started down the other side.

"Well, I waited for you to tell you that Erika and Jim have gone on to Woods Creek to set up camp. See you there." Before I could say, "What about Rae Lakes? What about Dollar Lake?" he disappeared down the other side of the pass. I knew Dionne and I were in trouble. I had never hiked fifteen miles in one day before, and at our pace, which had deteriorated to a mile an hour, we didn't have enough daylight left. There was no way we would make it all that way before dark.

Dionne finally reached the top. She was crying.

"Here. A surprise." I handed her four Advil, even though that would mean we only had fourteen left until Lake Edison. Who knew that ibuprofen would be such a valuable commodity?

"I don't think I'll make it."

"Yes you will. Jesse already decided we wouldn't. You, at least, have to believe we will. We both have to."

She nodded, and we limped our way down the pass. I pointed out Dragon Peak, and Dionne said, "That's it. That's how we have to be. Like dragons."

"Okay, Dragon Lady."

"That's better than the Turtles." We both managed to laugh. We descended below timberline and found hiking sticks, which seemed to help, and our knees began to feel better with the Advil. Our feet felt burning hot, though, so we decided to go skinny-dipping in Rae Lakes. If we had to hike in the dark later, we might as well give ourselves a short swim break.

Tiger lilies lined the banks of the lake. Painted Lady loomed overhead, the first mountain named for a woman, though an anonymous and possibly licentious one, that we had passed. Whitney could have been a woman's name, but in reality the mountain was named for geologist Josiah Whitney, who surveyed it in 1864. For some reason lakes are named for women, mountains for men. The early explorers had mountains named after them, while they named the lakes for daughters and wives, maybe even mistresses. Is it that mountains are majestic, lakes plentiful, common? Or is it that lakes can be entered, mountains scaled? The metaphoric possibilities are endless.

We set down our packs and took off our clothes. We both let out huge shouts as we jumped into the lake. The icy water made me feel more alive than I had felt in a long time. The water numbed my knee, turning the sharp pain into a dull ache. We pulled ourselves onto the rocks and lay there, breathing quickly.

Dionne had lost weight off her already slight frame. Her belly caved in, and her thighs didn't even come close to touching each other, like mine did. Her body would be viewed as fashion magazine ideal. I caught myself being jealous then remembered that if her disorder hadn't been so terrible, she wouldn't be out there in the first place. I felt a sense of shame for wishing that my thighs didn't touch.

Dionne turned to me and said, "I'll do it, if you do." She looked serious, determined. Her bottom lip quivered, but I couldn't tell if it was from the cold water or because she was wrestling with tears.

"Do what?"

"Finish." Dionne rested her head on her hand, bit her bottom lip.

"That's a deal. Even if it takes us two months." Dionne smiled, lay back on the rocks. I stared into the blue Sierra sky. This was the feast that Muir talked about it, a feast for the soul. I was amazed at how quickly I could go from hot, tired, and upset to cold, refreshed, and happy—hiking brings out conflicting emotions like no other activity I can think of, except maybe sex.

We dressed, helped each other with our packs, and hiked past Arrowhead Lakes, Dollar Lakes, and many other places that seemed like suitable camping spots, but we knew if we didn't catch up, that was it for us. They would go on without us, and we didn't have that much of the group food; plus, Jesse had the stove, and Erika carried both the water filter and the iodine tablets.

"Do you know we have no way to treat water?" I asked Dionne.

"We don't have the filter, huh?"

"No. And we don't have the stove to boil it. Or even the iodine."

"I guess we'd better get there then."

I hiked along, angry at Erika for taking off and mad at myself for not thinking about grabbing at least the iodine tablets. Luckily, Dionne and I had left with two quarts of water each, so we had enough, but if anything happened, we would have had to drink water without treating it. Even way up there, there was a chance of giardia, the unicellular parasite that causes "beaver fever," or explosive diarrhea and vomiting. I remembered when I visited Yosemite as a girl, I would dip my Sierra cup right into the stream and drink without a second thought. Now we had to treat all the water, even in the most remote places. Much had changed in just ten years.

After a thirteen-hour hiking day, the last part bumbling in the dark, we arrived at the campsite, which sat near a densely forested river, making it seem more like a South American forest than the rocky Sierra Nevada. It smelled of wet granite, pine, and moss.

"Look who's here," Jim called.

They had spent the early evening fishing and quite successfully at that. Dionne and I went off to filter water and then sat down to eat with everyone else.

"We found some spices on the trail," Erika announced. "Wild onion, and we added it to the meal."

"Great," I said, amazed that aside from the quick dip in Rae Lakes, Dionne and I had mostly kept our heads down and hiked, while the others had time not only to fish but to forage in the forest for vegetables. They had put together a feast of fish and mashed potatoes, and I knew I should have felt more appreciative than I did, but I wanted someone to say something about what might have happened if we hadn't made it to camp. Had they planned to leave us behind?

"And we found some mint too. I added it to my water." Erika showed me the water bottle with the floating mint. "Want to try it?" I took the bottle and tried her mint water.

"Amazing," I offered. I really wanted to say, "Would you have left us?" The mint water reminded me of sorority rush—water with mint, water with orange slices, and all the while no one talking about how Marcy Johnson had been dropped from rush because she had crooked teeth. Erika joined the sorority to compete in the sports, which she excelled at. I joined because I thought it would be a good way to meet fraternity brothers, and it was. Erika wanted to be like the boys. I wanted to be with them. We might have learned something, if we had paid attention, from the women who had joined for the sisterhood.

"What do you think of the onion? Good, huh?" Erika asked with her mouth full.

"Delicious," I said, trying not to sound sarcastic. The onion was hard and briny, but I hadn't done anything to contribute to the meal, so I wasn't about to complain.

The stars hid behind a screen of clouds. Jesse said he didn't think it would rain, so he slept outside with Erika and Jim. Dionne and I washed the group dishes, and then we began to set up my tent in the dark. As we pushed the tent poles through the nylon sleeves, Dionne said, "We're going to make it, aren't we, Zsa Zsa?"

"We totally are, Cassiopeia."

*A few minutes ago every tree was excited, bowing
to the roaring storm, waving, swirling, tossing
their branches in glorious enthusiasm like
worship.* / JOHN MUIR

Day 7

Blood Suckers

*Pinchot Pass (12,130) to the Fourth
Lakelet of Lake Marjorie (11,160)*   9 MILES

I woke to the rhythm of rain on the tent. Outside, a misty curtain
hung across the sky.

"Shit. Rain again," I said. Maybe we wouldn't make it, after all.

"What?" Dionne asked.

"Rain."

Dionne groaned and buried her face in her sleeping bag. Jesse
was outside, trying to shake the water off his backpack. Erika already busied herself, fetching the bear bags out of the tree. Her rain
pants swish-swish-swished as she walked past the tent. Industrious
as ever. I began stuffing my sleeping bag, and Erika swish-swished
over to our tent. "Let's do bars this morning," she said, pitching two
PowerBars into the tent. "We have thirty-five hundred feet of elevation gain to the pass. We should get going before it really starts
coming down."

I sat and ate my PowerBar in the tent while Dionne packed up
her stuff. Dionne unwrapped her bar and said, "I'll need the energy
today." I was glad she now looked at food as the energy her body
needed. At the time I thought maybe Geoff had been right after all—

a few weeks of hiking, and she'd be cured. I didn't realize Dionne knew all the tricks to make me think she was better without her actually being any better. She could make sure someone witnessed everything she put in her mouth, so we all thought she was eating enough; she could make comments, tell lies, bury food, though if I had seen her do this with our current food situation, I would have killed her. In short she would do anything to disguise her disorder.

"Do you think you're getting better?" I asked Dionne. I wasn't sure what I was looking for. The truth? Was I trying to empathize with her? Or was I trying to make her feel badly because I myself felt terrible?

"I feel better. How's your knee?"

"Bad," I said.

"Maybe you should consider quitting. I mean, it might just get worse."

As soon as she said it, I felt a pang of betrayal in the cage of my heart. We had been the Turtles together; we had made a pact. Now she was suggesting that I quit. I wanted to say, "Maybe you should," but I didn't want to go into full cry. I knew my voice would come out duck-squeaky, so I just left the tent and started packing my bag.

As we started up the trail, we passed two mule deer grazing on the hillside. Jim pointed his finger like a gun again and said, "Pshoot." Erika laughed at his joke, though I wasn't sure why.

We arrived at a suspension bridge that swung high over the river. I let everyone go first, watching the bridge waver with each step. The bridge slickened with rain. I stepped onto the wooden slats and held onto the sides. Erika took a picture of me. I knew not to look over the side. I had always suffered from vertigo. The whirling dizziness never happened going straight up or down as in rock climbing or skiing, but when I looked off a steep side, like from a hiking trail or a bridge, the ground trampolined up and down, reaching for me, pulling me toward it. At this point falling seemed so inevitable that the terrifying urge to get it over with and throw myself off would overcome me.

I remembered visiting Las Vegas as a young child, and we were staying at the old Sands Hotel. These were the days before high-rise hotels tried to prevent people from flinging themselves off by sealing all the windows, and balconies even graced top floors. We stayed in a room with such a balcony. My mother found me lying on my stomach, looking over the edge. "What on earth are you doing?" she had asked. I told her I liked the way the ground moved up and down. She just shook her head. The hotels were probably onto something when they sealed all those top-floor windows.

I was nearly across the bridge when Jim stepped onto it and started jumping. The bridge rolled in waves. "Stop it. Get off," I yelled. He kept at it and laughed. I became convinced that the bridge was about to flip over, so I sat down in the rain, clutching onto the railings of the bridge.

At this Erika came to my rescue. "Leave her alone," she told Jim. "We have to get going." He laughed but stopped, turned around, and followed her up the trail. I managed to get up and skitter across.

What Erika had called drizzle turned into true rain. I hiked more slowly than usual, and the others disappeared ahead. I ruminated on what Dionne had said. Maybe she was right? The trail followed a creek that cartwheeled in waterfalls, splitting into white feathers over the rocks. Ferns and corn lilies flocked the trail. I passed the gray, rain-spattered Twin Lakes, and then hiked up through the craggy rocks. The wind brushed across the cliffs; the dwarfed trees followed the wind, and I realized why the trees were small and gnarled like old women. They leaned with the wind, in what Muir would surely call "glorious worship" or some such thing. The trees looked exhausted to me. Thomas said that the views from here would be spectacular, with three glorious peaks. He liked the word *glorious* too. Everything, though, was shrouded with fog at the moment, so I just kept my head down, trying to avoid the stinging rain.

The ascent of Pinchot Pass proved to be the worst hiking day yet, but at the time the irony of it escaped me. Gifford Pinchot was the first chief of the Forest Service and a close friend to Theodore Roosevelt; Pinchot approved the damming of the Hetch Hetchy in

Yosemite National Park. Muir had helped launch Pinchot's career, and Pinchot showed his loyalty by going against everything Muir believed in by first allowing grazing in Oregon's and Washington's parks and then supporting the Hetch Hetchy dam; the reservoir drowned the Hetch Hetchy Valley, which had been as picturesque as the Yosemite Valley—full of waterfalls and glacial-carved rocks and home to the path of the Tuolumne River. But San Francisco wanted the water. Muir died during his fight against the project. I think that was what finally killed him—he died of a broken heart. Maybe a perpetual cloud hangs over Pinchot Pass, Muir's last stand against the man who had betrayed him. This projection, however, was mine alone. Muir himself adored mountain storms.

I climbed to the top of the pass, and the wind from the other side swept against me, almost knocking me and Big Heiny over. A group of Australian thru-hikers huddled together. The rain turned to a sleety snow. I believed my group had descended the other side but later learned Erika had waited, ensuring I made it. It felt cold enough to crack bone. At least, I reasoned, it was too cold for lightning.

"Heading to Whitney?" I asked them. A mineral smell seeped from the wet granite.

"Yes, you?" one asked.

"Yosemite." The wind had another go at me. I held onto a rock during the gust.

"How's Forester?" they shouted over the wind.

"Not too bad." I didn't want to sound like a wimp. "You can still mostly follow the trail."

"That's good," one of them said. "Mather's a bitch. Lots of snow."

"Thanks for the info. Have fun." I found the trail back down the other side and then realized how very strange it sounded to have said "Have fun." I was soaked through, lonesome, and starting to get a rash on my hips from the wet straps. Prickly stars of wind stung my cheeks. I picked my way down the cloud-shrouded pass, doing my best to hold it together. There was no fun in summiting that pass nor in the descent. I felt like Sisyphus or maybe his rock, up and back down. Up and back down, ad infinitum. Was there a point?

Later I would discover that the hard and lonely days would make me appreciate the beautiful days with an intensity I could not have predicted. Still, nothing faded the difficult times into nostalgic amnesia, nothing made the long hours of hiking in the rain seem glorious, even in retrospect.

The trail leveled out, the rain let up, and the clouds began to dissipate. I turned around and could barely make out Mt. Wynne. A smallish gray-haired man came skipping up the trail. He wore a small pirate hat that reminded me of Captain Hook, and he carried two metal walking sticks like ski poles. His backpack looked more like an inner tube around his belly. He wore running shoes with gaiters around his ankles.

"Well, hello there, lovely lady," he said.

"Hi. I'm not feeling so lovely."

"Ah well. You are, and where might you be going on this glorious day?"

"I'm not sure." I knew I looked like a rain-soaked cat, not a lovely lady, and the day seemed anything but glorious to me.

"Not sure?" He wrinkled his nose.

"My friends are up ahead. I think we're going to camp a little ways past Lake Marjorie.

"Delightful," this Puck-like fellow answered. "Well, I'm heading to Whitney. I left five days ago on the full moon, and I'll arrive to Whitney Portal day after tomorrow."

"That's more than thirty miles a day." Maybe I was having delusions or an acid flashback and I had dreamed this winsome fellow up. Or maybe he was the ghost of John Muir, there to haunt me. He had said the word *glorious*, after all. But he didn't look like the pictures I had seen of the tall, gaunt, bearded Muir, though I supposed a ghost could choose any likeness he wanted. John Muir as a middle-aged Peter Pan who had somehow managed to steal Captain Hook's hat? I didn't know why Muir would haunt me, though—he had written that he was happy to see women, or the "girl mountaineers," as he called them, in the wilderness. He thought women outdoors signified a "hopeful beginning." Perhaps this funny little man was Muir's way of welcoming me?

"That's right," he said. "I hike until dusk, sleep until the moon comes out, and then hike by moonlight. It's delightful. Bye now."

I watched him skip down the trail and felt annoyed by all this joy; then I wondered why I couldn't be that joyful. Maybe everything really was attitude. I had mastered self-pity and realized maybe it was time to work on joy. Doesn't the Dalai Lama say happiness is a decision? Pain is inevitable, suffering a choice. Could it be that I simply suffered from a bad attitude? Maybe I needed to try harder to enjoy all of it even if it wasn't exactly fun. I limped down the trail to Lake Marjorie and practiced smiling, which just made me feel silly. I found everyone near the lake eating lunch.

"You look happy," Erika said. She wasn't being ironic. I was still practicing my smile.

"Yeah," I said, "happy to stop for lunch." I threw off Big Heiny, changed clothes, and laid everything out on the rocks to dry.

"Crazy how fast the weather changes, huh?" Dionne asked.

"Yeah. Did you see that guy running down the trail?" I hoped he hadn't been a figment of my imagination.

"That airy-fairy guy?" Jesse asked.

"The one with the funny little backpack and hat."

"Yeah. What a freak," Jesse said.

"He's out to set the JMT speed record," Erika said. "Maybe next time I do it, I'll try to set the female record."

"Better not take these two," Jesse said, pointing to me and Dionne.

"Hey," I said.

"I'm keeping up today," Dionne said.

"Barely," Jesse answered, which made me feel better in a mean-girl sort of way.

"No," said Erika. "I'll go solo."

Before I finished eating, everyone started packing up. I told them to go ahead since we'd planned to camp just another couple of miles away at the last lakelet. Before they left, Dionne said, "I didn't mean anything by what I said. About you quitting."

"I know." I realized how I spent the morning angry for no real reason other than to make myself feel better through my suffering, which sounds ironic but happened more than I would like to admit. I knew I had to adjust my attitude, or as Dionne and Jesse both suggested, I might as well quit.

I finished up, drank some water, and put everything away. I tried to smile again and found that it was starting to work: I began to feel happy—the sun burned yellow in a blue sky and the post-rain air seemed elastic, smelled of wet earth and pine. No one was in sight, so I felt truly alone, and for the first time I was glad. Happy, I told myself as I hiked, a happiness more complicated than fun. But try as I might, I couldn't bring myself to glorious. Bliss, maybe, despite the new age connotations that I couldn't quite swallow. Despair to bliss—I began to feel like an emotional chameleon. I had never been so overloaded with so many opposing emotions at once.

The trail unfolded before me, and I followed it past a string of lakelets until I found our campsite, a sandy patch that sloped into one of the small lakes. We set up our tents, hung the bear rope, and went down to filter water. The water was much warmer than any of the other lakes we had passed, so we decided to swim. Erika wore bathing suit bottoms but not her top. As she probably anticipated, Jesse and Jim seemed to enjoy the gesture.

The warm water provided a perfect end to a long hiking day. Jesse asked me if I wanted to swim across the lake, and I said, "Sure." Erika heard us and said she wanted to go with us, which of course turned it into a race. Jim swam up next to Dionne, pretending to spit water on her, his attempt at chivalry.

"Ready?" Jesse asked.

"I'm ready," Erika said. She extended her arm in preparation for the big race, and I noticed a black slug-like thing on her shoulder.

"Erika, you have a slug or something on your shoulder," I told her.

"What? Where?" She craned her neck, trying to look behind her.

She probably just thought I was trying to throw her off, gain an advantage in the race.

"There," I pointed, and as soon as I did, I realized what it was. "Leech. It's a leech."

"What? Where?"

Rather than answer her, I took off swimming for shore, sure that if Erika had a leech, I probably did too. Erika and Jesse followed me—the only race I would ever win in my life.

"Leeches," I shouted to Dionne and Jim as I splashed by them. I checked my body and found one on my belly. As I tore it off, it left a petal of blood. Jesse had two, and Erika had another one. Dionne and Jim swam to shore, and Jim had one on his ankle. Dionne didn't have any; still, she kept screaming, "Oh my God, gross. Gross, oh my God."

"Do they carry diseases?" Jesse asked.

"I don't think so," I said, though I wasn't sure. I did know that sometimes they were still used medicinally, so I figured they had to be free of disease. We finished checking each other, and Jim continued to check Dionne's hair and back, brushing his fingertips along the back of her neck.

After we had all dressed and started getting our food together, Jim said, "Dionne did great today, I think." He looked in her direction and winked. She smiled at him. Erika and I were both disgusted. I guessed for different reasons.

"My knee is much better today," she said. "I'm still slow, but thanks for hiking with me."

"No problem, Cassiopeia."

I couldn't believe Dionne had told Jim her trail name. We had kept them mostly secret because Erika just rolled her eyes at us. Could Dionne really be flirting with the Murderer? So, now I was the only one hiking way behind? I felt something floppy in my stomach, like a dying trout. Something like the air being let out of my bliss balloon. Being slow is one thing. Being the only slow one is another thing entirely. Even on my high school track team, I had the other pathetically slow "speed demons" to run with.

I wasn't sure whether it was because Jim had paid Erika very little attention during the topless leech swim or Erika finally noticed how light the food bags had become, but Erika told Jim that he couldn't eat our burritos that night.

Jim offered to share his freeze-dried pad thai with Dionne. To my surprise she ate some. Erika asked, "Is it good?" but Jim didn't offer her any. I wished I had kept up on the trail just to know what had happened to facilitate this dramatic turn of events.

After dinner I went right to the tent. Erika and Jesse got into her tent, and I could hear Dionne and Jim chatting. Try as I might to eavesdrop, I couldn't make out what they were saying. When Dionne finally came to bed, I couldn't stop myself from asking, "What were you and Jim talking about?"

"He's having a hard time," she said. "He just got back from the Gulf War."

"Is that why he's so weird?"

"He's disturbed. He hiked with me and told me about it."

"So, you aren't afraid of him?"

"No, not really anymore. I just feel sorry for him. He said he doesn't care if he lives or dies."

"Is that why he doesn't treat his water?" I had been waiting for him to get sick so he couldn't hike with us anymore, but so far he seemed just fine.

"I don't know. Maybe," Dionne answered. "I just feel bad for him. We have no way of understanding what he's been through. I think maybe we've been too hard on him."

At the time I didn't make the connection between Jim's questions about killing and his career as a machine gunner. I didn't have the capacity to empathize with him. He scared me, so I wanted him to go away. We all had our reasons for being out on the trail; at the time I didn't see that his were more compelling than mine. We were nearly the same age, yet the war had given him years of experience, an edge that I had no way of comprehending.

"I don't know—it seems like he likes you" is all I could manage to say to Dionne.

"I know, but since Erika won't give him any more food, I think he's going to hike ahead by himself tomorrow."

"Why did she change her mind?"

"Because she waited for him twice today, but he said he wanted to hike with me. I think she got jealous."

"And then he didn't pay any attention to her even after she went topless. That explains it; he likes you now. Who knows if anything even happened with them, but if you're getting the attention, that will make Erika mad. She has a temper too. I'll tell you more tomorrow. I'm too tired now."

"You can't tell me now?"

"Too tired. Tomorrow. Promise."

"Okay. Good night."

"You too." It was true; I was too tired to worry about the snow on Mather Pass, my knee, or the types of disfiguring diseases leeches might carry. But more than that, I was too tired to tell a good story.

Another glorious day, the air as delicious to the lungs as nectar to the tongue. / JOHN MUIR

Day 8

Gossip with a Bang

Mather Pass (12,100) to Lower Palisade Lakes (10,600)   11.3 MILES

With the sun out, everything seemed better. That, and Jim really did take off.

"Where's Jim?" I asked Erika, when I emerged from my tent.

"Gone, I guess. Will you give me a hand with this?" She was trying to get the bear bags down, but they were too high up, so she couldn't reach them. I tried to help, but it was no use. When you counterbalance the bear bags, both end up high in the tree. To get them, you push one up with a stick, letting the other one down. Jesse came over to help, and he couldn't reach them either. Finally, Dionne got on Jesse's shoulders, and she could reach one of the bags with the stick.

"That's a relief," I said. We sat down to eat oatmeal, and this time Erika mandated Jesse's portion.

"That's too much, Jesse." We had enough oatmeal for one more breakfast each, two if we stretched it, but we had another week before our resupply at Lake Edison.

"Whatever," he said, but he put some back before pouring in the water.

Erika and Jesse hiked on ahead of me and Dionne, though I was fairly sure they didn't hike together. Day 8, and everyone was starting to tire of one another.

"This group of Aussies said there's a lot of snow on the north side of Mather," I told Dionne. I thought about a time when I had been hiking in Lake Tahoe's Desolation Wilderness with Jack and he decided to slide down the snowy north side of Dicks Peak instead of climbing over the boulders to the side. To make matters worse, he put on his rain suit so he would slide faster. Dylan barked, whined, and stomped his feet, trying to warn Jack of his folly. Fearless but not stupid, Dylan knew Jack was headed for danger. Jack took off, and within seconds he was flailing around like a rag doll, unable to slow himself down, screaming with woeful surprise. Somehow he managed to get himself onto his stomach, feet first, before he crashed into the boulders below. Still, he hurt his knee and his back, scraped up his hands and his face, and I had to carry all his stuff out. That marked the end of my adventures with Jack.

"I wish we had ice axes," I told Dionne.

"Do you know how to use one?"

"No, I guess not."

"Then it wouldn't do much good anyway. We'll be okay, Zsa Zsa."

A ranger hiked down the trail toward us.

"Hi there. Do you have your permit?"

"Our friends have it." Erika was the keeper of the permit, which we almost didn't get. Reserving a permit to hike Whitney in August wasn't easy. Erika's plan was to camp out near the ranger station everyday until we could get a permit to hike Whitney. There was no way we were going without a permit, Erika had said. Luckily, when we showed up at the ranger station in Lone Pine, they had four "first come–first served" permits available.

"Okay. I saw it," the ranger said.

"Are our friends very far ahead?" Dionne asked.

"Pretty far. Are you guys okay?"

"Just tired," Dionne said. The ranger looked at us. We must have looked as terrible as we felt.

"And we hurt our knees," I said, though this must have been obvious because we each had an ACE bandage wound around a knee.

"And you are hiking with your friends to Yosemite?" the ranger asked.

"Do you think that's stupid?" I asked, trying not to cry. The uniform gave the ranger the authority to either endorse or reject my passage into the wilderness, and I was sure we would be told that we had no business being out there.

"Not stupid. But if you decide to hike out, you can take the trail up ahead over Taboose Pass. It's about fifteen miles and then another five miles to 395. It's a brutal walk downhill, though, especially with bad knees—from the high country to the desert. After that the next pass is Bishop Pass Trail, and from here that's at least a two-day walk out. If you want to keep hiking, maybe your friends can take some of your weight for a couple of days."

"That's a good idea," Dionne said. Her pack was already the lightest, and I couldn't see Erika or Jesse offering to take any of our stuff.

"Well, good luck," the ranger said and waved good-bye. She seemed so at home out there, like she wasn't displaced, trespassing, proving that there really was the kind of woman I wanted to be out there. It didn't occur to me that people might see me, backpacking for a month, and think the same thing—that is, if I didn't happen to be in the middle of one of my crying jags.

"Thanks," we said and started hiking.

We came to the trail to Taboose Pass, and we both stopped and looked at each other. I said, "It's not like we can just leave and not tell them. Can we?"

"They were going to leave us."

"True. But do you want to do that brutal hike out and still not finish?"

"No, but if we keep going now," Dionne said, "we have to promise to make it to the end." She leaned on her walking stick, tilted her head, narrowed her eyes, and smiled.

"We'll do it, Cassiopeia." We shook on it.

We started hiking again, leaving behind the chance to hike out.

I felt a mixture of anxiety and relief—we had not given up yet. I wasn't sure either of us would make it the whole way, but for the moment we were still on the trail.

"Hey, what were you going to tell me last night in the tent, Zsa Zsa, about Erika and her temper?"

I had planned to tell stories about Erika, things that involved punched-in windshields, smashed mountain bikes, totaled cars. I had some really good gossip, yet I realized I wasn't up to it. This might have been the first time in my life I didn't jump at the chance to gossip about someone; I realized it wasn't my gossip to share. Instead, I told Dionne gossip about myself, about how I had made Erika so angry she wouldn't speak to me for days.

I told Dionne about the road trip Erika and I once took to Colorado, how we had been camping every night since we left California. We didn't have the money for a hotel room, and I was tired of sleeping at dingy KOAs, so after a couple of beers in a Fort Collins bar, I told her that if we met some guys, we might not have to camp. She laughed and said, "Good one." I was only half-joking—as it turned out, not joking at all. We did meet a couple of guys at the bar, and I arranged for us to stay the night at one of their houses. Erika went along with it, but her guy ended up going to his own house, so she slept on the couch alone while I slept in the other one's bed.

The next day Erika and I went backpacking in Estes National Park, and she would not speak to me, aside for essential communication, for two days. Finally, she said, "That was crazy. Those guys could have been deranged. Plus, that was really slutty, Suzanne. What were you thinking?" I told her it wasn't like I had sex with him, which had been true. I did, however, leave out the bit about the hand job. I told Erika that the hook-up wasn't just for the bed. He was cute; the bed just turned out to be an added bonus. For Erika this move disrupted her sense of decorum. She was so furious she didn't say another word until we had hiked out and were back on the road. It was a low point, I had to admit, making out with a stranger, no matter how handsome, for a night in a bed. And Erika was right; that little adventure could have turned out to be dangerous. I had reasoned that because they were graduate students, in literature no less, they had to be harmless. It hadn't occurred to me that most women are raped by men they know or have just met casually, not by the stranger who jumps out of the bushes. Ironically, I carried a fear concerning men, yet at the same time I continued to neglect my own safety.

"You're a foolish girl," my mother liked to say, and she didn't know the half of it. Maybe that's what I had been looking for: foolish. To be foolish means you get to erase so many other things. To be foolish means that the other stuff is there but no one gets to see it. It means people will like your stories. The problem is that when we don't get past foolish, there is no point to the story. Foolish is no more than a cliché. And even worse, foolish is an easy, dishonest way out. And sometimes foolish is dangerous.

"I haven't always been so good," I told Dionne.

"No kidding. Who has? Well, Erika talked to me this morning," Dionne said. "So maybe there really was nothing going on with Jim."

"Maybe."

Two good-looking thirty-something men approached us on the trail, and I was happy for the diversion.

"Hello there," they both said.

"Where are you going?" we asked. "Where have you been?"

"We're just doing a loop. We're hiking for ten days, but we've built in a layover day every other day. We came over Muir Pass, and it was spectacular," one said.

The other added, "You aren't supposed to, but we slept in the hut on top. You could see snow for miles and miles. And that night we had a meteor shower. We drank cognac, ate cheesecake, and watched the shooting stars. Fabulous."

"Have a great trip," they said when we parted.

I was jealous. They were hiking slowly enough to enjoy themselves, whereas we swept through so quickly we didn't have a minute to enjoy it. Cognac and cheesecake on a backpacking trip? They obviously hadn't heard of Ray Jardine and his go-light campaign either. I bet they had a whole stockpile of Advil, maybe even something stronger. I regretted that I hadn't asked. Then I thought about what they'd said about the snow. More snow to worry about. Also, Thomas said the descent would be knee shocking, and I thought about that too.

Dionne and I had begun the crisscross up Mather Pass when a loud *kaboom* shook the cliffs above us, followed by a cloud of dust and then small rocks tumbling toward us. The sound of pebbles beneath a retreating wave. The smoke smelled like the Fourth of July snaking black fireworks that my father had always been so delighted with—the smell of burnt sulfur. I told myself that if we didn't get buried by rocks, I would no longer do foolish things; I would change my ways. I never thought much about God until I needed someone to bargain with. "I promise I'll be a nicer person if you don't bury me in a landslide. I'll be good from now on."

Dionne and I huddled together. Another loud boom shook through us, and Dionne shouted, "What the fuck is that?" Another blast, and we both yelled, "Shit!" So much for being good.

Then a voice on a bullhorn said, "We're doing some blasting. Can your party wait for us to finish? We'll tell you when it's safe." My heart rattled against the cage of my chest, and I worried that the blasts would cause the giant rocks above us to slide down and bury us.

"Let's walk down here," I told Dionne. We both hated to go back down, but the blasts continued, and a big rock rested off to the side, which felt like a safer place to sit.

"Well, this is ironic," I said.

"What is?"

"Well, this pass is named for Stephen Mather."

"So? Who was he?" Another blast shook the pass.

"He was the first director of the National Park Service. And from what I've read, he loved dynamite." Another blast. I held my breath, hoping there would be no rockslide, no live burial.

"What do you mean?"

"Well, he loved to build roads, and he was responsible for hotels and stuff in the national parks."

"Well, isn't that a good thing?" Dionne asked. "I mean, people need places to stay."

"I guess it depends on who you talk to. Look at us—we're finding places to stay."

"Yeah, but a lot of people want to see the parks but don't want to sleep on the ground."

"I know. I'm just saying that some people think that there's too much development in national parks."

"Do you think so?" Another blast.

"I do right now. But it's a hard one. It's really complicated. And political. No one would support national parks if people couldn't visit them easily. They need to be accessible, but if they're too accessible, they're ruined, and then no one will want to visit them. I agree with Muir, and at the same time I can see where Mather was coming from."

"But it's so beautiful here."

"Wait until you see Yosemite Valley. It's beautiful too but overdeveloped and crowded to the point of being a real circus."

"Really?"

"Just wait. Clowns and everything."

"Really?"

"Well, maybe no clowns, but you know what I mean."

"But aren't you happy there's a trail here?" Dionne asked.

"Yes, but I'm not so happy that they're fixing it at this very moment." Dionne and I sat there for a minute, anticipating more blasts. After a few minutes the bullhorn man notified us that it was safe to ascend.

We reached the top, and the explosive-yielding trail workers were two guys about our age with mops for hair. They looked like stoners to me, and I worried that maybe we really were in danger.

"Sorry about the scare," one of them said. "Just doing a little trail maintenance."

"That's okay," Dionne said and smiled. When Dionne smiled, her whole face turned on like a light bulb. Obviously taken with her, both mopheads smiled goofy grins back at her.

The view from the pass made it worth the hike—old Stephen Mather got a good one. The snowy north side unraveled before us, and the Palisades jutted triangle tops into the sky's blue panels. We didn't spend much time on the pass because we had waited so long for them to finish the bombing. I felt cheated, especially since it was a warm, sunny day. And I was jealous that Erika and Jesse got to loiter on the top before the blasting. Palisades Lakes scattered blue in the otherwise green forest. Thomas said that the camping would be "poor" at Upper Palisade Lake, so we agreed to hike to the Lower Palisade Lake, where the camping was supposed to be "poor to fair." Erika wanted to continue the three-mile descent down a steep section called the Golden Staircase to Deer Meadow, but I told her we would never make it, especially because of the reports of all of the snow on the north side of Mather.

The Aussies were right. Snow obscured the trail so that in many places we were forced to climb onto boulders to avoid postholing, our legs sinking into the soft snow, our calves snow scraped. We lost the trail over and over, and it took us a long time to pick our way down. Dionne was scared, so she sat down on a rock and cried. Someone had to be the strong one, and the only someone left was me. Even though I couldn't stop thinking about Jack and his fabulous snow slide, I pretended everything was okay. We both couldn't plop ourselves down and cry. We had learned to take turns with that sort of thing.

"Go ahead," she said. She buried her face into her knees.

"Like I can just leave you here. I'll wait."

Two hikers approached us and asked if everything was all right. It started to seem that whenever one of us started crying, men would appear, thereby solidifying the wimpy woman stereotype. "Do you have any aspirin?" I asked. Usually, I was too embarrassed to ask, but I couldn't stand to see Dionne cry, so I had lost all shame. Besides, I wasn't sure how else to get Dionne moving off her rock.

"What's wrong?" they asked.

"We have both injured our knees, and we're having trouble making it down."

"I can do better than aspirin," one of the men said. He handed us each two white, oval pills. "Vicodin. Take half at a time. You aren't allergic, are you?"

"No," we both said, though I wasn't really sure. I knew taking prescription pain medication given to me by a stranger while out in the middle of nowhere was generally a bad idea, yet desperate times called for pharmaceutical measures. Dionne and I both took half a pill with water and some granola.

After taking the Vicodin, Dionne left her rock, and we made considerably better time. Dionne even giggled when she fell onto her backpack and couldn't get up until I helped her. "Erika would really call me a turtle if she could see me now," Dionne said.

We finally arrived at Lower Palisade Lake, and Erika and Jesse were having lunch—crackers with the last of our vacuum-sealed tuna.

"Are you sure you guys don't want to go to Deer Meadow?" Erika asked.

Even though my knee felt better, I said, "I'm sure. I think eleven miles is enough for today." I unpacked my stuff and went down to the lake to write in my journal. I took off my shoes to survey the blisters: big ones on my heels from going up, small white ones on my big and little toes from going down. I also had a rash on my hips and sores on my shoulders. The blisters and sores were pinpricks of sharp pain amid the dull ache of the rest of my body. I looked like I had been through a meat grinder. Jesse said I looked like a junkyard dog.

I wrote a shopping list in my journal for Lake Edison: moleskin, Band-Aids, athletic tape, bandages for my hips and shoulders, bug juice, sunscreen, Pop-Tarts, ibuprofen, Handi Wipes, chocolate, new socks, hard candy, another pencil for sketching.

Then, with my chewed-up, knife-sharpened pencil, I drew a picture of the lake, which seemed much nicer than poor-to-fair if you asked me, and Erika came down to filter water.

"I know your knee hurts. I can take some of your stuff tomorrow," she said.

"That's okay."

"No. There's hardly any food left, so I don't have that much weight. I don't mind. And we don't have a pass tomorrow, so hopefully, you guys will feel better."

"Thanks, Erika." With less weight and the Vicodin I planned to take, I reasoned that maybe the golden staircase wouldn't be so bad after all. Before going to help with dinner, Top Ramen noodles, I wrote in my journal, "I just might be able to do this."

Healthy mountaineers always discover in themselves a reserve of power after great exhaustion. / JOHN MUIR

Day 9

Just the Ladies

The Golden Staircase (10,600) to Grouse Meadows (8,020)   6.8 MILES

After a fitful night of sleep, I woke up to wind. The water in my Nalgene had frozen nearly solid. I had difficulty sleeping—strange dreams about a talking marmot. I had to go to the bathroom, but it was too cold to get out of my sleeping bag. Dionne was still asleep. I listened to Erika and Jesse talking outside the tent.

"I'm not feeling well, so I'm going to bail."

"Well, you can go out right here—Bishop Pass Trail to South Lake. Then you can hitchhike home. You should be able to get there tonight. It's only thirteen miles." I peeked outside the tent; Erika was showing Jesse her detailed topographic map.

"I think I'll need two days. But I'll get going and try to camp somewhere along Bishop Pass Trail."

I pulled myself out of the tent, pretended I hadn't been eavesdropping, and said, "What's up?"

"Jesse's hiking out," Erika said.

"Okay," I said and headed to the woods to go to the bathroom. I was glad he was leaving. At the same time I felt badly that he couldn't stand us. I knew his escape was not from the wilderness but from us.

When I got back, Dionne was up, and Jesse was packing his bag. He said, "I'll need food for today and tomorrow." I knew he could do the whole hike in one day, but I didn't say anything. He rifled through the remaining food, took a couple of granola bars and a whole package of macaroni and cheese—one of our dinners for four. We all hugged him good-bye, and to any outsider this little scene would appear to be a sincere parting, full of well wishes and fondness. He put on his pack and hiked off with our food and both his fishing poles. He also took Erika's tent since we decided we could make do with mine, which was just big enough for three, and neither Dionne nor I could carry the extra weight. He also finally agreed to carry out the trash, but for all we knew, he was going to throw it into a bush somewhere. We all stood there watching him walk away.

"I'll come with Mark to Reds Meadow to bring you guys food," he said, waved, and turned toward the trail. Mark was Jesse's roommate, and he had agreed to bring us our food and supplies at Reds Meadow. Erika gave him a shopping list before we left. I now had my doubts that either of them would show up, leaving us to resupply at the expensive camp store. That, or we would have to hitchhike into town, putting us even more behind schedule.

"See you then," Jesse called, without bothering to turn around. We packed up our stuff, and Erika took the stove, fuel, filter, and my tent, leaving me with very little weight. Since Dionne now carried none of the food or group gear, her pack weighed next to nothing too. With a Vicodin each, Dionne and I felt considerably better.

We descended the Golden Staircase, and I saw why this was the last part of the JMT to be constructed; the jagged, narrow trail etched into the cliffs of the gorge. I appreciated my lighter pack. A misstep would mean certain death. I tried not to look down, avoiding the pull of vertigo. For the first time the three of us hiked together. Erika suggested we sing, so we first botched "Tears in Heaven" and then warbled "Me and Bobby McGee" and "Truckin'" terribly off-key.

We followed the zigzagging trail to the bottom of the Golden Staircase and hiked under the largest Jeffrey pines I had ever seen. We arrived at Deer Meadow, and the larkspur and mule ears bloomed purple and yellow. I told Erika and Dionne that the Native Americans used the large leaves of mule ears for diapers.

"And this plant," I told them, "is mugwort. The Indians used to put it on their pillow so they would have good dreams. Doesn't it smell good?" I put it to their noses. For some reason the day didn't feel as rushed as usual. My knee ached, but the sharp pain was nearly gone. Or maybe I had just gotten used to it. "And it's supposed to repel mosquitoes."

"Does it work?" Dionne asked. We had also run out of insect repellent, or bug juice, as we called it.

"Not sure. Try it." Dionne reached down and picked some. We rubbed the mugwort all over our arms and legs. Even if it wasn't going to ward off the mosquitoes and flies, the scent was an improvement. We had been nine days without a shower.

We entered a shady lodgepole forest, completed our descent, and began climbing once again; the next day we would hike up Muir Pass. It would be our last big pass, and from what we had heard, snow buried the trail on both sides. Because we were only hiking about seven miles, it began to feel like vacation. Almost fun. I thought back to our first day, when a three-mile day seemed like torture. I felt a small bubble of pride.

Erika stopped and looked at the map. "How about camping halfway between Grouse Meadows and Dusy Branch? By the fork in the creek." I couldn't believe she was asking me rather than just telling me the plan. With the guys gone, we had seemingly become equals.

"Sounds good to me," I said, and Dionne agreed.

We found a campsite near the other side of Glacier Creek and took our dirty clothes to the water to wash them. We also bathed without worrying about whether Jesse would see us or not. We dumped the contents of our food bag onto a tarp and surveyed our provisions for the next week: Fruit Roll-Ups, lemon drops, one breakfast of oatmeal, tea, Tang, tabbouleh, hummus, a few tortillas, miso soup, pesto, cornmeal, flour, cornbread mix, dry milk, oil, one more macaroni and cheese dinner, and four PowerBars.

We decided on macaroni and cheese, the whole package for the three of us, and herbal tea with lemon drops for dessert, which seemed like a real splurge. Obviously, we were not thinking ahead.

I threw the bear rope, even though it took me five tries to get it. Dionne filtered the water, and Erika set up the stove. We all put up the tent together. Dionne volunteered to sleep in the middle because she was the smallest and thought it might be warmer. With everything done, I felt a strange satisfaction at having done it all without Jesse. He had accused me of reading, writing, and drawing all the time; he said I had not been pulling my weight around camp, and he had been right, but tonight I was happy to help. I knew it wasn't the man's job to do everything, and Erika certainly did a lot more than he did, but with him around I felt like I didn't have to contribute as much. I knew Erika had noticed my lack of help too, yet she never said anything, and I started to think that maybe I had been too hard on her.

"Where do you think Jesse is?" I asked.

"Eating pizza and drinking beer in Bishop," Erika answered. We all laughed.

Dionne said, "Let's have a toast."

"Okay," we all agreed.

"Here's to us, just the ladies," Dionne said, "finding our reserve of power and finishing the trail together." We clinked our mugs and drank our tea.

"I'm really happy," I said.

"That's because we hiked less than seven miles," Erika said, "and I carried all your weight."

Then it seemed to me the Sierra should be
called not the Nevada or Snowy Range,
but the Range of Light. / JOHN MUIR

Day 10

The Ghost of Muir Pass

Muir Pass (11,955)   14 MILES

Tom said camping in the Muir hut was illegal, but because we had met other hikers who had done it, we decided to break the rules and, as Edward Abbey says, "live dangerous." Even Erika agreed. Muir, we thought, would be happy to have us as guests for the night in a hut dedicated to him. According to Tom, it would be fourteen miles to the top of the pass, with a four thousand–foot elevation gain. Tom also said we would "assault Goddard Divide" and "search out Muir Pass." We felt an intimate bond with Thomas Winnett, the author of our guidebook, so he was no longer Winnett nor even Thomas. Now he was simply Tom.

"Sounds like we're going to war," Erika said, "to search out and assault." Dionne and I laughed.

I almost told her our trail name for her but instead said, "So male."

"The women will seek out and conquer," Dionne laughed and raised her cup of hot Tang. Erika and I met her cup with ours. We drank hot Tang and ate Fruit Roll-Ups for breakfast.

None of us said so, but we were happy it was just the three of us. Even Erika seemed more relaxed. We had a long hike ahead of us, but we sat around for a while, joking about war metaphors, the language of men.

Finally I said, "Well, we should probably get going." We got our things together, put on our packs, which were much lighter these days—I could even get Big Heiny on without anyone's help—and we started up toward the pass.

The trail left the grassy meadow and climbed along Dusy Branch, a turbulent creek. White water ruffled over itself in lacy pleats. Erika pointed to the evidence of great avalanches. Paths of smooth rock funneled down the canyon walls. Giant boulders and broken trees tangled into a heap at the bottom. I imagined a slab of snow tumbling down the mountainside, snapping full-grown lodgepole pines and aspens like mere twigs, leaving a fan of snow and rubble behind.

"Probably a wet slab slide. It looked like everything slid, right down to the dirt." In the Sierra the snowpack is generally stable, more stable than in the Rockies. But in the spring the snow gets soaked through from rain or just melting snow, and a slab breaks loose. This type of avalanche is especially dangerous. Most people ignore the signs—balls of snow coiling down the slope that look like jelly rolls—that precede them. When the slab breaks free, the heavy snow destroys everything in its path, human and otherwise.

"Scary," Dionne said.

"Yeah," I agreed, "it is." I thought about Jim and how I might have come up with this way of dying in our game, though it couldn't have been further from the truth. The only thing that scared me more than heights was enclosed places. Years later I realized just how terrifying this would be when I took avalanche safety classes and we practiced finding each other with our beacons. To do this, we had to take turns being buried in the snow. You can't imagine how black it is under white snow until you try it. And the snow melts and then hardens around your body, so you can't move. It's like being in Dante's ninth ring of hell, where the traitors are buried up to their eyes in ice, and it is so cold, even their tears freeze, sealing their eyes shut.

Our trail climbed through a canyon of granite. Chaparral and

Indian paintbrush clung to the rocky walls. We passed Little Pete Meadow. Aspens, sagebrush, and mountain strawberry grew along the edge of the grassy meadow. A week earlier we would have hurried by. Now we took off our packs and picked wild strawberries. Even though we still had our plan, Erika wasn't being as strict; maybe that was because finally it was just us, and no one was watching.

"After ten days of dried food, these strawberries taste amazing," Dionne said. Though a pathetic fallacy, I couldn't help but imagine these strawberries were gifts, especially for us.

We put our packs on and continued past Big Pete Meadow, which was actually smaller than Little Pete. We passed fern, pussy-paws, arnica, and western aster—the flowers burst a fanfare of green, yellow, and purple. Two men passed us without much chitchat. After a while two women came down the trail after them. One wore frosted pink lipstick. The other had a crown of frizzy hair and was out of breath.

"Where are you going?" the one with the lipstick asked.

"Muir Pass," I said, before Erika had the chance to tell her that we were hiking to Yosemite. Even though other hikers and rangers had responded to Erika's boasting with "Today?" and "That's a long way to go before dark," she kept on bragging.

"It sure is snowy. We were there yesterday. Surely, you aren't going all that way today?" Frizzy Hair put her hands on her hips.

"Sure we are," Dionne said. "We're going to sleep in the hut." Erika glanced sideways at Dionne. Erika had agreed to break the rules, yet she surely didn't want to broadcast it.

"In that drafty little thing?" Hair asked.

"It's a dank hole," Lipstick added.

"We heard from a couple of guys—other JMT hikers—that it's fine for sleeping," I said.

"What's a JMT hiker?" Lipstick asked.

"Someone who's hiking the whole John Muir Trail."

"How far is that?"

"It's 211 miles, but we have to hike a little farther to get food and stuff, so we're hiking about 230 miles, maybe 240." Now I was the one bragging.

"Whatever for?" Hair asked. I didn't answer her. Partly because if I had tried to explain, she wouldn't understand. Partly because I wasn't exactly sure myself. Hair didn't pursue the question. Instead, she said, "Well, you wouldn't catch me sleeping in that little hut for a hundred bucks."

Lipstick added, "I wouldn't for a thousand. People have died in there, you know. Campers were killed by lightning. Wait till you see it. It's a real pit."

"Well, we'll decide when we get there," I said.

They both asked us who we were with. Dionne, Erika, and I looked at each other, not sure how to answer. No one had asked us that until now, but we had been hiking with men. For the first time I felt a surge of pride. I said, "We're with each other. Us three women together." I pointed to Erika and Dionne and then to myself.

"So you girls are alone?"

"Alone?" Dionne asked.

"We're not alone. We're with each other. This is the 1990s, not the 1890s."

"You must have a gun?" Hair asked.

"No." Erika shook her head.

"You're brave," both women said. They hurried off down the trail toward their husbands. The women whispered. I could only make out the word *crazy*.

We continued on. I couldn't imagine carrying a gun. If I had had one, I wouldn't have known what to do with it. These women couldn't imagine being "alone," yet I felt much safer, so much less alone, than I did when we were with Jim or even Jesse. Hair and Lipstick couldn't imagine that three women—or girls, as they called us—would be wandering around out there without men. I did, however, wonder if these women had their facts straight about the hut. I felt safe enough with my two girlfriends, especially because we were so far away from a town or even a road. Yet I didn't necessarily want to sleep in a place where people had died.

We followed the trail through red fir, lodgepole pine, and weeping spruce. I looked around for another walking stick. Before this trip I had thought walking sticks were for old people. After hiking across snowy passes with an injured knee, I came to appreciate the value of a good walking stick. Dionne used one too. Erika still thought they were for old people, but she waited for me. I found one, and we started back up the trail.

The damp earth alongside the trail was broken by an emerging snow plant. The red plant erupted from the soil like a miniature volcano.

"Look at this, you guys," I called to Dionne and Erika. "It's a snow plant."

"Trippy," said Dionne. "It looks like something from outer space. How come it has no leaves?"

"It isn't green because it doesn't photosynthesize. The plant doesn't make its own food. It feeds off nutrients from the forest floor." I told Erika and Dionne that this red plant is usually the first flower of spring, that it breaks through soil and pine needles shortly after the snow has melted. Here, at eighty-five hundred feet, springtime comes late. Though the snow plant is ubiquitous in the Sierra, the plant is considered endangered, so it is illegal to pick them.

A hiker approached. He wore a ripped T-shirt, and gray hair peeked out from under a blue bandana on his head. He asked us, "Whatcha lookin' at?"

"A snow plant." I pointed to the crimson plant.

"Funny little things. Phallic as hell, if you ask me." He laughed. Men find their penises in the most unlikely places.

"Where ya headed?"

"Muir Pass," Erika said.

"You girls won't make it up there tonight." He shook his head and added, "No way, José."

"It's not much farther, is it?" Dionne asked.

"No, but it's covered with snow. And it's late." He looked at his wrist even though he wasn't wearing a watch. "No. You girls definitely won't make it up there tonight. No way, no how."

I wanted to tell him that we had hiked farther in a day, that we had come almost a hundred miles, that we had gone through puberty a long time ago and, really, we were no longer girls. I wanted to tell him that Muir himself had supported the idea of women in the wilderness, that he had even defied Victorian decorum by traveling through Yosemite with his female friend Jeanne Carr. I wanted to tell him that the snow plant's red, convoluted folds looked like a vagina.

Instead, we thanked him for his advice and kept hiking.

"What do you think?" Dionne asked. "About what that man said?"

"I think he doesn't know us," I said.

"It isn't that far. What's a little snow?" Erika asked.

"Yeah. He doesn't know that these women are out to conquer," Dionne laughed.

The trail crawled up the stony ridge, passing the last of the trees. Dwarfed whitebark pine hunched over like gnomes. The sky hung over us like a blue tent, and the scraggy land stretched gray and white across the horizon. We walked through the first snow patches. Farther ahead, snow drenched the mountains, the meadows, the rocks, the trail. A landscape of white. I began to wonder.

"I love it when we get above timberline," Erika said.

"I don't." The rocky landscape seemed so desolate to me, so lonely. I imagined we were walking on the moon or some other area unfit for humans. When we hiked down a pass and into a cool green forest, I breathed a little more easily.

The trail passed Helen Lake, which was named for one of Muir's daughters. I wondered how much Helen and her sister, Wanda, had gone traipsing around the wilderness. Muir's "Stickeen" is dedicated to Helen, and the inscription reads, "Lover of wildness." Although the story is about a little dog, it is also about overcoming fears, venturing into unknown, wild places. Muir, however, talks to the dog as if it were a small boy with him, not a little girl. Even an imaginary little girl on a glacier in Alaska would be too much of a stretch to ask for from his nineteenth-century audience.

I did know Helen married a cattle rancher and Wanda studied at

Berkley and married a civil engineer. And Muir's wife moved with him to Yosemite, but she had trouble adjusting. Muir may have been in support of women in the wilderness, yet the culture itself didn't support it. Few women mountaineers existed, and most of them were climbing mountains in dresses and corsets. In general a woman's place was in the home. I watched as Erika strode up through the snowy landscape. Definitely not the Angel in the House.

We followed dirty footprints through the snowscape. The snow had melted into sun cups, rippled blue-and-white pockets. The slushy snow moved under our boots like sugar. I carefully placed my stick and stepped. We hiked up the hill, our shadows following behind, stretching a ghostly gray. Water trickled under snow. I tried not to look into the deep holes where snow had melted away from granite, worn thin. Some of these mini-crevasses were so deep they appeared bottomless and large enough to swallow a foot, a leg, a hiker. I knew that a misstep could mean a sprained ankle, a broken leg, or worse. I dug my walking stick into the snow, chose steps with caution, tried not to posthole. We didn't talk to each other on this stretch of trail. I listened to sounds of boots on snow, to water and to wind.

Red stains stretched across the snow. At first I thought blood, danger, death, but then I realized I knew better. Hues of pink, orange, and red were created by snow algae. This one-celled organism contains a bright-red carotenoid pigment, and it thrives in freezing water. Other types of snow algae exist and can change snow to green or yellow, yet red algae are the most common in the Sierra. Some hikers refer to pink snow as watermelon snow. I tried not to think about how great real watermelon would taste right then.

The sun burned yellow and mirthless, so we went without shirts; we wore sports bras with shorts and gaiters on our bare legs. The valley below fell under the cast of shade, but we walked along in the still-bright sunlight. An older woman stood off the trail, looking at a map. We said hello. Erika and Dionne kept hiking. I asked the woman where she was going.

"Overland," she replied and pointed toward the surrounding mountains. Silver braids hung from underneath a floppy hat. She wore glacier glasses, pale-yellow wind gear, and a small orange backpack. Two ski poles had been stuck into the snow next to her.

"What about the trail?" I asked.

"No trail," she said. "I have my map. And my compass." She patted her pocket. "I prefer to go cross country." I looked again to the snowy peaks, white exclamations marking a cloudless sky.

"Where are you going?" I asked again.

"Overland," she said, as if I hadn't heard her the first time. She folded up her map and tucked it in her pocket. She grabbed her poles and started walking. I looked up the trail. Erika and Dionne were almost to the top. I turned back toward the woman. She was gone. She couldn't have made it over the ridge. I stood there and stared. I wanted to disappear into the late-afternoon sun, to go alone overland without a trail, as she had, without the usual fears. I hiked to the top of the pass, looking around for the woman. I could find no rational explanation for her disappearance. In my imagination she became the ghost of Muir Pass. Perhaps she had been struck by lightning one night in the hut, and now she prowled overland, across granite, snowy peaks, and sky. Not such a bad fate, I supposed. I debated about whether or not I should mention this woman's disappearance to Dionne and Erika. If I told them my ghost theory, Erika would roll her eyes, and Dionne would humor me with a smile. I decided to keep her disappearance to myself.

Erika and Dionne waited for me in front of the Muir Hut. Unlike the top of Whitney, we were the only people there. The granite hut mimicked the shape of the mountains that surrounded it. The hut was constructed after the pattern of huts used in Brindisi, Italy, built to shelter passing hikers, but Tom said, "Don't plan to stay there overnight except in emergencies." I was glad to find nothing about death by lightning.

Our guidebook called this hut "fairly old," yet native people had built huts in this area long before the construction of the Muir Hut.

The Monache, or Western Mono, a Paiute group, had migrated over the Sierra Nevada from the east near Mono Lake. Although the Monache kept villages in the foothills year-round, they sometimes came here in the summer to camp. Their huts, though, were not made of stone; they were conical frames of willow poles covered with the skin of cedar.

Erika, Dionne, and I left our packs on the rocks and walked through the splintered wooden door of the hut. A sooty gray from illegal fires stained the granite walls. Lipstick and Hair were not too far off—the dark hut felt drafty, Gothic even. I imagined the ghost of Muir Pass returning from her foray overland—ruddy cheeked, windblown, a little travel stained. She would lean against a ski pole next to the box of crumpled paper that sat in the corner, rake through scraps of paper that littered the floor, reading messages from hikers: "Flying high on Muir Pass," "Skiing down to Wanda Lake today," "Joey and Mindy slept here." She would understand that people felt the need to leave some sort of mark behind; she had seen names on mountain ledgers, the carvings in aspen trees, wrinkled scraps of paper in the stone hut. She would see these as tiny messages of hope.

Light from the setting sun glowed pink through the window. Erika read the plaque on the wall above the fireplace: "This building was constructed in 1930 by the Sierra Club in cooperation with the Sierra National Forest and dedicated to the Memory of John Muir. The Muir Hut was intended as a temporary shelter for hikers caught in storms on this exposed section of trail. Overnight camping and fires are prohibited." Next to the plaque was a picture of a bearded Muir.

"Well, at least we won't have a fire," I said.

We went back outside and found marmots on our packs. We clapped our hands and shouted to scare them away. These marmots must have learned to live off food they had stolen from campers, but we knew enough not to feed wild animals; besides, we didn't have enough to share.

We pulled on sweatshirts, pants, and windbreakers. We made tabbouleh with the last of our tortillas and ate our dinner on the steps of the Muir Hut. Erika told me it was my turn to give the toast. I raised my hot chocolate and said, "Wilderness for human beings, because it's home." We touched cups and drank. In truth I had borrowed the quotation from the writer Dave Foreman, but under the circumstances I didn't think he would have minded.

"What about wilderness for women?" Dionne asked.

We all agreed the modified quotation was much better, and we toasted again. "Wilderness for women, because it's home."

We sat in silence for a while, and then Dionne said, "Jesse is really missing out."

"Yeah, but to him this would have just been a hell hike with a nice view," Erika said. Dionne and I both nodded. For us it had turned out to be more. It wasn't just making it to the top when people didn't think we would. It was being there and finally feeling settled in the out-of-doors, at home in our bodies. I had been waiting for something to click, an epiphany, to feel connected to nature. Now I realized it didn't work that way. Only the ghost of Muir Pass could truly vanish into the landscape. Even the hut, built from the earth, stuck out like a beehive. Yet the hut seemed to belong there, even if it didn't exactly blend in. And that is the way I felt—that sense of belonging. Right there in that present tense.

I was not naive enough to think ten days without a shower or a bed made me an expert on all this, but I understood some of what Muir had been talking about. I finally felt a connection to those mountains, the place. The landscape was no longer just setting. I realized that the going and getting there were never the point—when we are always almost somewhere, we can't be happy where we are. I leaned against the stone hut and looked out over the lake basins, rocks, and snow. Not a tree in sight. I took out my journal and sketched the view. I wanted to study the landscape, to look at it long enough, until it entered me and I could carry it with me, inside my body, always.

Yellow and pink reflected in the lakes, mirroring sky. The mountains changed color—tan to yellow, pink to black. The sky blazed like fire, and I saw the mountains as Muir did, not only a great snowy range but a vast range of light. Dionne and Erika went into the hut to unfold their sleeping bags and pads. I wasn't ready to leave the view. I wasn't sure what the questions were, but I was certain these mountains contained the answers. Perhaps these mountains really were a passport to the self and its true nature?

When John Muir was asked to teach a Sunday school class, he offered his students instruction in botany instead of the Bible as a way to understand creation. That approach has always made perfect sense to me. Paying attention as devotion. Although I have always loved all kinds of books, I think more answers can be found by looking out at the world. That night my wall-less prayer offered thanks for the place, the body that got me there, and an imagination that believed we could relearn how to live with nature. As men, as women, as humans.

The warmth of the day left the granite. I finished my drawing and wrote, "In the range of light." I sat for a moment more in the near-darkness. The wind twisted through the canyon, crawled over the divide, rustled through my hair. I added the words, "Happy to be right here—Muir Pass, Planet Earth, the Universe."

I ripped the page from my journal, went into the hut, and left my message with the rest for the lady ghost of Muir Pass.

There is that in the glance of a flower which
may at times control the greatest of creation's
braggart lords. / JOHN MUIR

Day 11

Fantasyland

....

Muir Pass (11,955) to McClure Meadow (9,650)   9.5 MILES

....

Although I had wanted to sleep in the hut as much as anyone, I woke
up many times during the night, imagining that the ghost of Muir
Pass had returned from her trip overland, angry to find trespassers.
The wind had moaned all night through the stoned-up fireplace, and
we emerged from the hut just before six, happy to see the sunrise. A
hazy pink lifted from the mountains, reflected into the lakes below,
and the day unfolded before us.

We started the stove and made the last of our oatmeal.

"Why didn't you say anything to the boys about the food?" I
asked Erika.

She asked, "Why didn't you?"

"I don't know," I answered her, and it was true, I didn't know.
Because I didn't want to be seen as the bossy one? Because I hoped
to eat as much as I wanted, knowing we could run out of food? Not
only had I been relying on them to do everything for me; I had been
relying on her. "My knee feels better," I told Erika. "I can carry more
stuff today."

"I got it," she said.

I had a half a Vicodin left, and then that was it for painkillers, but my knee seemed better. We packed up our stuff and began down. We descended past McDermand and Wanda Lakes, both striking high-alpine lakes with stark granite shores. A few shrubby white-bark pines twisted through the granite.

Erika waited for us at the ford of Evolution Creek. She said, "Looks like we will have to take our boots off." We were still above timberline, so the land lay desolate, vacant of green life. I pulled my Tevas off my pack, took off my boots, put my sandals on, and strapped Big Heiny, who wasn't really big or heinous anymore, back on. We waded through the cold water holding our boots, and a group of packhorses passed us, coming from the other side.

"No wonder there's so much poop on the trail," Dionne said.

"I know," Erika said. "No bikes allowed but the horses do more damage."

"Maybe next time we should go with horses. They could carry all our stuff. We could bring more food." It wasn't even eleven, and I already felt the twinge of hunger. All we had for lunch were Power-Bars, so we tried to hold off for as long as possible.

"I'm in," Dionne said. "The next time we go with horses."

"No way," Erika said. "Horses are bad for the trail, and besides, that would be cheating."

We continued down past junipers and into Evolution Valley. The meadows shimmered green in the sunlight. The flowers burst with color—purple lupine, cow parsnip, yellow arrowleaf senecio, scarlet gilia. We decided to eat our bars there, by the stream. We chose a rock, and as usual, I let Big Heiny drop with a thud.

"You're going to break something if you keep doing that," Erika said.

"You have the stove and filter. What could break?"

It didn't take long before the mosquitoes and flies found us. A doe wandered over to the other side of the creek to drink. I could see that the flies were bothering her too because of the way she flicked her ears. I watched her drink and thought about how idyllic the scene could have been without the bugs. I began killing them and then dropping them off into the river, where trout would come to the surface for them. I probably killed fifty this way. I was feeling pleased with myself when Dionne said, "In Zen Buddhism those flies have just as much right to life as the fish or as us."

"Don't they also believe in reincarnation?" I asked, killing another fly.

"So?"

"So this one doesn't have to be a fly anymore." I dropped a dead fly into the creek and said, "Be a bunny." Then another one, "Be a deer." I turned to Dionne. "I'm doing them a favor. Plus feeding the trout."

"I was just saying. Justify it however you want." I could tell she thought maybe I would come back as a fly if I wasn't careful.

We gathered our stuff and headed another four miles or so down to McClure Meadow, where we hoped to camp for the night. As I walked, I realized that in addition to the throbbing ache in my right knee, my left knee had started to feel funny. I began to panic. There was no way I would be able to finish the trail on two bad knees. I had been favoring the left, trying to put as little pressure on the right as possible. How would I do that if both knees were injured?

I hiked along, worried I might be damaged for life, when it occurred to me I really wanted pizza, a classic tomato and cheese pizza. I had thought of fresh fruit and vegetables before, but this pizza craving produced a new kind of desire, one that filled my imagination. I pictured myself eating the tomato sauce and the stringy, melted cheese, even every last bit of the crust, which would be thick and chewy. And I would dip it into ranch dressing. Not the watery diet kind, the thick and creamy full of fatty goodness kind.

"Excuse me," a man said from behind. I was so far into my food fantasies that I hadn't noticed him behind me.

"Sorry," I said. "Lost in thought."

"Are you solo?" he asked. He wore long wavy blond hair that fell in front of his blue eyes. He looked about my age and was the very sort of boy I usually fell for. He could have been jobless and illiterate, and still with that long blond hair and those blue eyes, I would have called him perfect.

"You mean alone?" Of course solo was alone; was I stupid?

"Yes," he said and smiled. A row of white teeth, one front tooth just slightly crossing over the other making the whole set even more attractive. How boring, my father always said—perfectly straight teeth look like a set of piano keys. My mother's teeth are British crooked.

"No," I said. "My friends are up ahead."

"Where are you headed?"

"Colby Meadow or McClure Meadow, I think. One of those. Wherever my girlfriends decide to stop." I hoped he picked up on the word *girlfriends* and not *friends*. I thought I was so sly.

"I'm going to Yosemite." He brushed his blond hair out of his eyes. His forearms curled with short blond hairs. I wanted to touch one of the fuzzy arms. I knew I couldn't just reach over and do it, and no way to inconspicuously bump him presented itself, so I could not satisfy my desire to see how those curly hairs might have felt on the palm of my hand.

"Me too," I said.

"Are you doing the whole JMT?"

"I think so."

"You think so?"

"Well, that's what we're going for. And you?"

"I started out of Onion Valley because I didn't want to deal with Whitney, and I am going to Tuolumne. I don't want to face the crowds in the Valley."

"That sounds like a good plan. But then you aren't doing the whole thing?"

"I'm not so worried about that. I just wanted to hike."

I nodded. I liked his attitude. Not doing the whole trail and feeling fine with it hadn't occurred to me. I wanted to keep talking to him, but I knew he probably wanted to get on his way. I was glad Dionne and Erika were ahead; at least for a couple of minutes I had him to myself. All for one and one for all, as long as no cute guys were around.

"Where are you from?" I asked, hoping he would linger for a while longer and I would find my excuse to touch his arm. Maybe a fly would land there, I reasoned, and I could brush it away for him. Then, I realized, probably not with my fly karma.

"Alaska, originally," he said. "Now I'm at school at UC Davis. I'm studying to become a vet."

"Cool. You must like animals." Another stupid thing to say.

"I do." He smiled again.

"What about you?"

"I just graduated from Cal Poly in biology." I thought about how much we had in common—biology and veterinarian medicine. I imagined people asking us later how we met, and we would say it happened along the John Muir Trail. I always wanted a story like that to tell—so much better than if we had had math class together, met at a bar, or worked at the same delicatessen.

He then asked the dreaded question, "What do you want to do with that?"

"I want to write a field guide to the John Muir Trail," I said. "I want to write about the flora and fauna on the trail." I was glad to have said "flora and fauna" rather than "plants and animals." It sounded much more scientific. I wasn't sure how I made that come out of my mouth at that very moment, and certainly I had no intention to write anything about the John Muir Trail, yet I was pleased with myself, and, I reasoned, it wasn't technically a lie; I just hadn't thought it up until then. And it was a better answer than the truth: "With my biology degree, my goals are to move back to Colorado in the fall, be a ski bum, and waitress at night in a Mexican restaurant, where I will use my tip money to buy half-priced margaritas."

"Totally cool," he said. "Is this trip part of your research?"

"Research? Oh, yes. I mean, I'm taking some notes here and there, but I'll have to come back." I had been writing down which flowers I saw on the trail into my journal, so that wasn't technically a lie either. Maybe we could come back together, I thought, revisit the place where we had met. I imagined us on this stretch of trail, saying, "Here it is, the exact spot where we met." In my fantasyland he was the rare man who cared deeply about those sorts of things.

"Well, good luck," he said, passed me, and kept walking up the trail. And rather quickly, I might add.

"You too," I called to him and waved at his back. He didn't turn around. I was sad to see him go. Then I imagined him catching up to Erika or Dionne and telling them, "I met your friend, the field biologist, the one writing the book."

I cringed thinking about what they would say to him. I could hear Erika saying, "The field biologist? Is that what she said? The craziest things come out of that girl's mouth."

This wasn't the first time I had lied to impress a man. I could have killed one of my boyfriends with my storytelling. I had met TJ at one of the outdoor club parties, and he'd asked me if I rock climbed. I immediately said, "Oh yes. I love rock climbing." I had been a couple of times and liked it okay. The first time was in Colorado, and Erika and I had rigged a top rope and used a body belay—neither of us knowing anything about rock climbing. The second time was on the college climbing wall.

Because I loved climbing so much, TJ asked me if I would like to climb with him the following weekend. I said yes, of course. Before the date I studied the figure eight knot and reviewed how to belay a climber from a book I checked out of the library called *How to Climb*. I felt ready for the rock climbing date and tried to wear something functional yet as flattering as possible without making it seem like I had tried too hard. Truth be told, I spent as much mental energy on my outfit, maybe more, as I did studying the climbing book. TJ picked me up, and off we went to Bishop's Peak. The plan was that he would lead the climb, set up the top rope, and then I would climb, removing the gear as I went. I was happy that I had read the chapter about cleaning the route. I felt confident.

The route he chose wasn't difficult, but one move at the top, which TJ referred to as the crux, required climbing up an overhang. Everything was going well until I noticed TJ's leg twitching up and down like the needle of a sewing machine on high speed. He had asked for slack in the rope so he could reach for the next bolt. I loosened the rope, but it didn't take an expert to see that he was about to fall. He got to the edge of the overhang and then peeled off the rock and fell toward me. I hadn't known enough to tie myself in, so as he came down, I shot up into the air. He smacked against the rock. To my surprise and great relief, I saw that I had caught him. We were both hanging there in midair like the bear bags we were now counterbalancing. After that I took a rock climbing course, and our romance didn't last long enough for him to find out how inexperienced I really was on that first date.

I reached Colby Meadows, and Erika and Dionne were nowhere in sight, so I figured they must have gone on to McClure Meadow. I followed the trail through the meadow, crossed the creek, and found Erika and Dionne setting up the tent. I pulled out what was left of the food and went through it. I looked at it as if it were an empty refrigerator that would suddenly shelve food. Erika came over and said, "Looks like we'll have to get creative."

"Like how?"

Erika picked up the food bags and examined them. "I have an idea," she said.

"I'm glad." I left her to her creativity and went down to the creek to wash up. I found Dionne washing out her clothes.

"Hi. How's it going?"

"Good. Did you talk to that cute blond guy on the trail?" I asked.

"Dale from Alaska?"

"I didn't ask his name, but yeah, he was from Alaska."

"A little bit," she said.

"Did he say anything about me?"

"No. I don't think so. Why?"

"Just wondering."

"What would he say, that he has never seen anyone so pretty and he wants to marry you?" Dionne laughed.

"Something like that. Who doesn't want to marry me?"

"Erika." Dionne wrung out her tighty-whiteys and set them on a rock to dry.

"What?" I sat down next to her on a rock.

"We played your game while we were hiking. Fuck, Marry, or Kill."

"And you gave her me?" I washed my feet with my washcloth. The icy water felt good on my sore feet. I surveyed my bright red and white blisters.

Dionne smiled at me and then rubbed her washcloth over her face.

"Did she kill me? Never mind. I don't want to know." I finished washing up and helped Dionne filter the water.

By the time we got back to camp, Erika had cooked up her creation. She dished up three balls of what looked like dough and said, "Dinner is served." Erika mixed up the flour and the cornmeal, added the oil, the dehydrated milk, salt, and some of the cornbread mix. This resulted in a salty, spongy creation that tasted like the Play-Doh cookies I used to make and try to feed to the neighborhood children.

"Your turn for the toast," Erika told Dionne.

"Here's to being here together and having something to eat," Dionne said.

I knew I should be glad we did, indeed, have something to eat. I wondered what the toast would be the next night. Here's to being here with nothing to eat but our leather hiking boots?

Everybody needs beauty as well as bread,
places to play in and pray in where nature
may heal and cheer and give strength to
the body and soul. / JOHN MUIR

Day 12

Hungry

McClure Meadows (9,650) to Blaney Meadows (7,632)   11 MILES

Sleeping three in a two-person tent was going to take some getting used to. I tried to face out but ended up with the tent side sucked against my face like a giant jellyfish. We all got up and decided we needed to have a "conference" about our food situation. Originally, we had planned to hike the eleven miles to Blaney Meadows and have a layover day at the hot springs. Without food, however, this no longer sounded like an attractive option. Erika pulled out the topographic map that showed our area in detail. She had brought the correct detailed map for every inch of the trail. "We can do that," she said, "or hike the nine miles farther to Florence Lake and hope they have some kind of store."

"But what if they don't? What does the guidebook say?"

Dionne read from the guidebook, "It says here that you can mail yourself packages. It doesn't say anything about a store."

"Doesn't there have to be a store? Isn't there RV camping there and people with gingham tablecloths, Coleman lanterns, and Budweiser? There has to be a store," I said.

"Are you willing to hike the extra twenty miles round-trip to find out?" Erika asked.

Both knees hurt, and I had blisters on my hips, shoulders, and feet. My skin had burned, peeled, and re-burned. With all the bites scattered over the leathery, peeling skin, I looked like a pink toad in boxer shorts and a sports bra. "No," I said. "I suppose not. But what about asking the ranger? There's a ranger station here. The ranger would know."

Everyone agreed that this seemed like a good idea. We got our Tevas on and walked over to the ranger station. I imagined the ranger inviting us in for coffee and eggs. He would see how hungry we were and want to feed us. He might even give us some granola bars for the trail. Maybe he would let us use his solar-heated shower. In my mind Ranger X was certainly a man, and a handsome one at that. We knocked on the door, but no one answered. My dreams of eggs and coffee, a hot shower, and a hot man disappeared. I tried the door.

"What are you doing?" Erika shook her head, clearly outraged that I would try to break into a ranger's dwelling.

"Just to see," I said, but the door was locked. Erika looked relieved. We would have looked pathetic, standing there, admitting that we had planned poorly and run out of food.

"What if we wait for him to come back?" I asked. Erika shook her head again.

"Why don't we head to the hot springs and see how it goes. If we feel like going on, we go on," Dionne said. We all agreed.

We got back to camp and divided the last PowerBar three ways and ate it with tea. Erika had saved some of the cornbread mix for lunch, so she said, "We're all set." I tried not to think about it. We got our packs on, and I tried to look at the bright side—Big Heiny had become Little Heiny because, like me, she didn't have any food in her.

We followed the trail past junipers and cow parsnip and made good time through Evolution Valley. The meadow flashed an emerald green in the morning light. I was glad we hiked it early, or else the grassy meadow would be buggy. The mugwort we found did not repel the insects, as legend had it. Although I first resisted using the poisonous DEET, now I welcomed the noxious smell. I still tried not to put the insect repellent on before swimming because I knew it couldn't be good for the water, but otherwise, I would bathe in it.

Because the grade leveled on this stretch, we quickly reached the log crossing at Evolution Creek. I studied the picture in the guide-book, trying to determine how far off the water the log would be. By the black-and-white photograph I had guessed four feet. When we arrived, I saw that it was more like ten feet. Not as high up as the suspension bridge, I thought, but also no hand railings.

Not only was I afraid of heights; I've always been less sure-footed than most people because my right foot sticks out when I walk. Any-one who has seen me run or walk will know it is me coming from a mile away. I leave funny prints in snow and sand, the left foot straightaway, the right one off to the side like a penguin's. My foot has always been this way. It comes from my right hip, and when I was little, the doctors wanted to break the hip and reassemble me correctly. My father, not wanting his daughter put back together like a jigsaw puzzle, said no way, and I had always viewed his rejection of modern medicine as proof that he had protected me. But because I wasn't going to have the surgery, I was supposed to wear special shoes. Even at age three, I wasn't about to wear anything that didn't match the tutu I had taken to wearing. And those shoes were not just ugly; they were obviously built to fix a problem—an ugly cor-rective shoe. As far as I was concerned, I might as well have had a sign on my forehead that read: I AM DEFECTIVE. At one point I even wore my red Mary Janes to bed, with my tutu of course, so that my parents would not be able to sneak the ugly, corrective shoes onto my bare feet while I slept. No surgery and no special shoes meant that I would walk funny the rest of my life. And that was the upside. Chronic knee and hip injuries, the downside.

My first-grade teacher, Mrs. Firestein, noticed my abnormal gait and attributed it to being lazy. She took it upon herself to fix it so that I would not have such an unattractive and dysfunctional walk for the rest of my life. At recess she made me walk a painted line on the asphalt with her so I could learn to walk straight. All the other kids made fun of me. It was bad enough that I was in the special reading class with "the reversies," the term they used for dyslexia.

Now I was spending my recess walking a straight line, back and forth—I looked like a six-year-old who had been stopped for drunk driving and was given a roadside sobriety test over and over again.

Eventually, I told my mother about my recess remediation, and she made Mrs. Firestein stop. My mother told Mrs. Firestein that I walked like that because I was an excellent ballerina, which couldn't be further from the truth. My mother blamed my funny foot on so many pliés. I wondered how my mother accounted for the fact that only one foot went out, but I never asked. I did, however, memorize what my mother told me to say when my classmates teased me. I was instructed to say, "At least I can walk." Then to ask the following: "If I were crippled, would you still make fun of me to my face?" A yes answer would show a real insensitivity, one that even a six-year-old didn't want to claim. A no answer would imply that they would make fun of a cripple behind her back. Although my fellow six-year-olds could not verbalize any sort of response to my mother's manipulative question, they did learn to stay away from me. As a result, I spent most of the first grade with a boy named Milo, who had something the teachers called the "fragile X syndrome," which sounded wholly better to me than my own case of the reversies.

Because of the funny right foot, when I needed to walk anything in a straight line, including crossing a log, I got a little bit worried that my right foot would get caught up and the result would be a tumble off the log and into the rockbound creek.

"Are you coming?" Erika called from the other side. Erika could have walked that log blindfolded.

"Yes," I said. I stepped onto the log, put both hands out, and tried not to look down. Big Heiny was lighter but still off-balance due to my poor packing skills, so that complicated matters considerably. I made sure I firmly planted each step before I took my next one. Somewhere near the middle I looked down.

"I can't go" was all I could manage to say. I froze. I couldn't make myself go forward or backward. Dionne and Erika conferred on what to do. They decided on verbal encouragement.

"You're almost there," Dionne said.

"You've got it," called Erika.

I stood in the middle of the log and thought about sitting down, but with Big Heiny strapped to me, that too seemed impossible. I felt like I might start to cry. I thought about Muir crossing that sliver of an ice bridge across the glacial crevasse in "Stickeen," and I felt like such a wimp. Still, there was nothing I could do. I resembled the little dog before he makes it across, a howling crybaby. Finally, Erika saw that their verbal encouragement wasn't working, so she took off her pack and came to my rescue. She walked to me, quick as can be, turned around, and said, "Hold onto my shirt." I did as she said. She walked, and I followed. If I did fall, I wasn't sure the fistful of her shirt would help me much, or I might possibly pull her in with me, but having something to hold onto gave me the feeling of security. We got to the other side, and I said, "Thanks." Most people would have been ashamed at having to be rescued, but any embarrassment I felt was overshadowed by my relief to be on the other side. Certainly, no man would have allowed his friend to rescue him off that log, yet I wasn't a man, and trying to act like one wasn't going to get me anywhere. I tried to think about accepting help as another, different way of being strong.

We followed the trail down the canyon, and the San Joaquin River bubbled below, whipping into waterfalls. The white water reminded me of a vanilla milkshake. We passed Aspen Flat and came to a steel bridge at the crossing of Piute Creek. We stopped to take photographs. A couple coming from the other way stopped too. They pulled out a bag of trail mix and began eating it. We lingered on the bridge, hoping that they might offer us a little, but they didn't. I wanted to ask them for some, but I felt ashamed to. I remembered how I had gone home with the guy in Fort Collins for a bed, and I wondered what I would do for pizza. Or even a vanilla milkshake.

I thought about John Muir's travels. When Muir visited the Sierra, he never lived off the land. He didn't hunt or fish, so he must have been hungry, really hungry, though he never dwells on it for too long in his writing. Maybe he knew that no one would want to read about it—hunger isn't that interesting. But maybe he really was hungry. Maybe the hiking wasn't as glorious as he says it was. Maybe only later, in his writing, does Muir's hunger manifest into a clear-minded, unveiled vision of the world. I, however, felt sure I would appreciate everything more if only I had a slice of pizza.

Too ashamed to ask for food, we continued along the trail.

"Aren't you hungry?" I asked Dionne.

"Yes. But I'm used to hungry."

"So, it isn't too bad?"

"It's weird. I'm seeing food differently. Now I see it more as energy. I never looked at it like that before."

"Uh-huh." I had never talked to Dionne about her disorder before, so I tried to put my words into the right order before I asked, "What did you think of food before?"

"Well, I'm sure Geoff told you some of it. I danced ballet from the time I was little, and I always had to be thin. I started starving myself when I was about fifteen. Maybe fourteen."

"What about the throwing up?" I asked. I didn't really understand the difference between anorexia and bulimia. All I knew was that anorexics hardly ate at all, whereas bulimics ate a lot and then threw it up. Some people do one or the other. Dionne did both. She would go for a long period of time without eating much, and then she would go on a binge of eating and purging. Geoff told me that she would eat Twinkies, hot dogs, butter, whole cream—stuff that didn't even sound good—and then throw it all up. Once Geoff caught her mid-binge, and to get him to leave her apartment, she told him she hated him.

"I know it's gross," she said. "This is the longest I've ever gone without a binge since I was sixteen."

"Wow," I said. "I can't imagine." I didn't know if she was telling me the truth. I had no way of knowing whether or not she really went to use the restroom and not to throw up the little she had eaten, but I wanted to believe her. And I wanted to understand. I asked her, "What are you thinking when you do it?"

"I'm not. It's like my brain shuts down. Or I'm in a trance. It's as if I'm someone else."

"Have you tried therapy or anything?"

"Of course, but my parents picked the therapist, and I don't like him."

"And?"

"So, I lie to him. He isn't that smart, so it's easy."

"But that's a waste of money."

"My parents pay."

I couldn't imagine my parents paying for therapy. My mother's favorite three-word phrase has always been "get over it." She would never want a stranger knowing about our family's problems, much less pay to tell him.

"I also tried an Overeaters Anonymous meeting. But I only went to one meeting. It was too weird."

"I wouldn't think that would be the right place for you."

"It's for people with food obsessions, so technically it is," she said. "But everyone else was, you know, big. They looked at me like I shouldn't be there."

"There must be something else?"

"Well, I'm here, right?"

I was glad we were finally talking about some of this. It had been a difficult subject to bring up—the elephant on the trail. What do you say—"Tell me about your bulimia"?

"Don't you hate throwing up?" I asked.

"You get used to it, even addicted to it. The feeling of empty after the fullness feels good. Clean. I know it sounds so gross. God, I'm telling you more than I tell that asshole therapist. I'm sorry."

I couldn't imagine being addicted to throwing up, but people become addicted to even the most unpleasant things, like pulling out their hair or cutting themselves. Like Dionne said, it was a way of being in control of your body, destructive or not. Yet that wasn't what mattered. What mattered was the feeling of being in charge, not just thinking it but proving it to the world. We all had our own ways of asserting control over our bodies, our worlds, unhealthy as they were.

We hiked in silence for a while, and around the next bend a deer wandered by with a radio collar.

"Why would that deer have a collar?" Dionne asked.

"Maybe they're tracking it for some kind of study."

"Who?"

"I don't know. Scientists."

"I wish I could catch that deer and take her collar off. It seems unnatural," Dionne said.

"It's a strange thing to see all the way out here."

"But, look, we aren't that far from Florence Lake. There's the trail. Eleven more miles. Can you do it today?" Dionne asked.

"I don't know."

Erika waited for us at the trail junction. "What do you think, ladies?"

"I don't think I can hike eleven more miles," I said. Maybe Erika could hike another eleven miles today, but I couldn't.

"Why don't we go to the hot springs, and then we can hike the rest of the way to Florence Lake tomorrow?" Dionne asked.

We set off, and I wondered if we would see Dale again. Probably not. Surely, he was long gone. A couple hiked toward us. They smelled like soap and laundry detergent.

"If you're headed to the hot springs," they told us, "don't bother. It's a mud pit, and the small lake next to it had leeches, so we didn't go in either."

"Is there a store at Florence Lake?" we asked.

"Yeah. There's a resort there," the man said.

The woman, who wrinkled her nose, added, "Showers too."

This information elevated our moods considerably, almost enough that I was willing to hike there that day. I adjusted the socks that were cushioning my shoulder straps, and we started hiking again.

"Let's stop at the hot springs, anyway," Erika said once we started walking. "They could be wrong."

Erika was never one to believe trail gossip, whereas I treated it like gospel. We decided we would have lunch at the springs and check it out. We had already gone out of our way, and we were only about a mile away. I used that mile to fantasize about pizza.

124

I couldn't decide, though, if I would want a beer with it or a Coke. I debated the relative merits of each in my head to pass the time.

We arrived at Blaney Meadow and found a nice spot right near the river. I dropped Big Heiny, and we sat down, ready to eat lunch.

Erika said, "We can have cornbread mix with water, miso soup, or tabbouleh and hummus mixed."

It all sounded terrible, but we decided on the tabbouleh and hummus so we didn't have to set up the stove. We all received a little brown mound that looked like piles of sand in our dishes. Though I should have been appreciative of Erika's resourcefulness, I just stared at my mound, trying to decide if this rated better or worse than the previous concoction.

A couple of men who were camped nearby wandered over. "Hey, we heard you talking about food," one of them said. "And we have extra, if you need some." Erika told them we were fine. I was ready to commit trail murder.

"We're okay," Dionne agreed. Now I was ready to kill them both. I looked up from my brown mound and asked them what they had. Erika glared at me like I should appreciate her concoction and that starving was our little secret.

"We're just out here for a couple of days. We have way too much." One of them disappeared for a minute and then returned with instant mashed potatoes, crackers, oatmeal, pasta, and three granola bars. I felt so happy I thought I might cry.

"Are you sure?" Dionne asked.

"Of course he's sure. He wouldn't say he was sure if he wasn't," I said. "Right?"

"Sure, I'm sure. Less for us to carry out. I'm John, by the way. And this is John," he said, pointing to the other John. They were both mid-forties. One John was tall and thin and the other short and stocky. The short John seemed less sure about giving away their food.

"Two Johns?" I asked. They nodded, and we introduced ourselves.

"And if you're camping here," Tall John said, "we're right next door, and you're welcome to come over for pudding after dinner."

"Thanks," I said. "We're not sure what we're doing. But if we stay, we'll join you."

They walked back to their camp, and Erika threw us each a granola bar. It wasn't pizza, but it was a lot better than the hummus and tabbouleh mudcake.

"So girls," Erika said, "what's the plan now that we have food?"

"We still don't have a lot." I looked forward to the camp store and a shower—and maybe even a beer, which I had decided would be the more attractive complement to my pizza.

"It's nine more miles out and then another eleven just to get back to the JMT," Erika said. "Then we still have to hike out to Vermillion Valley Resort at Lake Edison to pick up our package there."

"How fast can we get there?" Dionne asked.

"It's about thirty miles," Erika said. "Two or three days, depending on how fast we hike."

"But this isn't three days' worth of food," I said.

"I say we skip Florence and go for it," Dionne said.

"Let's do it," Erika said. I had not agreed with the plan, but I was clearly outnumbered. Plus, we had fallen behind schedule, so the only way to make up the lost mileage was to forgo one of our two planned layover days.

"I'm going to check out the springs," Erika said, grabbing her towel. "Anyone want to come?"

"I'll go with you, sweetie," Dionne said.

They hiked off together to the hot springs, and I stayed behind. Dionne had always been a "sweetie" and "honey" kind of person, yet this was the first time I'd heard her call Erika one of her pet names. I would have liked a soak; instead, I swam back into self-pity. I went to the creek to wash up and write in my journal. I didn't feel like complaining to my journal, so I made a list of the food I wanted to eat at Lake Edison, with pizza at the top of the list, followed by salad, a hot fudge sundae, and beer.

Erika and Dionne were back before I expected. They held a box of instant cheesecake.

"Where did you get that?" I asked, as if they had run off to the 7-Eleven to pick up some sundries.

"A lady at the springs gave it to us. Said she didn't want it. Just asked us if we would eat it." We had become the seagulls of the trail.

"Awesome. And we even have some dehydrated milk to make it with," I said, reading the package. The cheesecake cheered me up.

"How were the springs?" I asked. They didn't look like they had gone in.

"A mudhole and a lake with leeches," Erika said. "But this three-mile detour was worth it—tonight we'll have cheesecake."

After Erika and Dionne washed off in the stream, we set up camp. Now that everyone had her boots off, it became clear we weren't hiking anywhere that night. We decided on mashed potatoes with pesto, which wasn't as bad as it sounds, and then we took John and John up on their pudding offer. We decided to save the cheesecake for the next night since we would be having a smaller dinner of miso soup. I still wasn't convinced we had enough food, though I didn't say any more about it. I tried to enjoy the present. I began to learn that I could not have guessed at the ways in which our tomorrows would take care of themselves.

We told John and John stories about our trip, about the bears and fishing, sleeping in the Muir Hut, and the dynamite blasting on Mather Pass. We left out Jesse and Jim entirely, as if they had never been with us.

The tall John showed us pictures of his wife and daughter. "They would never want to do what you girls are doing," John said. "My wife hates camping." We heard that a lot. It seemed to me that women have been taught to fear, even hate, the outdoors. Although I had spent the day hungry, I had to admit there was something to worrying about food and shelter, even aches and blisters, that made more sense than my usual front-country problems—getting a job, paying bills, finding a date, wondering why I had chosen the wrong man once again.

The last light shined a dusky orange in the creek. Everything quiet, everything still. And never in my life, before then or since, did chocolate pudding taste so good.

FIG 1. Dionne and Erika posing at the hot springs the night before starting the John Muir Trail.

DAY 2 Aug 4 We are
at 12,000 ft. There is
still snow patches on the
ground. The snow run off
is loud amongst all the
quiet.
    The sky is filled with
ominous gray clouds - but
it feels too cold for rain
    We have a huge hike
tomorrow. about 9½ miles
total with a 2,500 ft
elevation gain. thats the
kind of day that will
make me ask myself
if this month - long
journey is crazy.
    Too many people
on this trail, at this
camp. I feel like my
privacy is invaded.

FIG 2. (*opposite top*) Leaving Whitney Portal in the rain on Day 1.

FIG 3. (*opposite bottom*) Suzanne's journal: Day 2 sketch of Mt. Whitney from Trail Camp.

FIG 4. (*above*) Suzanne and Erika on top of Mt. Whitney.

FIG 5. Guitar Lake.

FIG 6. Suzanne navigating a log creek
crossing with an injured knee.

FIG 7. Dionne and Suzanne making
a pact to finish the JMT together.

FIG 8. Suzanne hiking over
Pinchot Pass in the rain.

FIG 9. Climbing the snowy Muir Pass.

FIG 10. The top of Muir Pass.

FIG 11. Self-timer in front of the
Muir Hut at sunset.

FIG 12. (*opposite top*) Suzanne's journal:
Day 10 sketch from the top of Muir Pass.

FIG 13. (*opposite bottom*) Evolution Lake.

FIG 14. (*above*) McClure Meadows.

FIG 15. Erika and Dionne taking a break
at the edge of the San Joaquin River.

FIG 16. Goofing off with our
self-timer on Day 14.

FIG 17. Our shadows on granite.

FIG 18. Suzanne's journal: Day 16 sketch of
Lake Thomas Edison and the two men we
encountered at Vermillion Valley Resort.

FIG 19. Dionne and Erika on the trail.

FIG 20. Devils Postpile.

FIG 21. (*opposite top*) Suzanne's journal:
Day 23 sketch of Ruby Lake.

FIG 22. (*opposite bottom*) Posing on the
footbridge over the Tuolumne River
(before eating too much ice cream).

FIG 23. Self-timer, looking out over
Cathedral Peak.

FIG 24. Suzanne and Erika climbing
the Half Dome cables.

FIG 25. Sunset on top of Half Dome.

FIG 26. Dangling our boots off Half Dome.

FIG 27. Sunrise on Half Dome. Photo
taken by our new German friends.

FIG 28. Suzanne and Dionne coming
down Half Dome in the morning.

The sign reads:

HIGH SIERRA LOOP TRAIL

	MI	KM
VERNAL FALLS BRIDGE	0.8	1.3
TOP OF VERNAL FALLS	1.5	
EMERALD POOL	1.6	
TOP OF NEVADA FALLS	3.4	5
LITTLE YOSEMITE CAMPGROUND	4.3	6.9
GLACIER POINT	8.2	11.3
HALF DOME	8.2	11.3
CLOUDS REST	10.5	17.0
MERCED LAKE	13.1	21.0
TENAYA LAKE	16.4	26
TUOLUMNE MEADOWS	27.3	44
MOUNT WHITNEY		
JOHN MUIR TRAIL	211.0	

NO PETS ON TRAILS

FIG 29. Completing the John Muir Trail
in Yosemite Valley. We made it!

The clearest way into the Universe is through a forest wilderness. / JOHN MUIR

Day 13

Without a Map

....

Blaney Meadows (7,632) to Sally Keyes Lakes (10,150)   7 MILES

....

When I woke up, I heard Erika outside the tent talking to a man. Dionne groaned, "I'm still tired." I felt the same way. Erika was laughing, and I could hear her saying, "No, way. What a coincidence seeing you here." I immediately thought, "Oh, no, not Jim." I dragged myself halfway out of my sleeping bag to peer out of the tent's mesh door. I could only see him from the back, but clearly, it wasn't Jim. He had dark hair but stood taller and with better posture. I was relieved.

I crawled out of the tent and saw that the stranger was a friend from college. "Hey, Matt," I said and gave him a hug. "What are you doing here?"

"Hiking with my dad," he said. "We do this loop every year."

We invited them to eat with us, and when they saw what little food we had left, they asked, "Do you need any more?"

"People gave all of this to us," Dionne said. "We were out."

"I have way too many PowerBars," Matt said. "I don't need all of these." He rifled through his bag and gave us two each.

"Wow, thanks." Things were starting to look better and better. Who knew you could set off on a hiking trail without food and freeload off other hikers? Although once I thought about it, that was exactly what Jesse and Jim did.

"And have some of this gorp," he said and poured trail mix into a plastic bag and handed it to Erika.

"Where are your food drops?" Matt's father asked.

"Edison, Reds Meadow, and Tuolumne," Erika said.

"So, none for over a hundred miles, and then three all together?" Matt asked. Erika's face went red. We hadn't planned as well as we had thought. It would have worked out if we were faster, but some of us weren't, so our first food drop ended up being more than two weeks away.

Matt and his father went back to their campsite to pack up.

"That was a coincidence," I said.

"I know," Erika held out her PowerBars like a gold fan and said, "A lucky one at that."

Now that I didn't have the lack of food to worry about, I concentrated on my knee. I limped along, so Dionne hiked ahead with Erika again. I felt another pang of jealousy. It wasn't like I gave a second thought to how Erika might feel when Dionne and I hiked together. I didn't feel like hiking alone, so I tried to speed up. I passed the Florence Lake Trail Junction and got back to the John Muir Trail. Erika and Dionne waited for me, and I was happy to see them.

"How are you doing, Zsa Zsa?" Dionne asked.

"My knee. It's killing me."

Erika let out a loud sigh.

"I'll stay back with you, sweetie," Dionne said.

"You don't have to," I said but hoped that she would.

"I will."

"I'll see you at Senger Creek for lunch," Erika said. "Why don't you guys take the topo map, just in case. I have the book."

"Put it in my pack," I said and turned around.

Erika shoved it into a pocket and said, "It won't zip. You have too much crap in here. No wonder you hurt your knee with all this extra weight."

"I'll get it. Don't worry about it."

130

Erika hiked ahead, and Dionne said, "You know, we have a twenty-five hundred–foot climb today."

"We do?"

"Erika told me."

"Jeesh. I thought this would be an easy day because we don't have a pass."

"I thought so too. But I have something that might make your knee feel better."

"Did you get aspirin from someone?"

"No." Dionne turned around and smiled. She took off her pack, reached into a pocket, and pulled out a small glass pipe and a baggie.

"I didn't know you brought any."

"I just brought a little, but it makes my knee feel a lot better. Do you want some?"

"Yes." I didn't normally smoke pot because it made me hungry and tired, but I was already hungry and tired, so what did I have to lose?

We smoked a couple of hits, and I said, "I don't really feel anything."

"Trust me. Your knee will feel better."

We hiked along the trail, and I stopped to get some water. I realized the sharp pain in my knee had dulled like the faraway ache of a lover who had hurt your feelings once and now you couldn't remember his name.

"It's working," I called to Dionne.

"Good," she said. We began climbing switchbacks past yarrow and manzanita. Time seemed to slow, and we walked for what seemed like miles, and we approached a hiker.

"Are we almost to Senger Creek?" Dionne asked.

"Halfway," he said and kept heading down.

"Well, if we're only halfway up," I said, "I need to get some water and a snack."

"What kind of snack?"

"I still have some lemon drops."

"Awesome."

I threw off Big Heiny in my usual manner, and she hit the ground with a thud then started rolling down the hill, passing one switchback after another. Dionne and I stood there and watched her go. She went head over end, things flying out of the pocket I forgot to zip up. Finally, Heiny hit a lodgepole and came to a rest more than two hundred yards downhill.

"Oh God," I said. Dionne was laughing. I started laughing too, though I wasn't exactly happy about walking all that way back down again. I climbed down, following the path Heiny took, trying to find everything that had fallen out of the open pocket. I found my Swiss army knife, nail brush, Band-Aids, sunscreen, and the bag of lemon drops. "I got the lemon drops," I yelled.

"Good," Dionne shouted back. I strapped a very dusty Big Heiny back on and began walking back uphill. Dionne was still laughing. We drank some water, each had a lemon drop, and started hiking again. We made it to the top fairly quickly. We were clearly farther up than halfway. Erika waited for us at Little Senger Creek, looking at the guidebook; right then I realized that among the items I had retrieved from the side of that hill, the map was not one of them.

"Hey guys." She looked up from the guidebook, and it may have just been my paranoia, but she seemed to stare at me and frown.

"Hi," I said.

"Your pack's all dirty. Worse than usual," she said.

"It fell down the hill," Dionne said and laughed. I looked at her and tried to will her to shut up. My telepathy, though, didn't work. Dionne kept laughing and said, "You should have seen it go. It was *so* funny."

"How did that happen?" Erika asked.

"Well, I went to put it down."

"In your usual way?"

"Yes, but—"

Before I had the chance to answer, Erika asked, "So, it rolled all the way back down the hill?"

"Not all the way," I said. "Do we need water? I'll filter."

Erika said, "Yeah. The filter is by my pack." Then she added, "Unbelievable." I grabbed the filter and hurried to the creek. I was glad she had not yet asked for the map, but I knew it was just a matter of time. Not only had I left my pack unzipped; I had thrown down my pack on the edge of a steep switchback.

"Need help?" Dionne called.

"Sure."

Once out of earshot, I whispered to Dionne, "I lost the topo map."

"It fell out of your pack?"

"I guess so. Don't tell Erika we got stoned, or we'll really be in trouble."

"Shit. Don't worry, I won't." Dionne handed me another bottle to fill. The flies started biting, and we smacked them off ourselves and each other. I was glad to have this secret with her, but I wasn't looking forward to the wrath of the Commander.

We joined Erika and ate granola bars. The wind picked up, which helped with the flies. We packed up our stuff, and luckily, Erika didn't ask to see the map. I rationalized that it didn't matter much because within the next day or two we would have hiked onto a new map.

We weaved through a forested area and arrived at another green meadow, speckled with wildflowers. I counted at least nine different types of wildflowers—larkspur, cow parsnip, corn lilies, columbine, mule's ears, scarlet gilia, prettyface, mariposa lily, and Jacob's ladder. A quilt of white, fuchsia, yellow, and purple flowers. The corn lilies and cow parsnip stood tall; others, like the yellow prettyface and scarlet gilia, grew low to the ground, making this wildflower patch look like a garden. Bees and butterflies flitted from flower to flower. I had never seen so many different species of flowers growing together. I told Dionne, "Muir says that 'the clearest way into the Universe is through a forest wilderness.'"

"I know what he means," Dionne said. Erika just looked at us.

Gray storm clouds piled like stacked dinner plates onto the horizon. The frayed clouds indicated rain in the distance. The wind carried a cold mist. We had enjoyed so many days of sunshine in a row, I had forgotten about the possibility of rain. "Let's get camp set up before this moves in," Erika said, so we continued on to Sallie Keyes Lakes. We hiked between the isthmus of the two lakes and found a site near the far lake.

Although our hiking day was shorter than usual, we hadn't gotten started until late morning, and now dusk's gauzy veil had already begun to fall. The clouds compounded the darkness. We set up the tent on the leeward side of a large boulder, hoping for a wind block. Erika prepared the miso soup, I put together the cheesecake, and Dionne filtered water. The rain held off just long enough for us to eat dinner. The cheesecake tasted better even than the pudding. Marmots and chipmunks watched us eat it, hoping we'd drop some, but we ate every last crumb. We made it into our tent just before the rain fell in earnest, slickening the earth and sky with a gray film. I felt happy to be dry and warm, listening to the rain on the tent, feeling like maybe for once Erika wouldn't ask to see the map.

Keep close to Nature's heart . . . and break
clear away, once in awhile, and climb a
mountain or spend a week in the woods.
Wash your spirit clean. / JOHN MUIR

Day 14

Found Out

Sallie Keyes Lakes (10,150), Selden Pass
(10,900), and Bear Creek (9,040)   7.2 MILES

Frost gathered on the tent, and our water bottles froze again. Erika got out of the tent, first as usual. She sat on a rock and began fiddling with the stove.

"Shit," she said. "It's broken."

We had enough food, but if we couldn't cook, we were left with only crackers, trail mix, and one PowerBar each. It reminded me of that *Twilight Zone* episode where the librarian finally had the time to read but his glasses were smashed.

"Well, let's eat our PowerBars, and then I'll look at it later," Erika decided. "By the way, where's the map? I want to look at the trail to Edison. It could be tricky finding the ferry, and the book doesn't say much about it. The ferry will cut off six miles each way."

"I lost it."

"You what?" She looked up at me. Her hands were coated black with soot.

"Well, you know how I dropped my pack?"

"You said you would zip up that pocket. You didn't, did you?"

"I was going to, but I forgot." I could see my breath as I spoke.

"Great. Just great. I should have never given you the map." Then she muttered, "Stupid," under her breath. While she was technically right, I didn't like being called stupid and started to feel a thickening in my throat, behind my eyes.

Dionne emerged from the tent and said, "Erika, she didn't mean to lose it."

"Well, that doesn't help us, does it?" Erika turned to me and said, "If you didn't throw your pack down every time you took it off, you wouldn't have lost the map."

I could stand there, looking the other way with my arms crossed, or I could apologize and be done with it. I would have rather been done with her, though I didn't have that option. "I know. Sorry."

"Well, hopefully, we'll be able to find the ferry stop. Hopefully, we won't have to hike the extra miles. I just can't believe you did that." Erika behaved like I had intentionally started a forest fire.

"Hopefully." I wiped my face with my sleeve. I didn't know what else to say. Erika walked away to get the bear bag. The trees were small, tangled whitebark pine. We hung our food, but any bear would have been able to reach up without any trouble and pluck the food bag from the dainty tree if he'd wanted. Our meager food supplies, though, must not have been interesting enough to attract the bears, so the bag still hung there. We ate our granola bars and got going. Erika was still mad, so she hiked ahead. My knees still hurt, so Dionne hiked faster than I did too. I watched them both climb Selden Pass ahead of me and then vanish into the red and gray rocks. I alternated between feeling badly about the map and being mad at Erika for being such a commander, such a tyrant, for proving to me that she wasn't going to be the friend I wanted her to be. Of course, at the time I didn't stop to think that maybe I wasn't the friend she wanted me to be either.

I passed Heart Lake, which lived up to its name, at least in shape. I looked out over the lake, granite slabs, and cloudless sky. I reminded myself that happy was a choice. A hiker practically galloped down Selden Pass. He hiked with long strides and carried two professional-looking hiking poles.

"Hi there," he said as he went by.

"Hi. How's the pass?" I looked up at him. He was dark-haired and wore mirrored sunglasses. I could see myself in the reflection. I realized I had not looked into a mirror in two weeks, and I had forgotten all about it. I was distorted in his glasses. I immediately wondered if I had pimples that needed popping, stray eyebrow hairs, or any other ugly thing I had been walking around with on my face.

"Beautiful," he said.

"Beautiful?"

"The pass, the view from Selden is beautiful."

"Yes, of course."

"Where you headed?"

"We're doing the John Muir Trail."

"South to north?"

"No," I answered. "North to south."

He looked at me with a strange grin and said, "Aren't you headed up Selden?"

"Uh-huh."

"That would be south to north."

"Yes, you're right. South to north. I have always been terrible with directions. Do you by chance have a topo map of this area?"

"You don't have a map?" It was clear that he thought he had encountered a clown who had run away from her circus, out there with no map, clearly lost.

"I lost it. I just want to look at it so we can find the ferry across Lake Edison to the Vermillion Valley Resort."

"Sure." He pulled the map out of his pocket and said, "It's easy to find. Here it is. You can't miss it. Just turn off at Quail Meadow. You have a food drop there?"

"Yeah. The first one in two weeks."

"That's a long time. I have a buddy hiking up over Bishop Pass and meeting me with my food."

"That's nice. We ran out of food. But people gave us some." Why was I telling him this? First, I told him I traveled in the wrong direction; then I admitted that I didn't have a map. Now I shared with

137

this stranger our food situation. What would be next? That our little group, composed of a bulimic, a bully, and a neurotic, wasn't getting along?

"Well, sometimes you have to live off karma," he said. He cocked his head and smiled.

"Well, thanks, and have a good day," I said.

"You too." He continued down the rocky trail, humming as he walked.

I had just read *Way of the Peaceful Warrior*, and I wanted to believe that karma worked, that my "way" was in my hands. I wanted to believe that the world could be a place that made sense. And that if I could fight my natural inclination to cynicism, which came easier at twenty-two than it does now, and hold kindness in my heart, everything, ultimately, would be okay. I wrote clichés in my backpacking journal and believed them, things like "We have to make the most of ourselves because that's all there is of us" and "Wherever you go, there you are."

But even then, I knew mooching off other hikers had to do with poor planning, not karma. While Muir didn't live off the land either, preferring bread and tea, he didn't sponge off other people in the ways we had, didn't depend so heavily on the kindness of strangers. Or maybe he left those parts out.

With my mind occupied, I reached the top of the pass more quickly than I expected. The valley on the other side scooped into a deep green V. The sky wavered in Marie Lakes. Dionne and Erika were sitting at the top, talking to two older women.

"It's so good to see girls out here. You are an inspiration," they were telling Dionne and Erika. These women were out on a weeklong hike but were impressed that we were hiking the John Muir Trail. No one told them we were hiking without a map or food. No one told them we were going the wrong way on the trail. They shared their m&m's with us. I didn't feel much like an inspiration, yet I was happy for the chocolate. And for some reason, with them, I didn't feel like I had anything to prove. Maybe that was karma.

We started the hike down past Marie Lakes. I had to totter down because of my knee, but I was tired of complaining, so I tried to think about other things.

"Do you think they have showers at the resort?" I asked Dionne.

"I don't know. But I could use one."

After passing Marie Lakes, we reached a stream crossing. I watched Dionne hop lightly from one rock to the next. She had lost so much weight that I could see the stones of her spine under her sports bra. As I watched her, I wished she could just cure herself. Just eat normally. I tired of worrying about her. I also knew worrying, and especially judgment, wasn't going to help Dionne. And I knew that the things we are most judgmental about are the things we end up being tested with ourselves, and we usually fail. At least I always seemed to.

We hiked through Rosemarie Meadow and began climbing again. The trail branched, and Erika waited at the fork. Even though I was still mad at Erika, I was happy to see her; without her, Dionne and I wouldn't have had a clue which way to go.

"I didn't want you to go the wrong way. We go this way." Erika pointed. Another log crossing, but this one was not as high up, and I walked across without any help. I was getting better at this. Plus, there was no way I would allow myself to be rescued by Erika at that point. The three of us hiked together and reached Bear Creek.

"Tom says there's better camping farther down," Erika said. We passed the trail to Mono Hot Springs, and I wondered why we didn't send our resupply package there, yet I didn't dare mention this to Erika, who had organized the food drops. We began to look around for a flat place to camp.

Erika didn't mention the map again, which was her way of forgiving me.

Because of our relatively short seven-mile hiking day, we had time at camp to relax, so we spent the afternoon goofing off. We took crazy self-portraits with our camera—one of us hanging upside down off the side of a rock, another of us doing handstands, a last one of our shadows. Then we attended to some serious sunbathing. Dionne and

Erika lay out naked. I wore my bathing suit. Bikini tan lines would be an improvement over my sports bra and sock tan lines. Dionne wrote in her journal, and I flipped through the wildflower guide, trying to figure out which wildflowers we had seen. So far, we had seen more than thirty species. The benefit of a big snow year was a big wildflower year. If I were John Muir, I would be drawing pictures of them, but since I had a book with color photographs, there didn't seem to be much point. Plus, I couldn't very well stop along the trail and take the time to draw each flower I saw. I could just imagine telling Erika to wait up while I drew the arrowleaf senecio.

Erika sat on the rock, fiddling with her stove, trying to fix it. She looked crazy sitting there trying to fix the stove in her Tevas with a bandana on her head, wearing nothing else. She would have made the perfect picture for a brochure advertising a nudist colony. Finally, she said, "Well, I can't get it. We'll cook over a fire tonight." She lay down and fell fast asleep. Being in charge of us must have been exhausting.

The shadows slid over our rocks, and I got up to start a fire. I had no idea if we were allowed fires there or not. Even though cooking over a fire would be a messy affair, the side benefit would be that fire would keep the mosquitoes away during bug hour.

By then Erika had woken up and said, "I think when I get back to the real world, I'll visit my parents for a while before going back to Colorado."

"The real world? I asked. "Isn't this the real world?"

"You know what I mean," she said. I did, yet it struck me as strange that what we had been doing was closer to "real" than what we usually did. Though we hadn't exactly been living off the land in any natural sense, we also hadn't been in a building, aside from the huts on Whitney and Muir Pass, or in a car for two weeks. We hadn't talked on the phone, listened to music, or seen a television. We carried all our own trash, which made me realize how much trash we produce in just one day, and that was after we had already taken everything out of the wrappers. It became clear to me that if we had to carry our own trash around all the time, we would not be so wasteful. We would also think twice about buying things with so much plastic packaging.

Also, we propelled ourselves only with our own bodies; when I looked at the maps, I was amazed to see how far we could actually travel without a car. And all the things we could see. Henry David Thoreau says, "Two or three hours' walking will carry me to as strange a country as I expect to see." From a car window this strangeness often escapes one's notice, but not so on foot.

I loved being outside all the time. True, I thought about food constantly, but my clothes fit looser, and I felt stronger, even if my knees hurt. I was dirty yet not in that grimy city way. I understood what Muir meant when he said nature washes our spirits clean. I realized I felt happy in a way I had not felt in a long time, maybe ever.

"What about you?" Erika asked us.

"I think I'll get a job at a coffee shop as a barista," Dionne said, "then apply to grad school."

I thought about what I would like to do. The looming question. I knew I'd be spending the winter in Colorado, but what about afterward? These were the questions I had started with, and I still couldn't answer them. And I couldn't go home. So, I said the first thing that came to mind: "I want to work at one of the San Luis Obispo wineries for a while. Wouldn't it be fun to work in a tasting room?"

"I guess," Erika said.

"I think it would be fun," Dionne said. "You could learn a lot about wine."

"You guys could come visit me at the winery." I liked the sound of that—much more glamorous than the last place I worked, which was a deli called Gus's Grocery, leaving me to smell like pickles and mustard all the time. Also, part of me wanted to prove to the world that I wasn't like my father. I could be around all that wine and not drink too much. Not cross the proverbial line between party-fun and desperation.

"We will," Erika said.

"You can ride your bike," I told Erika. She smiled because she knew what I was referring to. We had all taken a bicycle winery tour the previous year. After the first winery I opted to ride in the air-conditioned van. It was summer in Paso Robles, and it must have been 105 degrees out. After the third winery every one of us rode happily in the van, but not Erika. She bicycled out there, red-faced and sweating, determined to ride between every winery. Because of time, she had to bicycle past the fourth winery without tasting there and meet us at the fifth. She looked terrible, clothes and hair drenched with sweat, yet she reached her goal—riding between every winery. She called the rest of us wimps, especially me because I had only ridden to the first winery. Our friend Kristin, who got into the van after winery number 2, said, "Merlot tastes better when you aren't so sweaty. What's Erika out to prove?"

"That she can do it," I had said.

"But why would you want to?" Kristin asked.

"I don't know," I admitted, though part of me understood it. Erika had something I didn't—the ability to look forward to her future self and see what that self would have wanted to accomplish. How would she feel then? If her future self wanted to say, "I rode between every winery," then her present-tense self would do it. Delaying gratification became a gift from her present self to her future self. I, on the other hand, asked, How do I feel right now? What do I want right now? Why delay for tomorrow what I can have right this very minute? Therefore, my future self would receive no such gifts. So, the trail, where I would have to wait for air-conditioning, a beer, or a slice of pizza, proved more difficult for me than I had originally imagined. I cared only about the now-me, rather than considering the end-of-the-trail me—rather, even, than considering anyone else. But mile by mile the trail seemed to be changing some of that.

The night was full of strange sounds, and I gladly
welcomed the morning. / JOHN MUIR

Day 15

Flappy

Bear Creek (9,040) to Vermillion Valley Resort (7,750)   11 MILES

We climbed up and over Bear Ridge, and the valley descended before us. Volcanic Knob, which was more impressive than its name, hunched over us. We began our descent of seventy or so switchbacks; the trail was not as rocky as it had been, so I made better time than usual. We looped down through a diverse forest of mountain hemlock, silver pine, red fir, Jeffrey pine, aspen, white fir, and cottonwood. A purple carpet of lupine swathed the slope with an occasional clump of yellow black-eyed Susans or red Indian paintbrush. The diversity of the forest reminded me of the mystical Sherwood Forest; I expected Robin Hood and Maid Marian to jump out from behind a tree at every turn. Dionne, Erika, and I stopped to take pictures of each other in the filtered morning light. Though lovely at that time of day, I wouldn't have wanted to hike through there at night. I imagined the dense forest would be downright spooky. Nightfall would turn Maid Marian's playground into Dracula's wilderness.

We were all glad to come to the bottom of the switchbacks; we stopped for water and ran into an older couple that was about to begin hiking up. They both had tree branch walking sticks like mine. As we got closer, we could see that they were not just older; they were old—white-haired, wrinkled, and shrunken like dolls in a museum case. Though not without spunk. They told us they were seventy-seven and seventy-eight and that, like us, they planned to hike the John Muir Trail. I immediately felt a mix of awe and embarrassment. Here I had been complaining, and these two were out there doing it, and they each had more than fifty years on me. One hundred if you counted them both.

"How many days are you out here?" the woman asked.

"About a month," I said.

"Oh my. Well that's fast. Frank and I are taking two months." This was the first time anyone had said we were going fast. Many hikers average twenty miles a day, finishing within two weeks. People had even called our pace leisurely, though it had not felt that way to me.

"That's great," Dionne said. "How are you getting your food?"

"We have our daughter and grandson hiking in every so often to bring us supplies. I think they want to check up on us to make sure we haven't croaked," the woman said and laughed.

"Oh Ilene." Frank joined Ilene in laughing. They stood there together in their floppy hats and giant sunglasses, and they smiled.

"We wish we'd decided to do this when we were younger," Ilene said. "We've been on other long trips but never got around to this one. It's beautiful. Better late than never."

"God's country," Frank said, and we all nodded.

"Well, we better get to it," Ilene said. "Bye now, and God bless." I watched them hike off. The skin on Ilene's legs hung like the craggy hide of an elephant. Something about the early morning light made her wrinkled skin beautiful. I decided that I would keep on wearing shorts too. If my legs were strong enough to get me places like hers did, they should not be covered up in shame.

And then I thought of my father, who was about the age of Frank and Ilene, but I couldn't picture him hiking the John Muir Trail. He was fifty-three when I was born, so everyone always thought he was my grandfather, not my father. This was a source of embarrassment for me, and it angered and saddened him that I felt that way. He was now in his seventies, and despite the drinking, I thought he had held up well, though not well enough to hike hundreds of miles. Yet he had always talked fondly about the outdoors, the camping and fishing he had done in his youth. For the first time it occurred to me that my love for the outdoors had perhaps been inherited from him.

"I hope I will be out here doing this at their age," I finally said to Erika and Dionne.

"Me too," Dionne said.

"I know I will be," Erika said. "Just gotta keep doing it."

We hiked along, and I thought about aging. Certainly, it was all relative. At eighteen I thought I would never get to thirty, used to think, "Just kill me at thirty—that is so old." But here I was, almost twenty-three, and thirty no longer seemed quite so far away. The "never get to" or "just kill me" age keeps moving beyond our current age. Yet being a young woman has its own set of problems. In our society, a young woman's most important asset is her beauty. We can never get away from it—object to someone else's subject. As she ages, my beauty queen mother is losing the very thing that always defined her. Once when we went to try on bathing suits, I could hear her weeping in the dressing room next door. I have never had a fabulous bikini body, and in some ways that has made things easier. I didn't have as far to fall.

Erika stopped to look at the guidebook. "It says the trail should be right up here." I hoped she wouldn't mention the more detailed topographic map again. At least when we reached Silver Pass, we would be onto a new map. "There," Erika pointed. We all looked up from the book, and a hiker bumbled down the trail toward us. He wore round sunglasses that made him look like a beetle and gaiters around his ankles. A dirty orange T-shirt, wet with sweat, stretched across his large potbelly. He sported two full-sized backpacks, one on top of the other.

"That's quite a load there," I said. Both Erika and Dionne looked at me, wondering why I would initiate a conversation with him. I wasn't sure myself. The man came straight at us, and we jumped out of his way as if he were an angry bull.

"I establish a base camp," he said, still running, "and then I day hike." He then stopped and looked around and shouted, "Where's the trail? Where's the trail?" Because we weren't sure what he meant—we were, after all, on the trail—we didn't answer him. He threw off one pack and then the other, much like the way I used to throw mine down before I lost the map.

"The trail. The trail?" Now he was flapping his arms up and down like an overfed turkey who would sure like to fly but couldn't quite get his heft airborne. He ran one way and then straight toward us again. Dionne and I both ducked behind Erika. She said, "That way," and pointed. He nodded, outfitted himself with one pack and then the other, and started scrambling up the trail. We hurried the other way, toward the ferry, where he had come from. I hoped he didn't decide to turn around and flap after us down the trail.

"Well, we must be close," Erika said. "That guy couldn't have made it far with that load."

"What do you think he had in those two backpacks?" I asked.

"I don't know," Dionne said, "but he was crazy, flapping all over the place like that." We all laughed and began referring to him as "Flappy." I kept looking over my shoulder, however, in hopes that he wasn't following us. We kept hiking, and I began to imagine that he had dead bodies hacked into pieces in that second backpack. I didn't dare tell Dionne or Erika this hypothesis because they would have surely called me paranoid.

I looked up and saw Erika and Dionne stopped up ahead talking to a blond guy. Dale from Alaska. My heart did a funny thing in my chest, much like it did when Flappy started flapping, though my fantasyland in regards to Dale was much more fun than the idea of Flappy carrying around body parts. Maybe this was my chance to get to know Dale better? Maybe hike together for a while? Maybe exchange telephone numbers?

Then I noticed Dale's hiking partner, a petite woman with two long sandy braids. It became obvious to me that there would be no future tales about how Dale and I had found each other on the John Muir Trail.

"Hi guys," he said to us. "This is Penelope. She met me at Vermillion Valley Resort, and we're hiking the rest of the way together." He took her small hand, and she smiled at us. Freckles scattered across the bridge of her nose and her cheeks, and of course they were not ugly freckles but the cute kind, a constellation of small, brown stars. I was happy to know we were on the right trail to the ferry though not thrilled about seeing Dale with this woman. Hadn't he said something about hiking "solo"? I was too busy concentrating on what I wanted to say next or trying to find an excuse to touch his arm that I hadn't really listened to what he said.

"Great," we all said. "Nice to meet you."

"Penelope, this is the scientist I told you about," Dale said and looked at me. Erika and Dionne both looked at me too, but not in quite the same way Dale and Penelope did.

"Cool project," Penelope said.

"Yes, well thanks. Nice meeting you. We have to get going."

"The morning ferry left. The next one won't be back for a couple of hours," Erika said.

"Well, I'm sure Dale and Penelope here would like to get hiking along. Nice seeing you again. And nice meeting you." Now everyone looked at me in the same quizzical way. I was so getting caught. I imagined Penelope saying, "Really, tell me about your book project," and then Dionne and Erika would say, "What book project? We have never heard of a book project." Erika would laugh, getting back at me because when she'd told me she wanted to try out for the Olympics in mogul skiing a couple of years ago, I'd made fun of her to no end. My friend Jason and I even told her we were going to start ice skating and compete in the couples figure skating. She got so mad at us, especially when we went into the fabulous outfits with the flames on the sides that we were planning to wear for the competition. Jason and I even got into a fight about the color of our costumes. I had said blue, as in hot blue flames, but what with all the bluish ice there already Jason thought something in fuchsia would be better. Erika told us we'd better both shut up. I now regretted making fun of her, and the truth was Erika was an accomplished skier, and Olympic freestyle skiing would not have been entirely out of reach, whereas Jason and I were both clumsy, so anything involving blades and ice would be certain to end in a bloody mess. When Erika joined the logging team, we had all laughed, yet she had the last laugh when she went on to win the state championship in the female axe throw. Apparently, her performance in the logroll was also quite impressive.

"Well, have a great hike, girls," Dale said.

"Nice meeting you," Penelope said, though I couldn't imagine she thought I had been very nice. I pictured her saying to Dale, "That scientist was a weirdo." And he would reply, "That's how scientists are; they are peculiar that way because they are so interesting and smart."

"What's this project, Dr. Roberts?" Erika asked. I now had to face Erika and Dionne, with whom I would spend the coming weeks, but not Dale, a stranger I would likely never see again. Still, having people out there who thought of me as a peculiar scientist and not a lying fake seemed attractive to me. At least I might have been something interesting to someone.

"Well," I told Erika, "I said I wanted to do a natural history of the John Muir Trail someday. And I do. I mean, I could see doing that." This was a lie. I was neither detail oriented nor patient enough to ever write anything scientific. It was a miracle that I had completed a bachelor's degree in biology.

"Like what? The rocks and stuff?" Dionne asked.

"Yes, but mostly the plants and animals. Come back and check it out and write about it."

"Sounds cool," Dionne said. She was just being nice.

"Can't wait to read all about it, Dr. Roberts," Erika said. We hiked along toward the ferry. I was glad that this was all the teasing I got, even though I deserved more. And Erika was right; I liked to read and write but had no fortitude when it came to anything tedious, whether reading a map or fixing a camp stove. I had hoped nature possessed the ability to give me something to make up for my short-comings so that maybe I wouldn't dwell so much on my own dull psyche, making up stories to mask the truth. Yet waiting around for nature to deliver the answers, to fix me, wasn't exactly working.

I remembered visiting Kings Canyon National Park, and one of the park signs warned, "These mountains are indifferent to your survival." For some reason that felt to me a great relief. Nature wasn't out to get me, but nature also wasn't going to wrap her bountiful arms around me and squeeze me to her flowery bosom. The personification of nature, most often into some sort of good mother or siren lover, only seemed to make sense from afar.

Once on the trail, I began to see that neither construct worked—nature as threatening or nature as nurturing. John Muir may have found nature glorious, yet the glory was in Muir and in his response to the natural world. As far as I could tell, the mountains weren't going around trying to make me feel one way or the other. That was left to me. "Did you know Dale had a girlfriend?" I said, trying to change the subject.

"I'm not surprised," Erika said. "What did you think? He liked you?"

"Why wouldn't he?" I asked.

"Why do you think every guy you meet is going to like you?" Erika asked.

I didn't answer, so we all hiked on in silence. I felt betrayed. If I couldn't rely on nature to care about me, then surely I needed girlfriends who cared, who would prop me up even when I didn't always deserve it. At the time I couldn't see that the problem wasn't Erika; the problem was me and my desperate need for male approval. Like many young women, I believed my value could only be determined by a man. I had been following a narrative that went like this: if he likes me, I'm worthy, and then I'll be happy. I needed a new story-line, though I couldn't see that at the time, so knowing she would be kind, I asked Dionne, "What do *you* think?"

"I think you are cuter than that Penelope. I think he liked you."

"Thanks, Cassiopeia."

I had happily accepted the shams and delusions as reality, but if being out in nature did anything, it forced me to start to see things as they really were, which is why I needed girlfriends, like Dionne, to help me confront the truth. False peaks give us hope that we are almost there, yet soon enough, we reach the false peak and realize that our destination still remains a long way off. Sunny mornings make us believe the day will be fair. Before long clouds swallow the mountains, and we are hiking through a storm. That's where the story comes in. Is the windstorm glorious? Would I find a version of myself not dependent on the male gaze?

Erika stood near a big white sign with painted back letters that read FERRY. She had both hands out, palms up, in a ta-da magician way, pointing at the sign as if it were a white rabbit she had just pulled out of her hat.

"Yippee," Dionne shouted.

"Finally," I said. Erika took a picture of me, pointing to the ferry sign. We set our packs down, and I hoped that Erika took note that I had stopped throwing mine down. The wind chilled the sweat on my back, and I pulled on my fleece.

A couple of forty-something hikers were waiting for the ferry too. They were hiking the John Muir Trail but from Yosemite to Whitney, the way most of the other hikers had been going. They told us they were on their honeymoon. The woman smiled, and she had small wrinkles around her blue eyes. The man was balding but had a kind face. They both looked happy. I wanted to ask them how old they were, though I didn't dare. People in their forties generally didn't announce their ages like people in their seventies, like Frank and Ilene. I was impressed, though, that they were having a hiking honeymoon. I couldn't imagine a hiking honeymoon, or any kind of honeymoon, except in a dreamworld sort of way, a fantasyland where I married a man because I liked the way blond hairs curled on his forearm. I wondered if this was the first marriage for these two—did they wait until their forties to get married? I wished they would offer us more information.

At four o'clock the ferry arrived. We paid the skipper, and it felt strange to use money. We had not paid for anything since Whitney Portal, more than two weeks ago. We loaded the ferry, the *Edison Queen*, and the honeymooners talked between themselves, but I kept sneaking looks at them. I was intrigued by this forty-something woman who was on her honeymoon and appeared happy. I had thought of my sister as an old bride, not marrying until thirty. And I would have said that the idea of forty-year-old honeymooners seemed preposterous, almost as bad as the thought of my own parents having sex. As I watched these two whisper to each other and laugh at their secret jokes, these middle-aged honeymooners didn't seem ridiculous at all. They looked happy together in that unmistakable way people look who have just had sex. Erika and Dionne didn't seem to be as preoccupied with this couple as I was. They just seemed to be enjoying the boat ride, looking out as the forested shore whirled by. Maybe at the time part of me knew it would take me a long time to figure out my life, that I might have to learn how to be happy alone before being happy with someone else. Though at the time, if someone had told me that I, too, would end up a forty-year-old newlywed, I never would have believed it.

When we arrived at Vermillion Valley Resort, we headed straight for the store to see if our package had arrived. It was waiting there for us, and we ripped it open and found oatmeal, hummus, rice and beans, tortillas, tabbouleh, Top Ramen, pasta, and powdered milk—enough dried food to choke a marmot. And thankfully, we had had the forethought to include lemon drops and M&M's. We immediately opened the M&M bag and began eating them. Even Dionne. Erika had also included some spare clothes for herself, and I realized I hadn't sent any bandages, so I spent quite a bit of time in the section of the store called "Blister Care." I bought Band-Aids, duct tape, antibiotic cream, and moleskin. I also bought two bottles of Advil, along with more bug juice.

I headed to the restroom and washed my hands with soap. The

water ran black off my hands and arms. Even though we washed daily in creeks and lakes, we really were dirty. Just washing my hands made me feel clean. I also inspected myself in the mirror. I looked better than I expected. I was tan, and my chubby cheeks were less chubby than usual. My mousy brown hair had lightened in front from all the sun. I found Erika and Dionne in the restaurant, looking at the menu. There was no pizza, but they did have my second fantasy food, French fries, as well as salad, all kinds of sandwiches, and an impressive selection of fruit cobblers. I ate a salad, tuna fish sandwich with French fries, and apple cobbler with toffee crunch ice cream. I ate until I felt sick. I finally noticed Dionne doing the same. Erika ate at her usual slow pace, which was unimaginable to me.

While inhaling my bountiful fare, I noticed two men in beige uniforms staring at us from across the restaurant. One of them was tall and skinny, with a five o'clock shadow and greasy brown hair; the other was short, with a beard, round face, and ice-blue eyes. They both looked at me, holding their gaze until I looked away. I tried not to look at them, but I couldn't help myself from checking to see if they were still staring at us. They were. This was not the kind of male attention I desired. This was the kind that scared me. I drew that imaginary line through a series of calculations combined with intuition—were they college-aged backpackers like us? Or something else? These men definitely fell into the category of "something else."

"Look at those guys," I whispered to Erika and Dionne. "They're staring at us."

"That's because we all look so pretty," Dionne laughed. She shoved a handful of fries in her mouth.

"No, they're weird. I just know it." I tried to peer over at them nonchalantly to see if they were still staring. "No, really. They're still staring. And they have a look in their eyes."

"Suzanne, will you stop?" Erika said. "Why are you always so paranoid?"

"I'm not paranoid. Think of those two women who were attacked on the Appalachian Trail five years ago. They were shot by a psycho. One died."

"This isn't the Appalachian Trail. They were just a few miles from a road," Erika said. "And that was a freak incident."

"We are zero miles from a road now, in case you haven't noticed," I told her. "We're back in the front country, easy targets. We just need to be careful, that's all. And there's something wrong with those guys, I can tell."

Erika scraped her ice cream onto her spoon, little by little, and said, "Whatever. We're fine. We've come this far." Dionne finished with her fries and was busy with her pie, so she didn't look up again for a while. Every time I glanced over at the two guys, they were looking at me. Because I kept checking to see if they were staring at us, I see now that it's possible that they thought I had been flirting with them.

The waitress came over and asked if we would like anything else.

"Do those guys work here?" I said in a low voice so they wouldn't hear me. I pointed with the end of my spoon as inconspicuously as I could. Erika rolled her eyes and said under her breath, "My God."

"Those two?" the waitress asked in a much-too-loud voice. "No, they're part of the CCC, but I think those two are ex-cons. Don't worry, though, they're harmless." She laughed and brushed a piece of hair back into her messy bun.

"What's the CCC?"

"California Conservation Corps. They're here, working on projects around the lake." She handed us our bill. "Will we see you for breakfast?"

"You sure will," Dionne said.

"See," I said to Erika and Dionne once the waitress left.

"See what? They're CCC, working on trails and stuff," Erika said.

"Didn't you hear her? They're ex-cons. You know, ex-convicts. Prisoners."

"I know what an ex-con is," Erika said. "You're being ridiculous. They wouldn't have let them out of jail if they were dangerous." Dionne just shrugged and excused herself to go to the bathroom.

Neither of them thought much of these two men. I tried to think about other things, but my imagination got the best of me. Suppose Flappy was working with these two, carrying the body parts in his two giant backpacks, disposing of women's bodies out in the wilderness?

We found out that we would have gotten one free night in the hiker's tent cabin, but another thru-hiker was already using it, so we rode in the back of a pickup truck to the backpacker's camp, which was just a flat, overflow camping area with no bathrooms, showers, or anything else. No one else was there. We set up our tent, and I lamented not taking a shower or even having a beer. I spent the night worrying that those two ex-cons would find us. I imagined that neither of them had had sex for a while and they would rape us, maybe even kill us. And here we were out in backpacker's boonieland, where no one would be able to hear our screams. I couldn't talk anymore about my fears because I knew Dionne and Erika already thought I was being paranoid. So, I lay awake with a cold-boned fear, listening for the sounds of boots on the dirt. Every time I thought I heard something, I whispered, "What's that?"

Erika answered, "What's what?"

"That sound."

"Go to sleep."

Dionne's heavy breathing told me she was already sleeping. So, I kept listening without saying anything else. All night I hoped that nothing would happen to us and in the morning I would feel like John Muir did, "rejoicing in the abundance of pure wildness, so close to me." I remembered reading about John Muir sleeping out in a cemetery because he knew people were afraid of graveyards and no one would bother him there. I would have rather been in a cemetery that night, far away from those scary-looking guys. Ghosts were nothing compared to frightening mortal men. I stayed awake listening, waiting for the gray arrival of dawn.

The mountains are calling,
and I must go. / JOHN MUIR

Day 16

Yay-Man and the Crazies

Lake Thomas Edison (7,750) to Pocket Meadow (8,940)　　2 MILES

In the morning we held another conference and decided that it would be best to return to the backcountry and take a layover day there. Normally, I would have argued for the resort, maybe even paid for one of those fancy tent cabins at the edge of the lake, but I figured we had escaped harm from those crazies long enough, so now it was time to get back on the trail. I even quoted John Muir, told Dionne and Erika that the mountains were calling and we must go. I preferred that they thought I was anxious to get into the back-country, rather than running from a couple of men who hadn't even spoken to us.

We divided the food and supplies we had sent ourselves and real-ized we had way too much. We had planned on Jesse staying with us, so now we had more than we needed. "Let's just carry it," Di-onne said, "just in case." We all remembered the pesto with pota-toes, tabbouleh mixed with hummus, and Erika's doughy creation, and we agreed. We took another look at our dehydrated bounty and decided we would eat at the restaurant one last time before taking the afternoon ferry back into the wilderness.

We strapped on our packs and headed back to the resort. Big Heiny lived up to her name once again.

"Hi there, ladies," the waitress said when she saw us again. "What'll it be?" I decided on pancakes. Erika had eggs, bacon, and toast. Dionne said she had eaten too much last night and ordered a fruit bowl. We both looked at her. I was happy when she had eaten all that food, and I tried to convince myself that she hadn't thrown it up again. Although the truth was that I had been preoccupied with the stories in my head, so I hadn't been paying much attention to Dionne's whereabouts.

When our food came, I offered Dionne some of my pancakes, and she took a bite, which made me feel better, though now I see that one bite of pancakes does not guarantee health. I was just hopeful. I didn't want to see what was really going on. The night before she had practically inhaled her food; in the morning she cut up her cantaloupe into about seventy-five pieces before slowly eating each piece. We had all lost weight on the trip, but Dionne didn't have anything extra to begin with, so she was skinnier than ever. I didn't worry about it too much when she had no choice about eating, yet when we were sitting in front of a menu and she only ordered fruit, and then carefully dissected it, I couldn't ignore the fact that maybe she hadn't been cured.

A tall man about our age with blond curly hair came traipsing over to our table. "Are you guys thru-hikers?"

"We're doing the JMT," I said. According to the waitress, most of the Pacific Crest Trail hikers had already come through on their way to Canada. Now it was just the JMT hikers and a few behind-schedule PCT stragglers.

"Yay. I'm hiking from here to Florence Lake."

"Great," Erika said. I could tell she didn't want to talk to this goofy guy.

"We're going to take the afternoon ferry."

With her eyes Erika told me I should stop talking to him.

"Yay. Me too."

"Yay," I said, and now Dionne and Erika both looked at me.

"I'm hiking alone. Yay. I wanted to bring my dog. But she died. Yay." This time the *yay* sounded different. It wasn't the happy *yay* but a somber *yay*.

"Well," he said, "I'll see you at the dock."

"See you," Dionne said with a wave. She continued to work on her cantaloupe.

"Yay," he answered and walked away. This was yet another version of *yay*—a good-bye, hope-to-see-you-soon *yay*.

When Dionne passed me the syrup, I said, "Yay. Thanks."

"Yay. You're welcome," Dionne said.

Even Erika got in on it. When the waitress handed us our bill, Erika said, "Only twenty dollars. Yay."

I asked the waitress where the phone was, and she told me it was out of order. I would have to wait until Reds Meadow to call my parents.

I'm not sure why we didn't take showers while we were at VVR, but I do remember Erika saying, "We can use the natural hot spring showers at Reds Meadow. Then we'll have something to look forward to. And don't you want to be able to tell people you went three weeks without a shower?"

That seemed like a strange thing to brag about. I imagined getting to Reds Meadow, calling my mother, and telling her that I went three weeks without a shower. She would say, "Wow, honey. What an accomplishment. Did you stop brushing your teeth too?" My mother's idea of camping was staying at the Best Western.

We decided to hang around the dock, swim, and sunbathe until the afternoon ferry left. I caught up on my journal, and Dionne read a book she'd found at the book exchange. Erika got to work on fixing her stove. I went to turn over and even out my tan, and I noticed the two ex-cons on the other side of the dock. They were in jeans and long-sleeved shirts even though it was nearly ninety degrees out.

"Look," I whispered to Dionne. "There are those two crazies. Why aren't they in their uniforms?"

"Huh?" She looked over. They still stared at us. "Maybe that is their uniform. Maybe it's their day off. How should I know? This book's great. Have you read it?"

"Not that one. Only *Jitterbug Perfume* and *Even Cowgirls Get the Blues* and one more, but I can't remember the name, something about a roadside attraction. Do you think those men will take the ferry with us today?"

"Which book did you like best?" Two gulls screeched overhead, and I wondered if they were lost. We were a long way from the sea.

"*Jitterbug Perfume*, by far."

"This one seems like it's going to be good." She held up *Skinny Legs and All*. "I think it's his new one."

"What do you think about those men?"

"I don't know." She went back to Tom Robbins.

I decided to draw a picture of the dock, the lake, and forested hillside in the distance to get my mind off the men. I felt the net of a shadow cast over me and looked up. It was the short, bearded one with the ice-blue eyes.

"Do you have a light?" he asked.

"A what?" Erika said.

"A light." He held up a cigarette.

"No, we don't smoke," Erika said. Her hands were covered in soot from the stove, and it must have been obvious to him that we would have a lighter for the stove. Also, Dionne had a lighter for her little pipe, and I hoped she didn't say anything about it. She didn't look up from her book. The guy just stood there, hovering over all of us, licking his lips as if we were slabs of meat hanging in a butcher shop and he was in the mood for rump roast. He seemed especially taken with Dionne, who had not yet looked up.

"Okay." He stood there, pushed his stubby hands into the front pockets of his jeans, and asked, "You girls wanta party?"

"No," I said, "we don't party." Of course this was a lie, but I didn't want him to think we were rude and be angry with us. For some reason I always felt like if I was nice to scary people, they would be less likely to want to kill me. If I considered someone particularly threatening, I started to give him compliments like I did with Psycho-

Mike's driving. What could I have said to this guy? Those work boots of yours are quite fetching. Love the scrubby beard.

"Okay." He nodded and continued to stand over us. Erika said, "I think I got it." I knew she was going to try to light the stove, and that man would see that we really did have a lighter. He would know we'd lied to him, and this would solidify his desire to kill us. I pretended to be intent on the picture I was drawing. From the corner of my eye I saw "Yay-Man," and I invited him over with a wave. He saw us, waved, and headed straight over. Erika shook her head. I certainly didn't want to spend the rest of the afternoon with him, but as far as strange men went, I could tell he was of the harmless variety. He had sunscreen smeared all over his face, making him look like Casper the Friendly Ghost. He carried one of those blow-up flotation tubes. It was one of those little kid ones, decorated with Incredible Hulk decals, revealing the Hulk's various degrees of transformation. I couldn't believe that he lugged that around in his pack; then again, I wasn't one to talk, with my library of books.

"Yay, I was looking, like, all over for you, and I found you. Yay." He plopped down right next to Erika, and she moved her towel away. Blue-Eyed Crazy then said, "Well, be seeing you." He walked back over to his friend, who had been watching from afar. Be seeing you? What did that mean? I decided to draw a picture of them both, so if they followed us into the wilderness, the police would know who had raped and murdered us.

Yay-Man got into the water and splashed around on his tube, shouting, "Yay, yay, yaaay." I never thought I would be so happy to get out of there and back onto the trail, though I wondered where that Flappy was, and I hoped we wouldn't see him again. Erika lit the stove with a poof and said, "I got it, I got it." I hoped with all my might those men didn't see her lighter.

I spent the rest of the afternoon pretending I was asleep so no one else would talk to me. Really, I lay there imagining those men getting on the ferry and following us. I pictured telling Erika and Dionne that I wouldn't get on it if the men were there. Erika and Dionne would say they were going anyway and I could do as I pleased.

I went back and forth between being angry at myself for being so paranoid and wondering what was so wrong with trusting my intuition. Maybe I had just watched too many horror movies as a child. I liked to scare myself with *Halloween*, *A Nightmare on Elm Street*, and *Friday the 13th*. I had also made the mistake of recently watching the film *The Virgin Spring*, and I couldn't get the rape scene out of my mind. Maybe those guys had to work tomorrow, I reasoned. Maybe I had nothing to worry about. Maybe they preferred blondes.

When the ferry arrived, Erika, Dionne, Yay-Man, who was really named Todd, and I all boarded the boat. The other men were nowhere in sight. For a minute I convinced myself that they had hiked the six miles down the trail to ambush us on the other side, but I told myself not to worry. I told myself to get a fucking grip.

When we got to the other side, we said good-bye to Todd, who hiked off in the opposite direction.

"Bye. Have a great trip. Yay."

"You too," we said in unison. "Yay."

We hiked the three miles or so to Pocket Meadow; all the while I turned around, looking behind us to make sure we were not being followed. We found a campsite that I noted was sufficiently hidden. Years later a girlfriend who served as a backcountry ranger would tell me that she always made an attempt to hide her tent, proving that even women who work in the wilderness carry with them similar fears.

We had our choice of seven dinners, and we chose burritos with the fresh cheese we had bought at the store. "Living large, again," Erika said.

"I'll say," Dionne answered, though when it came time to make our burritos, Dionne made a tiny one with hardly any cheese. She said she wasn't very hungry because we hadn't hiked that far.

We all toasted to being back on the trail again. I breathed a sigh of relief that we were no longer in that vague terrain between front and backcountry, the glen where goblin men lurked. We were now six miles from a road, far enough, I convinced myself, to deter a rapist or murderer.

For me, and many women I know, the almost-away-from-it-all, or the side country, is the scariest place because it is desolate yet easy to get to. As a woman, I can never escape the fear of violation, and the gravity of that fear becomes something as real as the weight of my backpack. While it's true that my active imagination has always made things considerably worse, I think this fear is experienced on some level by most women, even backcountry rangers.

The fear of other humans presents a layer of experience that men don't often consider. Muir rejoiced in his freedom in nature, but at the same time he took his personal safety for granted. He could fall from a tree or into to a crevasse, though either way, he retained a semblance of control. Nature doesn't provide a proving ground to women in quite the same way as it does for men because we are often too wrapped up in wondering whether or not we will be threatened out there. Women cannot control what men might do to them in the wilderness. The women who were attacked on the Appalachian Trail couldn't do much about the man with the rifle. And it only takes one gun-wielding lunatic to ruin the idea of nature for us all.

Rather than relying upon the language of men, a language that doesn't take into account all the ways I felt about being in the mountains, I needed a language of my own to describe the landscape in all its complexity, but I hadn't found it. I had not yet read Mary Austin, Isabella Bird, or Rachel Carson. I hadn't heard of Annie Dillard, Gretel Ehrlich, Linda Hogan, or Terry Tempest Williams. I wouldn't discover Lorraine Anderson's *Sisters of the Earth*, which was like a revelation to me, until that fall when I went on a search for women writing about the wilderness. So, for the time being I continued to have imaginary conversations with John Muir. Although I had come to see the Sierra Nevada as *his* mountains, I hoped that I too might come to find that not only was I in the mountains but that the mountains were also in me.

Go where you will throughout the noble woods of
the Sierra Nevada, among the great pines and
spruces of the lower zones, up through the towering
Silver Firs to the storm-bent thickets of summer
peaks, you everywhere find this little squirrel of
master-existence. / JOHN MUIR

Day 17

Spa Day

Pocket Meadow (8,940) to Silver Pass (10,900) 6.5 MILES

Our morning routine consisted of getting the bear bag and starting the stove, Dionne filtering water, and me packing up the tent. My personal routine included taping up my shoulders, hips, and feet with duct tape. Band-Aids just got sweaty and came off, so I had been using duct tape to keep my Band-Aids on. I wouldn't win any fashion contests, but my method worked well. Erika said I looked like a dented car. Though Erika wasn't exactly one to talk—she wore the clean yellow shorts she had sent herself with her black sports bra, so she looked like a bumblebee flitting down the trail.

Tom said that the upcoming ford of Silver Pass Creek could be difficult and was at the head of a fatally high cascade. I imagined losing my footing and being swept off the waterfall. When we reached the crossing, however, we navigated it with no problem. I reminded myself to stay in the present tense, that most of what I worried about never happened.

Down the trail we had to recross Silver Creek, and a path of stones was scattered across so we didn't have to take off our boots. Erika and Dionne went first. I tried to keep track of which stones they said were loose and which ones were stable. When I followed,

I forgot, though, and I stepped on a loose rock. It tipped, and I dumped into the creek. The water only came to my knees but was deep enough to go over the tops of my boots and soak my feet. As I sloshed through the water and back onto the trail, I realized the squishy feeling wasn't going away. My boots were filled with water. At first I liked the feeling—a water bed for my feet. After about ten minutes, though, I felt new blisters forming. Some of my duct tape wrinkled up inside my boot. The pain became so sharp that after a while it gave me the gag reflex. "Go ahead, you guys," I called. "I have to deal with my boots."

I sat down to take off my boots and socks, and my heels looked like fried bacon. I wrung out my socks, and I thought about getting another pair from my bag, but I knew it would be of no use. They'd be soaked in a minute. I decided to hike in my Tevas. I re-taped my blisters, tied my boots to my pack, and started off down the trail. I was careful not to roll my ankles. I felt so much lighter, yet the trail turned steep and rugged, so I walked with caution. The last thing I wanted was to hurt myself, giving Erika the opportunity to say it had been my fault because hiking without boots was a stupid thing to do.

I continued up toward Silver Pass, enjoying the break from my boots. Ponderosa pines and hemlock wavered green and brown in the breeze. A Douglas squirrel crossed in front of me on the trail. John Muir dedicated an entire chapter in *The Mountains of California* to this squirrel. Muir calls him a "bright chip of nature." In truth I had skipped most of the squirrel, sheep, and water ouzel chapters. I realized that if I took the time to observe these animals, I might have wanted to read about them. The closest I had ever gotten to a squirrel previously was the one my dog Dylan killed. Dylan had the squirrel in his mouth, and I yelled, "Drop it." To my surprise Dylan did what I said, but by then it was too late. The squirrel swaggered around like a frat boy after a pub crawl. I didn't want to kill the animal myself, yet I wanted it to be put out of its misery. So then I yelled, "Get it, Dylan, get it." To any passerby I must have seemed heartless. Dylan obeyed, which was out of character, and shook the squirrel to death. The animal squeaked with every horrible shake. Why is it that our encounters with wild animals so often result in their deaths? I had seen as many road-killed deer as deer grazing on hillsides. I had only seen skunks dead on the road, never alive, scurrying around in the wild.

The trail edged Silver Pass Lake, the spot we agreed to meet for lunch if we were separated. Granite embraced the alpine lake except on the north end, where a boggy meadow climbed from the water's edge. Dionne and Erika sat on the rocks there, waiting for me. Clouds swooped over the pass like mares' tails. We ate lunch and decided we would all go swimming in the icy waters of Silver Pass Lake. When I jumped in, I felt like the air had been sucked out of my lungs. We didn't stay in long, and I put my clothes back on right away because we were in plain sight of anyone who happened up or down the trail. Erika and Dionne loitered naked on the rocks until the wind picked up and it became too cold for naked.

Dionne said, "Let's have a spa day."

"All right. I'll have the hot stone massage, followed by the spa lunch of tuna tartar with champagne spritzer."

Erika went along with my joke and said, "I would prefer the Swedish massage."

"Only if the masseuse is a hot Swede," I said.

"Always thinking about men," Erika said.

"No, really." Dionne grabbed her backpack, and out came a nail brush, tweezers, a mirror, a brush, a razor, and lotion. I evidently wasn't the only one carting around an assortment of luxuries.

"What are we going to do with all that?" I asked.

"We can pluck our eyebrows, shave our armpits, clean and file our fingernails, brush our hair, and put on face lotion."

"I'd rather have the hot stone massage."

"It'll be fun, you'll see."

We took turns plucking each other's stray eyebrow hairs and filing each other's nails. Dionne and I each shaved our own armpits. Erika said, "I'm letting mine grow out for the trip." Another thing she felt proud of. We finished up by brushing our hair and putting

Dionne's face lotion on. I tried to imagine what John Muir would think about this—three women with camp towels wrapped around their heads like genies from magic lamps, plucking each other's eyebrows. My mother would have been glad to see that finally we did something in regards to trail hygiene.

Although our spa day wasn't like a real spa day, I had to admit it was fun. And I really did feel better, almost pretty, which seemed silly because all I did was file my nails and pluck a few itinerant hairs. The only trail beatification projects I had tackled up to that point had been to clean my nails and my teeth and brush my hair, and those had more to do with hygiene than beauty. I might have forgone the hair brushing, but with the kind of hair that forms dreadlocks after two days without brushing it, I decided the hairbrush was worth the extra weight. I had white friends from college who ground dirt into their hair to start dreadlocks. If dreads had been my goal, all I would have had to do was to go without brushing it.

"That was fun," I told Dionne. She put all her beauty products back in their ziplock bag, and we got packed up. The plan was to camp at Fish Creek, which would mean we would be able to get as far as Lake Virginia or maybe even Purple Lake the next day, where we would spend two days. It would be our first official layover or zero-mile day. I wanted to wash my clothes, read, write, draw, and nap. Almost like vacation.

The view from the top of the pass opened into the green Cascade Valley below, splashing with aquamarine lakes. Big Heiny was food-heavy again, so I took four Advil and picked my way down the rocky trail. We descended and reached what is now called Nüümü Hu Hupi, a smallish rockbound lake on the other side of the pass, and found a spot near the outlet. Because we had spent so much time getting beautiful, we had to hurry to set up camp before dark. We had hoped to camp at Fish Creek but only made it as far as Nüümü Hu Hupi because dusk's curtain had already begun to descend. Although we had only been on the trail two and a half weeks, the days were noticeably shorter than when we began.

We decided on a fast Top Ramen dinner. I never ate Top Ramen at home, but I loved it on the trail, always happy to see it come up on the dinner rotation. We ate our salty noodles, drank hot chocolate, and watched dusk toss its diaphanous folds over the valley, the orange alpenglow pulling off the distant peaks, leaving everything, except a pale western sky, in shadow.

Tourists make their way through the foot-hill
landscapes as if blind to all their best beauty, and
like children seek the emphasized mountains—the
big alpine capitals whitened with glaciers and
adorned with conspicuous spires. / JOHN MUIR

Day 18

A Cowboy's Visit

Nüümü Hu Hupi (10,550) to Purple Lake (9,900)   7.5 MILES

Although Erika had managed to get our stove back into working order, our water filter was now broken. This meant boiling or iodine.
I didn't mind using iodine, but Erika claimed it was unhealthy, and
she couldn't stand the taste. I brought along vitamin C, which neu-
tralized the iodine after it had purified the water, but Erika said she
could still taste the iodine. Dionne agreed with Erika on this one,
so we were now boiling our water.

After boiling and cooling the water, we began our descent. We
finally reached a steel bridge and took pictures of each other. While
the creeks bubbled white and wonderful at these particular spots,
I couldn't help wondering why we—and everyone else—seemed
to stop for pictures at every one of these bridges. Was it the jux-
taposition of the human made and the natural that we found so
appealing? And if so, why? Was this Stephen Mather's fascination
with good eats and plush accommodations in so-called wild places?

The trail followed the meandering creek past hemlocks. Although
most people were impressed with the high mountain passes, I preferred the rushing creeks, pine forests, and abundant wildflowers.
We followed Fish Creek and then passed Tully Hole, and the creek

swished over itself, and wildflowers of every color bordered the trail. But what a terrible name. Tully Hole sounded to me like a derogatory nickname for a high school girl, as in, I can't believe what Tully Hole did with White Waters last night in the Circle K parking lot. Then I thought, why is it always the women who pay for their indiscretions?

Erika wanted to hike ahead and meet us at Lake Virginia, our designated lunch spot. I asked Dionne if she wanted to hike ahead, but she told me that her knee wasn't 100 percent and it was probably best for her to stay back with me. I hadn't been sure if she should have come on this trip or not; now I realized how glad I was that she was there.

We started up hot, dusty switchbacks. "Are we supposed to be going uphill?"

"Unfortunately," Dionne said. "Erika said we gain about a thousand feet to Lake Virginia."

"Well, I guess that's not so bad."

"It's all relative," Dionne said.

"You're right. It is."

We reached Lake Virginia. The water shimmered a glossy blue, making it one of the loveliest lakes we had seen so far. Our guidebook said the lake would be crowded, but no one was there. Erika was waiting for us; she had her stove out and was boiling water. I wandered down to the lake, filled my bottles, dropped a few iodine tablets in my water, and sat down. We decided on tortillas and cheese with M&M's for dessert. "Two more miles to Purple," Erika said. "I say we continue on and camp there."

"But it's beautiful here. And no people." The craggy peaks surrounded the large lake, creating what felt like a natural amphitheater. The wind smelled of fresh water and pine.

"It's too windy. Don't you want to spend our layover day sunbathing?" The wind swirled white caps across the lake and tousled the tree branches.

"It won't be windy there?" Dionne asked.

"Well," Erika said, "according to the book, it's at 9,900. We're at 10,314, so Purple's lower."

"But the wind keeps the bugs away," I tried.

"We have bug spray," Erika said.

Dionne said, "Well, it is a little cold here." I was outnumbered again, so after eating, we packed up our stuff and continued to Purple Lake. We hiked up a few more switchbacks, crested, and then started the descent down many more switchbacks. I stopped to take a few more Advil. I was starting to feel like an addict, dependent on my next fix.

We followed the winding trail to Purple Lake, and Erika was right; it wasn't windy at all, yet Purple Lake didn't have half the charm of Lake Virginia. The wildflowers fluttered in the afternoon light, yet the water wasn't purple, just a churned-up brownish color from erosion. The scrubby peaks hovering above the lake, though, seemed to have a purple tint. Because so many people had camped there, dirty patches with blackened fire rings littered the forest, and almost every single campsite was filled with people. Up the trail a cowboy led a horse and five mules. Atop the horse sat a blond boy who couldn't have been older than five. We stopped to talk to them.

"I'm Mike," the cowboy said. "And these are my pack animals. And this is my grandson, Sky. He's riding Blackie."

"Hello," we all said and waved to the boy on the horse. Sky wore the tiniest Wranglers, cowboy boots, and hat I had ever seen. He didn't smile. He was all business atop the big black horse.

"What are you doing?" Dionne asked.

"Getting my crew settled for the night. We just dropped off some folks here. We bring the tourists, then we camp a little ways away with the animals so the tourists can have their privacy."

"What do you mean?" Dionne asked.

The cowboy laughed, "Well, these here mules brought in some folks and all their stuff too. And boy did they bring in a heap of stuff."

"Like what?" I always liked the details.

"Like a radio and a Ping-Pong set, beach chairs and rafts, and I don't know what all else."

"Wow," Dionne said. "That sounds like the way to do it."

Erika, who hated horses on the trail, sighed. We had taken to calling people with pack trains "cheaters" or "tourists."

"You betcha. And they get eggs, bacon, and coffee for breakfast and steak for dinner."

"You make all that?" I asked.

"Sure do. Me and my two nephews and little Sky here—he helps too. Where are you girls camping?" He smoothed his moustache.

"Here at Purple Lake," Erika said.

"I have a nephew about your age. I'll send him over to say hello later."

"Okay," we all said. It was about time we had a cute cowboy to talk to.

We walked around the lake, looking for a place to camp. We passed a Boy Scout troop, Mike's people, and a couple. We chose the spot farthest from the Boy Scouts. There were a few unoccupied campsites on two sides of us, so it seemed like the most private spot. A torn bear rope hung over our heads. It felt strange to be around all these people. It reminded me of Trail Camp at Whitney. We started setting up camp, and Erika said, "This isn't so bad." Lake Virginia would have been better, but I didn't say anything.

We all agreed to start a fire since bug hour was approaching, so we made use of the big blackened fire ring. Just as we unfolded our camp chairs around the fire, no fewer than twelve college-aged guys came hiking up the trail toward us. Normally, I would have welcomed such a sight, but these guys were moose-like, all neck, chest, and groin, and they were hooting and hollering—a walking Animal House party. Besides, we were there first, so we felt like we owned the place, and we had not invited them to camp next to us. It was like at the beach. Once you set down your towel, you might as well own the real estate; the land might as well have been in your family for generations because you have claim to it, and anyone who happens by with his beach blanket after you've arrived is a trespasser on your land. I had to admit, this wasn't a very generous attitude; however, it grew stronger each day we were out on the trail. We felt as if all the hiking we had done had earned us our space. We believed that those who had hiked in for the weekend were nothing more than tourists, out for a quick jaunt into our mountains.

I could tell Erika felt territorial because she stood there looking out at them, with her hand to her forehead as if she were on a boat and had finally spotted land. Then she did something that amazed me. She called to me, loudly enough that they would hear her, "Suzanne, I wouldn't worry about it. I don't think your genital warts are contagious." The boys huddled together as if on the sports field and then headed straight over to the other side of the lake. They walked away, and the three of us laughed so hard that Dionne actually peed her pants and had to change. I may have laughed as hard as Dionne had I not been the one assigned the communicable disease. Maybe Erika also wanted to make certain that I didn't end up sleeping on one of their cushy air mattresses.

We cooked our macaroni cheese, and I wondered what was taking our cowboy so long. Should I have changed out of my dingy, oversized purple turtleneck? I asked Erika to braid my hair since I could never make my own braids look good. Erika tugged so hard the braids stayed in for days, and my eyes eventually relaxed out of the pulled squint. The price we paid for beauty, on and off the trail.

We determined that it would be a chocolate pudding night, and Dionne said, "I have something that will make that pudding taste even better." She took out her tiny pipe and smiled. I hoped that Erika wouldn't make the connection between the pot and the lost map, but if she did, she didn't say anything about it.

Instead, Erika smiled and said, "Why not?" I didn't want to be stoned for the cowboy, but it was getting late, so I had given up on his coming. We all passed the pipe around.

I didn't feel anything at first, and then Dionne said, "I hope your herpes is okay." I told her it had been warts, not herpes, and we all laughed like we had just heard the funniest thing ever. Amid our laughter a family of four arrived with two llamas. They decided to camp right next door. We couldn't stop laughing, so no one came up with anything to say to stop the encroachment.

Dionne finally said, "Erika, I hope you can get your farting under control." We all laughed again, thinking we were so funny. The family ignored us. They were tying up their animals and putting up a condominium-sized tent. The mother was preparing to light a four-burner stove.

"Tourists," Erika said. But that was all relative—to PCT hikers we were tourists, rather than the backcountry travelers we saw ourselves as.

The littlest boy did something to make the father angry, and the father shouted at the boy, calling him "a little bitch." His insults made me shudder. The mother kept her hands busy with her cooking. The little boy cried.

"That wasn't very nice," I said, hoping they would hear me. I couldn't think of anything else to say, but I felt like I had to defend that little boy.

"What a dick," Dionne said.

"Doesn't he know," Erika said loudest of all, "'bitch' is a compliment." That got us laughing again. The big-tent family continued to ignore us.

A teenager in a cowboy hat and Wranglers walked toward us. He had a pimpled baby face and couldn't have been more than sixteen years old. I guess to a fifty-year-old, sixteen and twenty-two are just about the same age. His uncle probably had given him a hard enough time, so he finally agreed to visit us.

"Hi ya'll. I'm Dan. My uncle told me to come for a visit." He tipped his hat at us in a charming boy-cowboy sort of way. We offered him some of our pudding, but he said he had already eaten brownies for dessert. We ran through the usual where have you been, where are you going; all the while Erika, Dionne, and I were trying to act as sober as possible, and then Dan told us he was a cowboy poet, so we all begged him to recite something. He agreed, even stood up and took off his hat. I couldn't believe his composure. He told us that his poem was called "The Cowboy's Home," and he began reciting:

Nothing like the open trail for solitude
Riding my horse in the yellow morning light
Puts me into a mighty quiet mood
The open range, creeks, and pretty sights.

But nothing, nothing is so grand
As all the mountain passes, peaks, and granite domes,
My horse Blackie and me, riding open land.
The wind, the sun, the sky—a cowboy's home.

After a long day of riding trail,
We round up the horses, settle for the night,
Start the campfire, drink some coffee or some ale,
And the old-timers, they tell stories by the fire's light.

After the last story, it's off to bed at last,
Sleeping outdoors, listening to the coyote's song,
Dreaming of the open trail, sleep comes on mighty fast,
It's up at dawn, and that's all right 'cause coffee's on.

A can of beans on the fire, hotcakes too.
Welcome to the cowboy's home,
The horses, the open trail, all the solitude.
O' how all the world's the cowboy's home.

We all clapped, and Erika whistled through her fingers. The family looked over at us, annoyed, as if they were the ones who had been there first and we had trespassed on their real estate. Dan tipped his hat again and sat down. I was amazed at his bravery. Although admittedly not an aficionado of cowboy poetry, I found this the most honest poetry performance I had seen. In reality I had only attended a couple of poetry readings in college and mostly because some English professor gave me extra credit for doing so. The poet always seemed like she couldn't be bothered with the audience, like we were not important enough to be listening to her verse. Or the poet hid behind glasses, a podium, a microphone. This performance, though, was something else entirely.

I had always been one of those nerdy girls in high school who actually read poetry for fun. Unless you were reading Homer or Dante, books of poetry were small enough to hide in other books. I would tuck poetry inside a science textbook so I could pretend that I was using extra lab time to study. I had seen it done in a movie, but the girl had a *Cosmopolitan* magazine, not Emily Dickinson's *Selected Poems*. It was a source of embarrassment: What high school student read Emily Dickinson for fun? I knew there were other students like me, yet I would not have anything to do with them because I didn't want to be teased. I couldn't do anything about my funny walk, and adding poetry to that would have solidified my outcast status. I graduated from high school before *The Dead Poets Society* made being intellectual seem cool.

"That was great. It made me understand how it feels to be a cowboy. I loved it," Dionne said.

I started to think maybe I could find myself a cowboy. If this one were about ten years older and read a poem like that, I would have been hooked. It's the performance thing; I had always been a sucker for musicians as well. Most men know this about women, which is why so many of them take up the guitar, talented or not.

If I really were to find a cowboy, I would probably have to get over my squeamishness about farm animals and eating meat. And I would have to learn to ride a horse. The only time I had ever ridden a horse, I couldn't get him to stop grazing. The cowgirl had said, "Show him who's boss." I was doing just that—the horse was obviously boss. I was too afraid to pull his head up because I didn't want to hurt him, but mostly, I didn't want to make him mad. So, he stopped whenever he pleased to enjoy a snack, and we fell way behind. Then he would gallop to catch up, finding low branches to run under, so I had to duck in order to avoid being decapitated.

"I like to write poetry too," I told Dan.

"Will you recite one?" he asked. Dionne and Erika looked at me. This time I told the truth. I did write poetry, very bad poetry, and at that point I had never actually shown anyone my poems, much less recite them.

176

"I don't have any memorized."

"Well, I had better get back. Early morning," Dan said. "Nice to meet you."

He walked away, and Dionne said, "Too cool." She turned to me and said, "I didn't know you write poetry. I write some too."

"I do, but it isn't very good."

"Will you show me sometime?"

"Maybe when we get home."

"Okay," Dionne said. "And I'll show you some of mine."

"I think tomorrow I'm going to spend our layover day writing." I hoped Erika and Dionne wouldn't laugh at me.

"Feeling inspired?" Dionne asked.

I nodded. My mouth felt sticky, like I had been eating clay. I took a drink from my water bottle.

"If you write about me, make sure you make me beautiful," Erika said.

"Don't worry. I will. Pretty and strong as a mare. Beautiful and a pain in the ass."

Erika laughed at my joke.

"I would like to see something you've written," Dionne said, "especially if you write about this trip."

Then I made Dionne a promise I kept, although it took me nearly fifteen years: "It's a deal. You'll be the first to read anything I write about this trip. Maybe the first and only."

The power of imagination makes us infinite. / JOHN MUIR

Day 19

On Writing

....

Purple Lake (9,900)   0 MILES
....

The thing about being on the trail is that you have hours and hours to think, so at first you review the things you had been thinking about. Then you have the thoughts you were planning to have. But after that you still have thinking time and no planned thoughts, so you start to think about things you never expected to think about. It's new territory. For me being on the trail had been the first time I thought seriously about writing. I wanted to capture the landscape, how I felt out there. I tried drawing pictures, yet without much talent, my sketches bore very little resemblance to the land. So every day in my tiny journal, I wrote.

When I was little, I wanted to be a writer like my father. I loved listening to the tapping of the typewriter keys. It was Daddy who bought me ice cream, took me clamming, called me "kiddo." It was Daddy who prevented the doctors from breaking me in half. He was kind. He was a drunk who ignored me or crashed the car or shouted at me. I couldn't reconcile the different versions of Daddy, so they sat separate like boxes on a shelf. Like most little girls, I loved my Daddy, despite the shouting. When he was kind, whether he was making ice cream cones for me or driving me to the mountains so I could ski, Drunk Daddy disappeared in the shadows of my imagination. Children are the masters of forgiveness, of forgetting. Teenagers, however, aren't.

By high school I no longer wanted to be like Daddy, no longer wanted to be a writer, and decided I would become a doctor—that is, until I realized I hated blood, especially someone else's. I wanted to be the sort of person who was good at science in the same way that I wanted to be an early riser who drank protein shakes for breakfast and practiced yoga as the sun came up. I wanted to be someone else, to escape the core that held both Daddy and my own writer self.

So, I forgot what I was, forgot that I had wanted to be a writer before I could write. On the trail I began to remember. I spent so many hours alone, walking and thinking, that I could no longer distract myself from myself. I remembered reciting stories to my mother, who dutifully wrote them down. I then drew lopsided pictures to go with my stories, and we made little books out of them, some of which my mother has kept. Yet my father, who was proudest of me when I wrote stories, also seemed somewhat relieved when I announced I would study the sciences. He figured that maybe he hadn't passed the burden of a writing life onto me. He knew what it was like to tell people at cocktail parties that he was a writer and then get the inevitable follow-up questions: "Do you publish?" or "What's your career? How do you make your living?" My father did end up making a career out of writing; he wrote soap operas, which he considered selling out. But even that didn't last long. It's hard to know whether the failure led to the drinking or the drinking led to the failure, though I suspect it was the latter. Years later my mother would tell me that he used to say, "I feel like I'm living in a black hole."

And being a poet? That's worse-sounding than being a writer, unless of course you are a cowboy poet and your real job is to carry rich people's ice chests and Ping-Pong sets into the backcountry. In any other circumstance you cannot announce that you are a poet if someone asks about your career. Being a poet went out with the nineteenth century. If you say you are a poet, all anyone can picture is Tennyson droning on about the charge of the light brigade,

Whitman contemplating grass, or Wordsworth wandering around England's foggy Lake District, wondering if the world really is too much with us.

Writing, and especially poetry, became so mixed up with my family history that it felt like a secret I had been charged with keeping. It wasn't until I went out into the woods, with all that time to think, that I realized I had inherited a love of nature from my father and also a love of words. It was in the woods that I could go back to the child Suzanne, the one who had forgiven him for the parts of himself that he couldn't help. I finally began to feel compassion for the man who had struggled with writing, the man who felt like the harsh world—a world of wars and the Holocaust, which had claimed the lives of his cousins—rubbed at his skin like sandpaper. Maybe I couldn't see the world through my father's eyes, no more than I could wholly adopt Muir's perspective, but I realized that I, like Walt Whitman, was large enough to contain multitudes.

Journal Entry, August 21, 1993

PURPLE LAKE

Alpenglow's fire on the ridge—
a yellow rind. Our destination,
the deep space of blue.
The sun settles before us,
a pink mouth. The moon swells,
white, cratered and whole.
Granite peaks bear the names
of forgotten men. But the animals—
frogs and deer, bears and marmots,
squirrels and mice—gather
in the nests of our imagination—
a web of memory and of meadows,
decorated with wildflowers,
like bits of colored glass
cut into a green mosaic.

The worlds that we contain.
Meanwhile, we remain anonymous
like lizards breathing in
the afternoon, breathing
out the dusk. We hitch a ride
with the sun, sink with it
below the mountains,
into a remembering sky.

When we try to pick out anything by
itself, we find it hitched to everything
else in the universe. / JOHN MUIR

Day 20

Disordered

....

Purple Lake (9,900) to Deer Creek (9,120)   9 MILES

....

The noises from the mare's bells, dogs barking, and people yelling in
an attempt to scare away bears filled our two nights at Purple Lake.
Because of the crowds, I was ready to leave, though I loved having a
day to do nothing all day but swim, sunbathe, write, read, and draw,
not anticipating when Erika would say, "Haven't you packed up your
bag yet? Have you completed your camp check?"

We waved to Dan, Mike, and Sky on the way out. Whatever they
were cooking smelled delicious. I hoped their people appreciated
them and tipped them accordingly.

We followed the glaciated Cascade Valley, and I asked Dionne and
Erika, "Do you know Muir was the first to realize Yosemite Valley
was formed by glaciers?"

"Are you sure you have your facts straight?" Erika said.

I wasn't really sure—I just thought I remembered reading that
somewhere—but I said, "Oh yes. Well, you know that Josiah Whitney, the geologist Mt. Whitney was named after? Well, he thought
that Yosemite Valley was formed by some random catastrophic
force, but because Muir had spent so much time here, well, he had
a better idea—a better intuition—about the land. He knew there

had been glaciers, and he convinced Whitney that he was right. Then he published a paper or something about it." I wished I had had a better memory when it came to all that stuff. That was why I had earned a D in evolution. I had probably written on a test that the Muir finches in the Hawaiian Islands had proven the theory of evolution, what with all their different beaks adapted to each island insect or seed. Erika, on the other hand, would have known it was in fact Darwin who had come up with his theory of evolution by looking at the Galapagos finches. She had a brain for facts and figures.

Erika said, "Look at that carved rock wall. Who wouldn't know that was the result of glaciers?"

We passed Duck Lake and carried on the six more miles to Deer Creek. Our hope was to pass it and stop somewhere called Deer Crossing. We weaved through a forest of Jeffrey pine and red fir, greeting hikers and animal pack trains along the trail. This was the busiest section of trail yet and the one most filled with horse manure.

We came to Deer Creek, crossed it, and began looking for a place to camp. The creek sauntered through a forest of lodgepole. Groundsel and lupine created a patchwork of color in the green and brown forest. And it was quiet. But I asked, "What if we hiked the next five miles to Reds Meadow tonight?" Erika and Dionne both looked at me in shock since usually I was the one who wanted to stop, yet with a shower and real food waiting, I was up for more hiking. Besides, we had already hiked fifteen miles in one day, so fourteen miles didn't seem quite the feat it had earlier.

"It's four o'clock now. We wouldn't get there until around six," Erika said.

"We've come into camp much later than that before."

Erika glanced over to Dionne, who shook her head and said she was tired. I was about to protest then remembered how many times I had been the one begging to stop. After not showering for three weeks, I was motivated to get to the hot spring showers. But I supposed I could wait another day. And after spending the night with all those people at Purple Lake, I had to admit this quiet spot near the meandering creek felt peaceful.

"There are probably a million people there anyway," I said and put Big Heiny down. We went off in our usual directions—Dionne's job of getting water was now considerably easier because she only had to fill up the Nalgenes since the filter was broken. Erika threw the bear rope and started the stove. I put up the tent. No matter where we were, we always fell into routine. I realized they were right to want to stay. It gave me time to write and draw. A thru-hike doesn't have to be the Bataan Death March. We could enjoy ourselves.

After I set up the tent, I walked down to the creek to find Dionne washing up.

"Hi." I put my washcloth into the cool water and rubbed it onto my face—almost as good as a shower.

"Hi. Sorry I didn't want to go."

"That's okay. Usually I'm the one who wants to stop. And it'll be nice to have a quiet night after all that ruckus at Purple Lake."

"It's just hard."

"Tired today?" I dunked my washcloth in the cool water again.

"No." She put her feet into the creek. "I actually feel good after having a break. It's hard because I know we'll eat in the restaurant and go to the store with all the food. It gets harder around all that food. It's easier out here."

"Really?" I immediately realized that was a stupid response. Of course it had been more difficult for her around all that food. I had been too wrapped up in thoughts about a hot shower and using the pay phone to think about what Reds Meadow might have meant for Dionne. "I mean, yeah. I guess it would be, but when we go back, you have to deal with all of that again," I said. Dionne nodded. I realized that in the course of three weeks I really started to see her, to know her.

During college I had always been a little afraid of her, the way I'm afraid of all strange, beautiful women because I imagined that they must be so confident, so unlike me. Geoff had parties at our house, and Dionne would come over wearing something super-slinky like a fitted black minidress with platform heels. She teetered around our house in her high heels with a glass of red wine, calling everyone sweetie and darling. In my memory that Dionne had very little to do with this girl now sitting next to me.

"An alcoholic can stop drinking. I can't stop eating entirely," Dionne said.

"No. I should hope not."

"I try, but then. Then. All I can think about is food, and I eat it so fast, I can't even really taste it. It's like I'm in a trance. And then, well, it's just gross. I mean, even anorexics think bulimia is gross. My dentist says I'll lose my teeth if I don't stop."

"Your teeth? Why?" I sat down next to Dionne and put my feet in the creek.

"The acid."

"Oh." I tried to imagine Dionne with no teeth. She had a small face already, so without teeth she would look like one of those shrunken apple people I used to make when I was little—the faces shriveled. "That wouldn't be good." Nothing like stating the obvious.

"No, it wouldn't."

"But aren't you getting better? You seem better to me."

"I think so. It's easier out here when we're hiking all day. I can set my intentions and stick to them. At home I set intentions in the morning, but by afternoon I'm on my way to the doughnut shop. Or I don't eat at all. All or none is easier."

"I guess so." I tried to understand it, but I didn't. I probably ate more than I should, and like most women, I worried about my weight, counted calories, tried to exercise, and gave the occasional fad diet a whirl. Luckily, I had never followed the slippery slope from fad diet to sickness. I could have been thinner for sure, but that had always been one of those things on a long list of concerns. It had never been the primary worry. Rather, it hung there like a dress between the others in the closet: if I said some stupid thing to a guy at a party or if I would ever find a career that would pay off my student loans. For Dionne food was the only dress, the single obsession, above all else; I began to understand that most of her decisions had somehow been connected to her eating disorder. Of course she would not have wanted to spend two nights at Reds Meadow. Of course she wouldn't want to be faced with all that food.

"Is there anything I can do?"

"No, you've already done a lot," she said. "I told Erika."

"You did what?"

"I said I was disordered when it comes to eating."

"What did she say?" I pulled my feet out of the creek.

"She said she figured." Dionne and I both put our Tevas on.

"What else did she say?"

"Nothing."

I was sure Erika imagined that Dionne just dieted a lot. Dionne obviously didn't tell Erika the whole story. And Erika was one of those rare women who had never been on a diet. In truth she viewed diets like most men did; she just didn't get it. I couldn't begin to imagine what Erika thought when she heard "eating disorder." When our friend Toni stopped eating in college, Erika said how good she looked. Then, when Toni became so thin that her body seemed burdened by the weight of her head, Erika said, "She's a little too skinny. She should probably stop dieting." That was all. The rest of us worried, and rightly so, that Toni was headed for a slow death. Erika thought we were overreacting. "Who starves themselves to death on purpose?" Erika had asked. I wasn't sure what planet Erika was living on, I had told her; people did it all the time, thousands a year in the United States alone. According to Erika, Toni was at first a little too fat, then just right, then a bit skinny. It was as if as much were at stake as if she were judging the ripeness of a melon.

"She didn't say anything, which is fine by me. As soon as I told her, I realized that I didn't want her to say anything. What could she say?"

"She didn't ask if I knew, did she?" Erika didn't have much of a reaction because Dionne hiked as well as I did, if not better. If Erika had known from the beginning, she never would have permitted Dionne to come with us. Erika would not have wanted to risk having her trip ruined, but because Dionne was doing fine, it didn't bother Erika one way or the other. Erika wasn't one to take on other people's problems.

"Did you tell Erika you had never been backpacking before?"

"Are you kidding? I'm not stupid."

Like Dionne, Toni had begun flip-flopping between starving herself and purging. She also tried diet pills, laxatives, and wrapping cellophane around her body underneath her clothes. She wasn't much fun to be around—wired and flushed, running to the toilet every five minutes. It was as if she wanted attention and to disappear both at the same time. I started to watch her every move. What was she doing in the bathroom? I would put my ear to the door to make sure she wasn't throwing up, but she ran the water so no one would hear her. And then she would lie—nothing so important as protecting the food addiction, the disorder. Finally, the friendship became too exhausting. I couldn't keep up. By the time Toni had decided her nose was too fat and her mother had paid for a nose job, I had to get out of the friendship. I realized I couldn't save her. I lost track of her completely, and maybe this hike with Dionne was a way to relieve my guilt over giving up on Toni. When I wondered what Dionne was up to, I caught myself. I tried to remember that if I became obsessed with fixing her, the same thing would happen. I knew I would eventually tire of trying to save her, and I would have to let her go altogether.

I told Dionne about Toni, and she said it was rare that someone had both anorexia and bulimia. But maybe it happens more often than we think. Bulimia is one of those things that most people don't admit to. Not eating is almost admired. Bulimia is another story, a story full of shame, even more so than other addictions. As hard as it is, admitting that you are an alcoholic is far easier than saying you are bulimic. Society understands a problem with alcohol. You say you got drunk and passed out. Someone listening might even one-up your story with his own alcohol-related tale. He might say, "Oh yeah, well I got drunk, danced on a table naked save the lampshade on my head, fell down, and then passed out." If you tell someone you binged and purged, no one is going to try to one-up you.

"Nope. She just said she figured. That's it. But now I have both of you watching me."

"Do you think I'm watching you?"

"Aren't you?" We gathered up the water bottles and headed back to camp.

"Well, maybe sometimes," I admitted. "But I don't think you have to worry too much about Erika."

Years later, when I asked Erika if she had known about Dionne's eating disorder, she said, "Yeah, I knew. But I didn't know how serious it was." Then she added, "But I certainly didn't know that Dionne had never been hiking before."

Never, before making this trip, have I found
myself embosomed in a scenery so hopelessly
beyond description. / JOHN MUIR

Day 21

Dirty Dirk and Cute Mark

Deer Creek (9,120) to Reds Meadow (7,400)   5.2 MILES

I stood at the trail with Big Heiny on, waiting for Erika and Dionne. Erika said, "I've never seen you move so fast. That is, when there's no lightning involved."

"Or leeches," I reminded her.

"Or leeches."

"But there are showers waiting and a phone and surely ice cream."

"Go ahead," Erika called. "We'll catch up."

"I'll wait." I sat down and let the heft of Heiny rest on a rock.

"Did you do your camp check?"

"Twice."

Finally, they finished getting their stuff together, and we started down the trail. I made a note of all the things I would have to do. It was strange how no matter where I was, I compiled a "to-do" list. I went through the order in my head: eat at the café, peruse the store, shower, call my parents, drink a beer? And then there were all the things we had to do as a group: call Jesse for our food, dump our garbage, buy fuel, see if we could do something about our broken water filter.

I asked Erika, "Do you think Jesse will come meet us?"

191

"Meeting back up with us was just talk. Don't you think? Besides, how can he face us?"

"So, you don't think he'll show up with our food? And what about your tent? And the money he owes us?"

"I'll get the tent somehow. But we can probably forget about the money. Maybe Mark will come with our stuff."

"Mark?"

"Jesse's roommate. Don't you remember? We met him at the springs the night before our trip."

"Hardly." By the time Mark had gotten to the springs, it was dark, so I never got a close look at him. "Do you really think a stranger would go out of his way for us?"

"Yeah," Erika said. "He seemed like a nice guy."

Dionne added, "And sure cute."

We hiked beside a long meadow and stopped to watch the bees at work in the flowers. An appropriately named mountain called the Thumb sat on the other side of the meadow. I took this as a good omen, a sort of "thumbs up." I thought about what Dionne had said about Mark. If he was so handsome, I would surely remember him. We kept hiking and passed Upper Crater Meadow.

"That's Mammoth," Erika said and pointed to the hulking mountain still snow buried.

"Hard to believe we were skiing there last month."

"You guys were skiing there in July?" Dionne asked.

"On the Fourth of July. When we were here, planning the trip. We went skiing with Jason's stepbrother Neil."

"And Jesse," Erika said.

"Really?" Dionne asked. "I didn't know you could ski in July."

"Yeah, you can in a big snow year. That's how we met Jesse. And after skiing, we went to the bar, which was where Suzanne here convinced Jesse to come with us on the hike." Erika pointed at me with her own thumb.

"Yeah," Dionne said. "I remember something about that. Whatever happened to Jason's brother Neil? Wasn't he originally supposed to bring our stuff?"

Erika gave her signature eye roll, and I cringed.

"Might there be a story?" Dionne asked.

"Do you want to tell it, or should I?" Erika asked.

I couldn't decide if it was better to tell the story myself with Erika's interruptions and corrections or just let her have it. "You tell it."

"It's better that way," Erika said. "Suzanne always leaves out something important when she's telling a story."

"Not always."

"Most of the time. Or you exaggerate. How many people did you say we saw at Purple Lake, fifty million?"

"I think I only said twenty million, but it seemed like fifty million. So, let's hear your version."

"Well, Suzanne got together with Neil on the Fourth of July."

"But they hardly talked that night in the hot springs. What happened?" Dionne looked at me.

Here it comes, I thought.

"Well, it turned out that Neil already had a girlfriend," Erika said.

"He had said he wasn't dating anyone seriously," I said.

"And that's not all. Serious or not, his girlfriend was pregnant."

I might have left out the pregnancy part.

Dionne asked, "If pregnant isn't serious, what is?"

"I don't think he knew she was pregnant in July. Maybe she wasn't even pregnant by then. We didn't find all of this out until August, when we came back up for the trip," I said.

"That's why Neil isn't bringing our stuff to Reds Meadow," Erika said. "That was the original plan before we ever met Jesse. Jason arranged it. Originally, Neil was also going to pick us up from Yosemite and bring us back to our car in Mammoth too."

That wasn't as bad as I thought it would be. I expected to take more of the blame for screwing up the original food delivery and car retrieval plans, for moving in on a poor pregnant woman's man. Neil was one of the reasons I kept to myself that night at the hot springs. I hardly talked to Jesse or his roommates because I figured they all

193

knew what had happened with Neil. I didn't want to be known as the slutty hiker, so I just drank my wine coolers and kept to myself.

"But now Geoff's picking us up, and we all get to go water-skiing at his dad's house at Bass Lake," Dionne said.

"See. It all worked out for the best," I said.

"Except for Neil," Erika said. "Twenty-one and a kid on the way."

"How was skiing on the Fourth of July?"

"Fun. We wore shorts and bikini tops." The bikinis were Erika's idea, and I had to admit, it had been fun getting whistled at from the lift. We just had to be careful not to fall.

We entered an area of blackened trees. We walked through without a word. The charred trees, brown pine needles, and ash gave the forest an apocalyptic feel, like the aftermath of a nuclear holocaust or environmental catastrophe. I knew many trees actually needed fires in order to reproduce, but walking through the blackened area felt unsettling. This charred section of forest had been the result of the 1992 Rainbow Fire, the previous year. By the look of it the fire had burned right to the fences of the resort.

We made good time and arrived at Reds Meadow in time for breakfast. Our first stop was the pay phone. We called Jesse, and no one was home. Erika left a detailed message, explaining that we were at Reds Meadow and Jesse could bring her tent, the box we left with Mark, the items on our grocery list, and our money. Good luck, I thought, as I listened to her leave the message.

We then went to the Mule Horse Café, and I wondered how Dionne would do. I ordered a fried egg sandwich with cheese and tomato, a salad, orange juice, and a chocolate shake. The waitress didn't blink an eye at my weird order. She was used to hungry hikers.

Dionne looked up from the menu and said, "I will have exactly what she's having." I was horrified. Had I known that would happen, I would not have had the shake. Was my breakfast large enough to constitute a binge? Was it so much food that Dionne would want to throw up? I excused myself and went to the restroom to compose myself and also wash up. Again, the soapy water ran a grayish black off my hands. "Stupid, stupid," I scolded myself in the mirror. Then I tried to convince myself that it wasn't my job to take on Dionne's problems. I knew one of the benefits of being a woman was female friendships, yet the line between benefit and burden can become blurred. I couldn't imagine a group of male backpackers dealing with this.

When I came back to the table, a tall gangly man in his midtwenties stood at our table, talking to Dionne and Erika. He had a long red goatee and chipped teeth. Over his pear-shaped body stretched a T-shirt with a cross-eyed Thanksgiving turkey who held a sign that read, "Eat pizza." His arms, legs, and face were smudged with blackish film. He looked like he had been rolling around in a fire pit.

"Yeah, yeah. I'm doin' the whole JMT too. Came from the Valley. Yeah, cool. That's where ya headed? Yeah, yeah." He gestured with his whole arms, not just his hands. He swung them around like the blades of a windmill. Before we had a chance to say anything, he said, "My partner couldn't come, so I'm solo. They had to work. Yeah."

The waitress came up and said, "All right, it looks like these girls need to eat."

"Well, look for me at the backpackers' camp. Yeah, yeah?" he said.

"Wow, who was that?" I asked.

"His name's Dirk," Dionne said.

"Dirty Dirk's more like it. I hope we don't have to camp near him," I said.

"What do you think his story is?" Dionne asked. We had been on the trail so long that we started to speculate about every person we'd met, since we didn't meet many and everyone was in transit. It gave us something to talk about, a way to escape our own thoughts. It was like being between flights at an airport bar and wondering about the couple at the next table—could she be a show girl from Vegas? Could he be her secret gangster lover? This fascination was weird but fun.

"What does it matter?" Erika asked. She wasn't one to partake in our speculation games.

"Why would he say 'they' after saying 'partner' and not 'partners'?" Dionne asked. Only an English major would have caught that. This was before the use of *they/them* pronouns was more commonplace.

"Maybe he meant business partner," I said.

"Do you really think that guy has a business? I mean, come on. Maybe he has a boyfriend." It was like she was searching for the final clue in order to solve a murder mystery.

"That guy? So not gay," I said. "No gay man I have ever met would be caught dead in that T-shirt for one thing."

"That's such a stereotype. Besides, he just meant hiking partner," Erika said. "You guys are so weird. He probably just has bad grammar."

It didn't matter one way or the other whether Dirty Dirk had a hiking partner, boyfriend, girlfriend, or conjoined twins as business partners, but it gave us something to talk about. You would think women would never run out of things to talk about, yet after spending twenty-four hours a day together, we had.

"You ladies like anything else?" the waitress asked.

"I have a question," Erika said, tapping her long fingers on the table. "Now, there's backpacking camp and regular camp, right?"

"Yes," the waitress said, "and to tell you the truth, they are both the same price, as long as you don't need RV hookups."

"We don't."

"Well, just pay for one of the regular spots. They're bigger and cost sixteen dollars, same as the backpacking sites, which are smaller." The waitress took our bill up to get change.

"Looks like we won't have to worry about Dirk." Erika smiled. She thought to ask all the logical questions, which, I had to admit, made up for a lot of her faults. If it were just Dionne and me out there together, for the first thing, we wouldn't be at the Mule Horse Café at all. We would be lost on the trail somewhere, walking in circles around Mt. Whitney. And if we ever managed to arrive, we would be camped right next to someone like Dirty Dirk because we wouldn't have thought to ask about the various camping options.

Dionne excused herself to go to the restroom, and I had to stop myself from following her. I couldn't trail behind her every time she went to the bathroom. Erika was still licking her plate, so I went to look at the store, and I wondered what we would need to buy if Jesse didn't come with our stuff. When Dionne came back, we went out and took turns using the pay phone. Dionne called Geoff, and I called my parents.

"We're all set," Dionne told us. "Geoff will be in Yosemite to pick us up one week from today."

"And then he can take us to my car in Mammoth?" Erika asked.

"Yup. Everything's set."

My father was out at the grocery store, but I talked to my mother, who asked me question after question about safety and hygiene. I told her to tell my father hello for me. "He'll be so happy you called," she said.

While Erika called her parents, Dionne and I headed to the showers. The Reds Meadow bathhouse smelled like sulfur, and the water was scalding hot, but I didn't care. I shaved my legs, scrubbed my nails, and washed my hair twice. I also washed out all my filthy clothes. Erika came in with three Sierra Nevadas. We toasted, and beer never tasted so delicious.

We found a great site with a picnic table under a shady tree and a bear box for our food. We all set up the tent together and pulled out what was left of our food to put into the bear box. Just as we were hanging our clothes up to dry, we heard someone say, "Hey, hey."

He found us, I thought. Dirty Dirk found us, though the call sounded more like "yay" than "yeah." Could it be Todd from Lake Edison?

"No way," Dionne shouted and ran over to hug a guy with a baseball hat on backward. He had brown hair, brown eyes, and the muscular body of a rock climber. I didn't recognize him at first. Then I realized he was Jesse's roommate Mark. I looked around, and he was alone. No Jesse. I felt relieved. We all hugged him, and Dionne was right; he really was cute. Gorgeous, in fact. I was glad to be clean.

"I'll go get my truck. Do I have some groceries for you!" We all jumped up and down in anticipation and joy, and Dionne shouted, "Yippee!"

Mark drove to our campsite and started unloading groceries. He also brought our box of supplies, including fuel, so we didn't have to buy anything. We started pulling everything out of the grocery bags and stocking it onto the picnic table. In addition to our stuff and the groceries we'd requested, he had bought us brie, French bread, grapes, a magnum of wine, and marshmallows, graham crackers, and chocolate. This was better than anything we'd ever expected. Even though the goodies were for all three of us, the gesture felt oddly romantic.

Just as we were about to have a wine toast, who should be bumbling through the thicket but Dirty Dirk. He waved his arms around, reminiscent of Flappy. He wore a towel around his neck. "Hi. Yeah, it's me. I just wanted to see if you want to share a campsite. But you have one. Yeah. That's cool." We were frozen with our wine-filled camp cups raised, and then Dirk noticed Mark. "Well, okay. See you're busy. I mean, the campsite is sixteen dollars, and it's an awful lot, and I thought you girls might want to share the cost, but I see you have one here already. And a friend. Yeah."

"Yeah," we all said.

"Okay. I probably need a shower, so I'll get going." He headed off toward the bathhouse.

"What was that?" Mark asked, and we all laughed.

"Here's to you," I told Mark and smiled at him in a way that I hoped was flirtatious enough for him to notice yet would escape the notice of everyone else. Dionne and Erika both smiled at him too. We clinked our camp cups and drank.

We all sat down to the wonderful picnic Mark had brought, and we proceeded to tell him about our trip. First, I described all the characters we had met, then Erika told him about the mountain passes, lakes, and meadows we had seen. Dionne told him about how we ran out of food and had to rely on handouts from strangers. We talked and talked until we finally asked, "Where's Jesse?"

"He wasn't home, but I got your message, so I went to the store and hoped I would find you."

"Jesse said he wanted to meet us and hike to the Valley with us. Finish the trip." Erika made quotation signs with her fingers and added, "When he was feeling better." She picked up her wine, took a sip, and asked, "By the way, did he give you my tent?"

"I don't know anything about your tent. Jesse didn't plan on meeting you because he said there was no way in the world you would be here. He said you girls would never make it," Mark said. He smiled and added, "But he was wrong."

"Can I come by after the trip to get my tent?" Erika asked. "I have to come back to Mammoth to pick up my car."

"Give us a call when you finish. I'll try to find the tent by then."

"Thanks. I will." I could see that Erika was already scheming on how to see him later.

"I'll go with you, Erika. So you don't have to drive home alone." I smiled at Mark, and Erika looked at me like I had just told her that the glass slipper would never fit. Hadn't I already moved in on enough of her dates?

"What did Jesse say about us?" Dionne asked. She took another bite of brie and bread. We all leaned in.

"He said you guys were a mess. That two of you had hurt knees, that there was a lot of complaining and crying, and you would never make it. He thought Erika might finish alone." At this Erika smiled.

"Well, we showed him," Dionne said. We all raised our cups and cheered again. We finished our brie, bread, and grapes and took out everything to make s'mores. Mark started a fire, and I stole looks at him whenever I could. He had one of those chin lines cut at a perfect angle, like a shape you study in geometry but can't pronounce. And his brown eyes seemed to sparkle with intelligence. When he reached for something, his triceps tightened. And what a nice person, I kept reminding myself. He didn't know us, yet he had done all of this for us. There were nice guys out there, after all. And those arms.

"Your marshmallow is on fire," Mark said. I looked down and

noticed a small bonfire at the end of my stick. I blew it out, and the marshmallow bubbled a charred black.

"I love them black like that," Dionne said. "I'll eat it." She pulled it off my stick and popped the black mess into her mouth. I started anew with another one.

Erika said, "Let me take a picture." Dionne squeezed right in close to Mark, and I sat next to her. He put his arm around both of us, though, so that his hand rested on my shoulder. I sucked my breath in. I acted like a thirteen-year-old, clipping pictures of the latest heartthrob out of *Teen Beat* magazine. I acted like I had never seen an attractive man before. Something in me, even then, knew how pathetic I was, so I reached for the wine and poured myself another heaping cup.

"So, tell me about your job," I said. My mother had always told me that men loved to talk about themselves. Because I followed her advice, I was unable to really connect with any of the guys I met. I spent my energy worrying about how to get them to like me, rather than getting to know them.

"I work at a climbing shop in Mammoth, selling ropes, harnesses, shoes, that sort of thing. Do you climb?"

"Oh yes. I love to climb." There I went again. I pulled the marshmallow off my stick, this time perfectly browned. I tried not to think about my climbing date with TJ. I had done a fair amount of climbing since then, though the verb *love* was still a bit strong to describe my feelings about climbing.

"Suzanne gets the award for best commentary when we climb because she says the craziest things," Erika said. I hurled her an ugly look, but she kept looking at Mark. I put my marshmallow between two graham crackers with a piece of chocolate.

"I didn't know there was an award for that," I said.

Erika ignored me and said, "She says things like, 'I'm going to fall, falling now, almost fell.' It's really funny. And that's on a 5.7."

"Sometimes a 5.8." While it was true that I didn't climb the more difficult routes, like Erika did, and I did talk a lot while on belay because of nerves, Mark was talking to me about climbing, not

Erika. We began roasting our marshmallows, and every time Dionne reached for a marshmallow to roast, she popped another raw one into her mouth.

"What's a 5.8?" Dionne asked with her mouth packed with marshmallows.

"It's the rating for a super easy climb, like a beginner climb," Erika said. I tried to think of something clever to come back with, but everything I thought of sounded stupid. Instead, I asked Mark where he liked to climb.

"There's a great place nearby called Clark Canyon and the gorge in Owens Valley. I also like Benton Crags. For big wall stuff, mostly the Valley."

"Yosemite Valley?" Dionne asked.

"Yes." He smiled at Dionne. I finally thought of a rebuttal to Erika, but I lost my chance. Like Proust's "wit of the staircase," I was always too late with the perfect response; whether three minutes too late or the next day, a response only sounded clever with perfect timing. I had always been too slow for witty.

Mark turned his attention to his own roasted marshmallow, and Dionne popped two more raw marshmallows into her mouth. Then three. I went from catching glances at Mark to watching Dionne. Erika was telling a story about climbing a 5.10, and Mark was nodding at her. I snuck in another look at Dionne. She shoved three more marshmallows into her mouth, and they filled up her cheeks, making her look like a chipmunk preparing for winter. Erika flirted with Mark, so she didn't notice. I wanted to flirt with him too, yet I was too busy monitoring Dionne's marshmallow intake. She held the bag in her lap, shoving her already full cheeks with one marshmallow after another. The most wonderful evening of our trip was being spoiled fast.

"Well, I have to work tomorrow, ladies," Mark said. "I'd better get going."

"At the climbing shop?" Dionne said, after she'd swallowed most of the marshmallow wad. They didn't even taste good raw, but I had learned enough to know that what she was doing had nothing to do with taste. And for the bulimic marshmallows made the ideal binge food: easy down, easy up.

"Yes," Mark said and smiled, showing a row of orderly white teeth with a small boyish gap in the middle. If Patagonia put a face like that on their catalog, I guarantee they would sell a lot of gear. I imagined women coming into his shop, leaving with climbing harnesses, chalk bags, and shoes they would never wear.

Mark stood up to go, and I felt both sad and relieved because his parting broke Dionne's spell. "But maybe I'll meet you girls in Tuolumne if I can get off work. Hike to the Valley with you. This has been fun." I had come to hate it when the men on the trail called us "girls," but coming from Mark, it seemed like a compliment. We thanked him, hugged him good-bye, and watched him leave.

I wish I could say that I'd realized then how ridiculous I acted that evening with him, trying to flirt with him, competing with my girlfriends for the attention from a man, still desperately searching for male approval. But that would take years.

I felt woozy from the wine, and I told Erika and Dionne I needed to go to bed. They went to put our new food into the bear box, and I walked over to the tent to get my toothbrush.

Dionne started screaming.

"What?" I shouted and ran over. "What's going on?" I nearly knocked into a bear at the edge of our campsite. Erika pounded on the metal bear box to make noise, which probably sounded like a dinner bell to the bear. Dionne continued to scream, and I just stood there, toothbrush in hand, tipsy from all the wine. Eye to eye with a hungry bear, but he, or she, just looked at us, seemingly annoyed, and wandered off. As the bear lumbered away, it looked back every so often to see if we were still there, finally disappearing around the corner.

"Better a bear than Dirty Dirk," Erika said. We all laughed. Dirk may very well have been watching us, waiting for Mark to leave, so he could swoop in for a visit. One thing was sure, we would have probably been stuck talking to Dirk if Mark hadn't come.

We heard people screaming at the bear in the next campsite. "This could be a long, noisy night," Erika said.

"Can you believe Jesse said that stuff about us?" I asked.

"What did you expect?" Erika shut the bear box with a clang.

We all got into the tent after brushing our teeth, and like usual, Erika fell asleep immediately.

"I have to go to the bathroom," Dionne whispered.

"Again?" You just went."

"Yes."

"That bear is outside."

"She won't hurt me," she said. "She just wants our food."

Since Dionne was no longer afraid of bears, I said, "Those marshmallows have already been digested. Simple sugar. They're gone already."

"Really?"

"Totally," I said, making it up as I went. "I learned that in one of my biology classes."

"I feel so gross. So full," she said but lay back down. In a couple of minutes she was asleep too. Crisis averted. For the moment. Dogs on the other side of the campground began barking, and their humans banged together pots and pans. Then something that sounded like a Renaissance faire chimed in from the distance, or maybe it was just the wine.

Day 22

Devils Postpile

....

Reds Meadow (7,440) to Rosalie Lake (9,350)   10.5 MILES

....

When we sat down to breakfast, I was thinking of having one of everything: eggs, toast, a hotcake, a waffle. I wasn't feeling great because of the wine, and I hoped some grease and starch might help. Dionne and Erika both looked at their menus, and when Dirty Dirk sauntered over, neither of them looked up.

"Yeah. Too bad we didn't hang last night. Hope you had fun with your friend. I found two dudes to share my space. That was cool, yeah, 'cause I charged them eight each, so it cost me nothing. Cool, yeah?"

I knew I shouldn't engage, but as usual, I couldn't help myself. I said, "Not cool for them. Didn't they know it was only sixteen dollars total?"

"No," he shook his head, "I didn't tell them. But I, like, found the spot. I so arranged it."

"And they didn't know they could just go get another one together?"

Erika and Dionne both studied their menus like they were the recovered Dead Sea scrolls.

"Nope. Cool, yeah?" Dirk looked around the restaurant, and I could tell he wanted to be the fourth at our table. Dirty Dirk looked considerably cleaner after his shower, and he even wore a different T-shirt. This one said, "Follow me to Soledad."

The waitress came over, gave Dirk an enough-is-enough look, and asked for our order. I was about to give her my one-of-everything order and then realized Dionne might end up ordering the same thing. I told the waitress I needed more time to look at the menu. Since Erika and Dionne had not taken their eyes off their menus, they were ready. Erika ordered a tall stack of pancakes, and Dionne ordered granola and fruit. Now that I was free to order the way I wanted to, I started to second-guess my order. Maybe it was too much food. Maybe I shouldn't eat that much. I had been thinking about food and the various implications of eating more than ever before.

"I'll have one egg, one pancake, one piece of toast, and tomatoes on the side." The waitress nodded, and I took that as an approval of my order. Dirk still stood there, fiddling with his long goatee, waiting for an invitation. Dionne, Erika, and I just looked at each other.

"Yeah. It's too bad I'm not going the same way as you guys. I mean, it would be cool to hike together, yeah?"

"Yes, too bad," I told him.

"Yeah, man, I wanted to play my lute for you girls last night."

I said, "I may have heard it."

"Oh so cool. Did you like it?"

"It reminded me of a Renaissance faire."

"So cool you liked it. Hey, I got a question. I got some food, and I hope it will last all the way to Whitney. I mean, do you think I'll make it there with what I've got?"

"You can stop at Lake Edison or Florence Lake if you need to," Erika said.

"No, man. I don't have any money left. See." He pulled out the pockets of his cutoffs to prove it.

"What about the sixteen dollars you charged for your camping spot?" Dionne asked.

"Well, that made up for the sixteen I already paid."

"But you have the money. You have the sixteen dollars," I said.

"No, man. I spent it on weed. The guys camped with me—they had the good stuff, you know what I'm sayin'?"

"So, you gave the money back?" I asked.

"No. We just, like, called it even."

"Well, good luck," Erika said.

Part of me wanted to tell him there would be no way he would make it to Whitney without a food drop. People did it all the time, of course, but they had to plan ahead. And hike fast. I couldn't see Dirty Dirk doing either. But as we had learned, there was always freeloading off other hikers, which we were guilty of, so I really had no room to talk.

"Yeah. You too. Peace."

"Yeah," we said. "Peace."

He left, and Erika said, "Do you have to strike up a conversation with every crazy person we meet?"

"He was standing at our table."

"You didn't see me or Dionne talking to him."

Dionne nodded.

"Well, I just didn't want to be rude."

After we paid the waitress, we asked her take a picture of us in front of the restaurant. We decided to reroute so that we would be able to pass Devils Postpile. This meant walking on the road for a little while and finding the trail to the monument. Then we would cross the river and join back up with the trail. Erika didn't want to cut out the mile and a half of the JMT, but I convinced her that we would be making up the distance on the other trail.

We stood on the shoulder of the road, arguing. "We get to the paved road," I said, "and we turn right."

"No, we go left," Erika said.

"But don't we want to go north?"

"Yes, but I'm positive we go south a little bit first to the trail and then north," she said.

"Well, I'm positive we go this way. I would bet on it." Dionne stood there, waiting to see which way we would be going. Erika pulled out the map because she didn't believe me. A shuttle bus passed, and we choked on the black exhaust.

"See. Turn left, then right onto the trail."

"Oh," I said, looking at the map. "You're right."

"Too bad we didn't bet."

After a short while we turned onto the trail to the Devils Postpile National Monument. Families with strollers and old ladies with sun hats admired the formation.

"It looks like dominoes," Dionne said.

"Or a rock wave," Erika said.

"Or microscopic split ends on a shampoo commercial."

Dionne and Erika both laughed at me. Without metaphor it was difficult to describe this structure. The basalt posts stacked together on one side but pulled out vertically on the other side. Stone beams leaned against each other with deep fissures between them. Though the monument resulted from volcanic eruption, cooling, and cracking, it looked as if the columns of rock swayed with an earthquake and froze that way. Pieces had broken off the columns, and a huge rock pile of broken basalt gathered around the remaining columns like a skirt. It looked more like an ancient Greek ruin than geologic phenomena. I imagined more than one little boy or girl seeing this structure and deciding to become a geologist just to figure out how stuff like this worked. We had seen many interesting rocks on this trail but nothing like this.

"Cool," Erika said, "Now let's go."

I could have stared at the Devils Postpile for hours, but I knew we had a long way to hike, and as Erika had said, we had dillydallied enough. We crossed the bridge and joined back with the John Muir Trail. Erika sighed with relief. Being off course made her uncomfortable.

After climbing a while, we came to another trail junction, and I knew better than to argue when Erika said we needed to go to the right. We passed Johnston Lake and meadows and then began the climb to Gladys Lake.

Once we reached Gladys, an array of lakes draped across the landscape, and we could camp anywhere we wanted, except for Shadow Lake. This lake, one of the oldest and lowest of the existing glacial lakes, was one of Muir's favorites; even in his lifetime, however, he had seen the meadows surrounding it trampled by grazing livestock and noted, "The money-changers are in the temple." Tom said Shadow Lake showed a classic case of chronic congestion and not to camp there even if it was open, and we would take his advice.

The hot, dusty climb weaved into the underside of the cloudless sky. Dionne and I soon lost Erika. We hiked together for a while before she said, "Sorry I got so weird last night. I know you saw."

"Saw what?"

"With the marshmallows. All of a sudden I couldn't stop. Do you think Erika noticed?"

"No way, she was too busy bragging about her climbing expertise to Mark."

"He was cute, huh?" Dionne asked.

"Uh-huh." We kept walking, and then I added, "I just want you to be okay."

"I know. I feel this thing is who I am. I can no longer separate myself from it. I just want to wake up one day and have it be over."

"I know," I said, though I really had no idea what it must have been like. "It's like a sickness. It's not your fault. And it isn't all that you are. You are other things too. You are Cassiopeia, the hiking wonder."

"Thanks, but I don't feel much like a hiking wonder. And I have to take the blame, or how will I overcome it?"

"I don't know. I really think you have to talk to someone."

"That's what I am doing, Zsa Zsa."

"No, someone real."

"You're a figment of my imagination?" she asked and laughed.

"Zsa Zsa and Cassiopeia may be figments of both of our imaginations. But you know what I mean, right? Real help. All I can do is hope for you to get better, and that's not much help at all."

"It is help. It is." She started crying again. I wondered if we could become dehydrated with all our crying. "I wanted so badly to get rid of it last night."

"I know, but you didn't. Isn't that a start? No one said this was going to be easy." I started sounding like my mother, though she would have added her favorite peppy phrase: Get over it. Instead, I told Dionne what Muir tells the little dog on the glacier to get him to cross the ice bridge: "No right way is easy in this rough world."

"Thanks. You're right."

"That last bit was Muir."

"Thanks, Muir," Dionne shouted to the sky. We walked for a while, and then she said, "I think Mark liked you."

"Really? I think he liked you."

"Even with my sexy marshmallow cheeks?"

"I don't think he noticed. He's just nice. I think he felt sorry for us because of everything Jesse told him, so he came to help us." Some men were nice and expected nothing in return.

"But he was impressed that we made it this far," Dionne said.

"You're right. Do you think he'll come to meet us in Tuolumne?"

"Maybe." The trail curved into switchbacks, weaving into the sky. "Did you notice those arms?"

"How could I not? But he isn't as cute as Geoff."

"Each to her own."

Two fishermen passed us; one held a deflated rubber boat. We said hello.

"You have a long way to go," they said, though they didn't have the foggiest notion of where we had been or where we were headed. We nodded and kept going. We had hiked over 175 miles. I was fairly sure that fisherman did not lug his little boat anywhere nearly as far as that.

After a short while we passed Trinity Lake and its small lakelets scattered between lodgepole and silver pines. We reached a saddle, and started the two miles down to Gladys Lake, our lunch spot. We found Erika, who sat under a hemlock, looking at the map. She pointed to the jagged mountains behind us and said, "Those are the Minarets." Snow-skirted granite spires poked into the blue belly of the sky.

"Amazing," Dionne said.

Gladys Lake, a dark-green lake with a sandy tree-lined shore, settled in front of mountains that looked like the haunches of an elephant. Erika had bought a spare filter at Reds Meadow, so we could use the water filter again. I had never been mechanically minded, so I paid very little attention to those sorts of things. I was glad, however, that Erika did. If not, we would be without both a stove and filter. We ate cheese and tuna with crackers and then drank filtered water.

"We can hike to the next lake, Rosalie, and camp, or we can go on another four miles to Garnet. Shadow is between, but we can't camp there," Erika said.

"Let's see what Rosalie looks like and decide," Dionne said, and we all felt like this sounded like a fine idea. We packed up, and within half an hour or so, we arrived to Rosalie.

"It's beautiful." I dropped Big Heiny. I already decided I wasn't going anywhere. This wasn't just because I was tired. Rosalie glowed cerulean blue in a granite basin, and snow-covered mountains surrounded us in every direction. A black-tailed weasel scampered by. Columbines splashed red and yellow on the backdrop of granite, manzanita, and pine. Rosalie made the perfect place to stay the night. We agreed to set up camp.

After dinner I went down to the water to draw a picture of the lake. Erika came down and sat on a rock next to me. We talked about where we might camp the next night, but neither of us mentioned Mark. Even then we both knew on some level that the situation was a comedy of errors—we were in competition for a man who thought nothing of either of us, not a Prince Charming, just a nice person, doing a favor for strangers.

"This has been good, Zsa Zsa," Erika said.

I smiled at her. "You're right. It has."

Two yellow braids peeked out from her hemp sun hat. She looked out at the lake, and the light reflected in her pale blue eyes. I looked from her to the rockbound horizon, the sky now a deep purple. Together we watched the sun dip beyond the mountains.

"Do you ever imagine hitching a ride on the sun? To the other side of the world?"

"No," she said, "I never do."

Nature saw to it that besides school lessons and church lessons some of her own lessons should be learned, perhaps with a view of the time when we should be called to wander in the wildness to our heart's content. / JOHN MUIR

Day 23

Getting Muir

Rosalie Lake (9,350) to Ruby Lake (9,840)   6 MILES

Soon after we started hiking, we followed switchbacks down a cool slope. "Look," Erika said, "Ritter and Banner Peaks." Below, Shadow Lake settled into its basin. A large flat meadow speckled with small boulders surrounded the lake. I could see why ranchers and campers alike had been drawn to this lake. Signs advised us that the lake was currently closed to camping for re-vegetation. It looked like Tom was right again. We crossed a bridge over Shadow Creek, started uphill, and crossed a trail to Ediza Lake.

"This is where we'll really start to climb," Erika said.

"I thought we were climbing."

Erika didn't answer.

We agreed to see how we felt today, most likely hiking the seven miles to Thousand Island Lake, which was a compromise anyway because Erika thought we could get up over Island Pass. I enjoyed the shorter hiking days, and this was my favorite area of the entire trip. Muir Pass was undeniably scenic, but in an on-the-moon sort of way. The Ansel Adams wilderness boasted swimming lakes of all sizes, forests, meadows, wildflowers, and streams, all with mountains like the impressive Banner Peak and Mt. Ritter in the background. As the day wore on, the sky deepened into Sierra blue. The Sierra sky casts a deeper blue than anywhere else in the world, except maybe Mongolia, which is known by its people as "the land of eternal blue sky."

A small cirrus wisp that looked like a feather or a veined aspen leaf floated in the sky. I decided the wispy cloud must be a good omen.

"Doesn't that cloud look like a fish skeleton?" Erika asked. I admitted that a fish skeleton was one of the things it looked like. I gave up hopes of the cloud as a good omen, but the truth was, the cloud wasn't a symbol of anything; it was just a cloud. We were always attaching our ideas to natural objects, assigning some meaning that made us feel better or explained the unexplainable, when really, an albatross is a seabird, not a symbol.

We stopped, and I asked, "Can I see the map?" I could tell Erika didn't think I would be much help, but she showed me anyway. She humored me more and more lately. She even demonstrated how to clean the stove, as if I would remember the various steps, as if I could tolerate soot-covered hands.

"Hey, I didn't realize the JMT and the PCT go two different ways at Reds Meadow."

"They do," Erika said looking at the map. "So?"

"They meet back up again at Thousand Island Lake. So why would anyone hike the PCT when this trail ends up in the same place but goes by all these pretty lakes?" Aside from crossing a few streams, no bodies of water lay on that stretch of the Pacific Crest Trail for ten miles, whereas the John Muir Trail passes seven lakes, not counting all the lakelets.

"Because if you're going to do the PCT, you would want to do all of it," Erika said.

"Well, that seems dumb to me. Look how beautiful it is here."

We had stopped in a grassy saddle strewn with rocks, moved thousands of years ago by glaciers. Alpine daisies scattered purple and yellow across the green meadows. A small pond sat in the middle of the saddle. This seemed like the landscape of shepherds and nymphs, pastoral meadows with the sublime mountains in the back-drop. I could explore this area for a whole month, maybe longer.

"Let's stop for lunch at Garnet," Erika said. "There's supposed to be a panoramic view of Ritter and Banner over the lake. It's one of the places where Ansel Adams took some of his famous photographs."

"Sounds good," Dionne said.

The trail now switchbacked down to Garnet Lake. As soon as we stopped hiking, we had to put on our sweatshirts because of the wind. The storm-stunted trees grew from cracks in the granite, the reflections of the snow-draped Ritter and Banner rode the waves of the wind-chopped water of Garnet Lake.

We looked at the map again, and Erika said, "Thousand Island Lake is only another 2.6 miles. Easy. That will put us in position for Island Pass." She always looked ahead to where we would be next. I had just started to enjoy the present, there with my crackers and tuna and a feathered cloud, now a bit windblown, above my head.

"Hard to believe this trip is almost over," Erika said, still in the future. "Just a few days, and we'll be in Yosemite." We all sat for a while, looking out at the wind-whipped lake and the serrated peaks beyond.

"Do you think Mark will meet us in Tuolumne?" Dionne asked. She flashed a smile at me.

"How would I know?" Erika asked.

For the last couple of days I had been thinking about that very thing, hoping he might be there. But what then? Was he going to hike into Happy Isles with us? Didn't we want to complete the trip together, just us three women? What happened to our girl power? Was I that quick to give it up again? The three of us had been through so much together; still, I couldn't help but think that if Mark joined us for those last three days, it would be an awfully exciting development. One thing was sure: I didn't have anything nice to wear. My flowered boxers were almost as bad as Dionne's tighty-whiteys, which we had gotten so accustomed to seeing that they didn't seem strange anymore. Erika had finally asked Dionne why she was wearing Geoff's underwear. Dionne said that they weren't Geoff's underwear, that she had bought them new, especially for the trip. At this I had to say, "But why?" She said she thought they would be comfortable, and they were. I didn't care how comfortable they were; you wouldn't catch me hiking in them. For one thing everyone would see how my thighs touched.

As we hiked, I went back and forth between wanting to see Mark, wondering what I should wear, and hoping to finish the trail with just Erika and Dionne. Around and around like a carousel that plays the same boring song every time. We followed the stony trail along the ridgeline. Mountains surrounded us in all directions. I stopped, looked out over the landscape, and realized that while it was nice to encounter an attractive man on the trail every once in a while for a thrill, for the first time in my life I was happy to be on my own. In college, if I went to a party and didn't happen to meet anyone, I would consider the evening a failure. I realized now, more than ever, that if I kept up this sort of thinking, my happiness would always be beyond my control.

I thought about the times I felt happy because of someone I liked or, more appropriately, lusted after. If that someone seemed to like me, I would be ecstatic. The problem with that paradigm was that if my happiness depended on a man, what happened when the man went away? When he didn't want me anymore, even found someone else, I became desperate for that feeling again, so I would ignore all my good intentions and do anything to get the feeling back. I had been like a rat in a cage who got drugs when she pressed a lever—pleasure, repeat. Pleasure, repeat, until she ignored the food lever entirely and starved to death.

We arrived at Ruby Lake, and I could hardly believe how peaceful it was, even more so than Rosalie. Charcoal-colored mountains fell right into the small lake. Snow patches flung across the north side, and bluish ice floated on the shadowy corners. Whitebark pine, red fir, Douglas spruce, and a few junipers swayed in the breeze.

Mountain chickadees sang their three-syllabled song. I called them the laughing birds, but Erika said it sounded like they were saying, "Cheeseburger," so she called them the "cheeseburger birds." They flitted gray, black, and white along the bark of the trees, oblivious to their various names. I dropped Big Heiny in the dirt.

"It isn't far to Thousand Island," Erika said.

"But, I'm sure it isn't nearly as nice. What's another mile tomorrow?"

"I guess you're right. This is a pretty nice lake." Even Erika had been seduced by the landscape. That, or my opinion was beginning to count.

"I love it here," Dionne said. We all agreed Ruby was one of our favorite spots on the whole trail. I told Erika that although we had only hiked six miles, it was mostly uphill. For her twelve miles was a hiking day, not six, uphill or not.

When we began the trip, Dionne and I had averaged one mile an hour over the passes. We were now up to two or sometimes even three miles an hour, so the hike to Ruby Lake only took four hours with lunch and picture taking. Though Erika called that half a day of hiking, at least we arrived with enough time to enjoy it. We found a great spot, set up, and still had plenty of time before the sun set. I grabbed my journal and headed to a rock on the shore.

I was finishing up a drawing of the lake, trying to decide if I should add columbine to the foreground even though none really grew there, and Dionne walked over. She looked over my shoulder and said, "Hey. Nice picture."

"Thanks. Do you think I need some columbine in the foreground?"

"What's that?"

I pointed to one behind us. "There's one. The flower with the red and yellow petals hanging upside down. It's the state flower of Colorado. Aren't they pretty?"

"Yes, but there are none in front of you."

"That doesn't matter. It's okay to add things."

"I like the picture as you have it. I don't think you should add things that aren't really there."

"Okay. I'll leave it. Do you want to read something? It's a poem I wrote." My heart started to beat quickly, and I felt embarrassed because Dionne had studied English literature in college, so I figured she must be a far better writer than I was.

"I'd love to. Do you want to read it aloud?"

"No, I don't think so." It was bad enough having someone read something I'd written while I was sitting right there. I gave her the journal and opened it to the poem I had written at Purple Lake. She sat down to read it. I busied myself by cleaning my fingernails.

"Fantastic," she finally said. "Really beautiful. I love it."

"Really?"

"Really. You could publish your poetry."

"Get out." I felt a chill. We were now in the shadows.

"No, I'm serious, you're an excellent writer." Dionne stretched her sweatshirt over her knees.

"Thanks." I was happy she liked my poem. I realized it meant more to me than I had thought. Even if she was just being nice.

"I came down to ask if I could borrow your John Muir book," Dionne said.

"Of course."

"I've never read him. But I'd like to."

"I bet most people who hike this trail never read Muir. I'll warn you, there's a lot of description, but he's good." The sun rode lower in the sky, casting yellow dashes into the lake. "And being here, you can see why Muir loved the Sierra."

"Tell me something else about him."

"Well, he was originally from Scotland, and his family moved to Wisconsin, and he thought of that as a great adventure. He loved running around the woods with his brothers. And he invented all kinds of things."

"Like what?"

"Thermometers and all sorts of clocks. He made a clock that would measure how fast a plant grew and another one that was an early rising machine—it would shoot him out of the bed in the morning."

"How cool," Dionne laughed.

"I know, huh? So, he went to Madison to enter his clocks in their science fair, and everyone was impressed, so they let him go to the university there. And then he worked in a factory, but he left because he was almost blinded in an accident of some sort."

"No wonder he appreciated all the beautiful things in nature."

"True. And he loved botany and went on all sorts of adventures to Alaska, the Grand Canyon, the Amazon. He came to the Sierra because he worked as a shepherd, and he followed his sheep into the high country. Can you believe that? An actual shepherd. That's what his book *My First Summer in the Sierra* is about."

"I thought writing about the shepherd's life went out with Christopher Marlowe," Dionne said. "Is that the book you brought?"

"That story is in this anthology, and so is some stuff on his boyhood, along with *The Mountains of California* and some essays about Alaska. You have to read 'Stickeen.' It's a cute story that takes place in Alaska about a dog."

"Sounds good. Do you know anything else about Muir?"

"Well, I already told you that he helped form the national parks system. He also started the Sierra Club and led trips. He took President Roosevelt on a trip for a few days around Glacier Point, and that convinced Roosevelt that Yosemite should be a national park. It's more complicated than that, and I'm sure I'm leaving a lot out, but he did a lot of important things. You'll learn a lot more from the book."

"I'll look forward to reading him tonight in the tent."

"Of all the places he explored, I think he loved the mountains of California best. He called the Sierra Nevada the 'Range of Light.'"

"So, we've been traveling through the Range of Light?" Dionne rested her elbows on her knees, her chin in her hands, and looked out over the lake.

"More like bumbling through in the Range of Light." We both laughed. Dionne's face blended in with the gray landscape. The half-moon rose into the dusky sky. By the time we'd reach Half Dome, it would have completed its cycle, would be full again.

But the Ouzel never calls forth a single touch of
pity; not because he is strong to endure, but rather
because he seems to live a charmed life beyond the
reach of every influence that makes endurance
necessary. / JOHN MUIR

Day 24

Naked Man and a Water Ouzel

Island Pass (10,492) and Donahue Pass (11,056)   10.5 MILES

To my surprise I woke up before Erika and Dionne. I decided to take advantage of being there, so I headed out of the tent to watch the view. Plus, being the first one up implied a sort of morality I certainly wanted to claim. This early morning business, however, required me to layer all my warm clothes because frost carpeted the ground, and the air crackled with ice. I tiptoed down to the lake to filter water and write in my journal. Across the lake lay a patchwork of blue tents. They must have arrived after dark because I hadn't seen them there before.

I wrote for a while and then had to go to the bathroom. I got my toilet paper and Handi Wipes out of my bag and looked for another trash bag since my personal baggie still dangled from our tree. I reassigned my camera bag and set off to find a suitable bathroom spot. Dionne and I would laugh about how talented we had gotten at squatting. Although other cultures don't use sit-down toilets and squat all the time, it took us some getting used to. Dionne came up with a plan where you press your butt against a rock or tree for balance and aim for the hole you dug. I tried it but scratched up my backside, so I didn't use that method, even though Dionne swore by it. Erika was more private about her bathroom business and made it clear she didn't want to discuss it. Once she came back from the bathroom with a piece of toilet paper stuck on her socks, and Dionne and I were both too afraid to say a word. Eventually, she saw the toilet paper and plucked it off her sock. She didn't ask us if we had seen it, but I was sure she hoped that we hadn't.

On my way back from the bathroom I ran into a twenty-something dark-haired man with glasses. His little shovel and roll of toilet paper told me he had been on a similar mission. Thank God I had all my personal hygiene items in the pocket of my windbreaker rather than out for the world to see. "Hi there," he said. He didn't seem bothered by the fact that I could see his toilet paper. I tried not to look because it seemed like it should have been private.

"Hi. Are you camped with all those tents over there?" I pointed.

"Yes, those are my kids."

"Your kids? You must have a lot of kids."

"Well, not technically my kids. I'm a teacher, and this is my outdoor education class."

"What a cool job."

"It's pretty cool," he agreed. He had sparkly green eyes beneath his glasses. "I'm Michael."

"I'm Suzanne." I decided it was better not to offer my hand, considering where we had both been. And I didn't see him holding any Handi Wipes or hand sanitizer.

"What are you doing here? I mean, I know you must be camping." He seemed nervous, which made me feel more sure of myself.

"Yes, my girlfriends and I are hiking the John Muir Trail. We're almost done. We came from Whitney." I carefully avoided the subject of north to south or south to north because, quite frankly, I was still mixed up about that. I couldn't get it straight because though Whitney lay to the south, it was colder, more snowy, higher, making it seem to me like it was to the north.

"Wow. Really cool."

"It's been great. It's our graduation trip."

"So, what are you going to do now?"

"Did you have to ask me that?"

He laughed and said, "You could apply at one of the outdoor education schools. They're always looking to hire women. Outward Bound would probably hire you."

"Really?"

"Sure, why not?"

"Well, thanks. Have fun with your kids."

"Have fun with your girlfriends."

We parted, and I felt excited about the idea of working for an outdoor school. I could get paid to hike, and here I had been doing it for free. Maybe that's what I would do for a while. Maybe I had become the sort of person an outdoor school looked to hire. Maybe I had my in-between plan—between this and I didn't know what— but at least I would have some sort of idea of my future. I really wouldn't have to move back home. I could hardly wait to research the opportunities. Who knew a trip to the bathroom would help me figure out my future?

By the time I got back, Erika and Dionne were up, puttering about camp.

"Where have you been?" Erika asked.

"The bathroom."

"That took a long time," Dionne said. "Are you okay?"

"I met the guy who's camped over there." I pointed to the compound of tents.

"He's with a lot of people," Erika said.

"He's a teacher at an outdoor school, and those are his kids. He's being paid to hike. Wouldn't that be such a cool job?"

"Yeah," Erika said. "Like getting paid for kids' camp. What's the difference?" As soon as she said this, I felt deflated like a popped tire, but I had to admit Erika was right. We had both worked for a summer at a kids' camp in Colorado, which sounded great and turned out to be just the opposite. We took the kids horseback riding, rock climbing, and rafting. We taught them archery. All of this seemed fun until you actually did it with a group of twelve children. When Johnny had just hit Peggy over the head with his paddle, and she lay howling at the bottom of the raft right before a rapid, and you were the one in charge, it wasn't so much fun. The more exciting the sport, the worse it was. Kids would drop one another at the rock climbing wall and shoot at each other at the archery range.

Sometimes I had to work the family events, which were the worst. My job at the family duck races was to sit in a metal boat in the middle of the lake, tossing rubber duckies into the lake; the object of the game was for the competitors to paddle out to me, fish out the rubber ducky I had just thrown into the lake, put said rubber ducky into my boat, and paddle back to shore. The fathers would yell at their sons for not paddling fast enough, and they would yell at me for tossing their rubber ducky farther away than the competitor's ducky. It was as if their lives depended on winning this rubber ducky game.

One race day I sat out in my boat as usual. I kept an eye on the quilted clouds, watched them congregate into giant thunderheads by afternoon. None of the competitors thought to look up at the sky; they were too focused on their duckies. Just as I was supposed to throw their duckies out—the afternoon race was particularly close—I saw the first flash, heard the first rumble of thunder. I paddled to shore, past the competitors, who were on their way to their duckies, which still sat safely in my boat. They shouted at me: Where was I going? They wanted their duckies; I had ruined their game; they were going to win this one.

My boss later said I should have stayed out in the middle of the lake in my metal boat until the race was over. I told him that he could keep his six dollars an hour, that I would rather serve cocktails at a dive bar, so I spent the remainder of my summer breaking up bar fights. I didn't have the sort of personality to work in outdoor education. I would rather wander around, daydreaming.

We waved to Michael and his kids on the way out, and instead of feeling envious, I felt sorry for him. But unlike me, he probably came equipped with a personality well suited for being in charge of children who ran amok in the wilderness. Other counselors at the camp where I worked managed to handle it better when the children aimed for one another with the bows and arrows. They'd tell the children, "Not so cool to shoot at Mary Ann when she's retrieving her arrow from the target." I, on the other hand, went into full panic mode whenever the kids shot at each other, sometimes screaming profanities that didn't tend to go over very well with the parents. I argued, however, that the F word, as my boss called it, was perfectly justified when you are trying to save children from puncture wounds or possible death if the kid shooting was an accurate enough marksman. When I told people I had earned a certification in archery instruction, they never believed me. For a time I listed it on my resume, until I figured out that it might just be working against me.

We hiked past Emerald Lake, between the views of the Ritter Range to the west and the lower Sierra crest to the east, and then past Thousand Island Lake, aptly named because of the a thousand little islands strewn across the large lake. The views made me feel like I was wandering through an Ansel Adams photograph. We climbed a ridge through lodgepoles and hemlocks to pond-speckled meadows with panoramic views. The mountains interrupted the blue horizon with shades of gray, white, brown, and green.

"We're at Island Pass," Erika said.

"What? Really?" I looked back; behind us were sweeping views of Thousand Island Lake and Banner Peak.

"That didn't feel like a pass," Dionne said.

"We must be in really good shape," I said. "Either that, or we're on a false pass."

"No, we're on it, but it wasn't much of a pass," Erika said, consulting her map, "but I feel sorry for north-to-south hikers who go over that, thinking it's a pass, and then they have to climb Pinchot and Forester."

We took some pictures on the pass that didn't feel like a pass and then began our descent, and after a little while we had to take our boots off for multiple creek fords. Tom said to leave your boots off, so we all hiked in our Tevas. My blisters had healed, but it still felt freeing to walk in sandals. And then I realized that this was the first day in three weeks that neither of my knees hurt. Pain is strange that way. It grates on you day after day, and when the burden of it is lifted, you know something's missing, but it takes a little while to figure out what it is. Then, you realize, what a difference in the world. Your mind is no longer fettered to the pain; you are free to think about other things.

We followed switchbacks up through an alpine environment—tundra, stone, and dwarfed whitebark pines. Snow patches clung to the ridge, and some obscured the trail. We decided to stop for lunch.

"So, what's the plan?" I asked Erika.

"Well, it looks like Donahue is another two miles away. We could go over it and camp somewhere in Lyell Canyon."

"Two passes in one day?' Dionne asked.

"Well, if Donahue is anything like Island, I don't think we have much to worry about. It's almost a thousand feet higher, but it shouldn't be much harder."

"How many miles will we have hiked today?" Dionne asked.

Erika counted them out on her map and said, "If we hike just to the other side of Donahue, we can find a campsite at the base of the Lyell Cirque. We'll have hiked ten miles, eleven tops."

"Sounds good to me." I felt fast and strong, and I realized that this was exactly how I wanted to feel about myself and that finally I did. After a few short hiking days and adequate food, I had more energy than I had since before we started the trip.

"We're rock stars," Dionne said. "Two passes in one day. Woo-hoo." "Rock *and* pass stars," Erika said.

We climbed the gradual trail up Donahue Pass. We came to a saddle, and at first I thought we had reached the top. Then I saw that we were not at the top; rather than a false peak, it really was a false pass. We followed the trail across the tundra, and steep steps confronted us, more like the passes we had come to know. My legs ached yet not in the sharp way that my knee had hurt earlier.

If there was such a thing, it was a good pain. I would have never thought I would modify the word *pain* with the word *good*.

After a while I began counting my steps and decided to allow myself a short break every hundred steps. I reached the pass this way—one hundred steps at a time. Or really, one step at a time.

From Donahue Pass the Yosemite high country opened before us. Erika pointed out Mt. Lyell, which at 13,144 was Yosemite's highest peak. The Lyell Valley cut a deep green V between domes of granite. The afternoon sun reflected off snow-covered peaks. I saw why Muir had loved this valley.

We were careful to avoid hiking down a steeper trail that Tom advised us against doing with heavy packs. We picked our way down, but even the better trail seemed no more than a steep animal trail, strewn with loose rocks, so I lost my footing a couple of times, ending up on my butt. I wondered what the other trail must be like until Erika finally figured out that we had, in fact, taken the steeper trail. "That wasn't so bad. Plus, it was probably faster than the other one," Erika said, making me wonder if taking this trail really had been a mistake. We finally reached the first dwarfed trees, whitebark pines, and then a small alpine meadow and the Lyell headwaters. A naked man waded into a small pond. He shouted, "Won't you join me?" We kept walking.

"No thanks," Dionne called. "It's a bit too chilly for a dip." The man waved and smiled. We found a campsite near a bubbling creek, far enough away from Naked Man, so we could no longer see him or his camp. Mt. Lyell, Mt. McClure, and Simmons Peak hovered above us. The Lyell glacier formed a snowy apron around the jagged peaks of Mt. Lyell. A family of four mountain quail, two big ones and two little, waddled by. Two black-tailed deer sauntered through our campsite. They grazed on the meadow and didn't seem bothered by our presence—a sign that we had reached Yosemite.

Dionne walked over to the cascading creek to filter water. As I set up our tent, I also set about convincing myself that Naked Man was perfectly safe. I realized that as the landscape became more familiar, the more comfortable I felt in it, more at home, so my usual fears were mitigated.

Then I heard Dionne shouting.

I threw down my tent poles and ran over to her. Dionne pointed at the creek. "Look."

Erika ran over too and asked what all the commotion was about. Dionne put her finger over her lips and then said, "Shh. He'll come up in a minute." Right then a bluish-gray bird popped out of the water and shook off his wings. We all squealed, even Erika. The bird seemed intent on what he was doing and paid no attention to us. He bobbed his brown head around, let out a little chirp, and then dove back down into the churning water. We leaned in for a closer look, and he seemed to be flying under water, overturning small rocks with his beak; he disappeared under the white veil of a small cascade.

"It's a water ouzel, the bird Muir writes about. He flies underwater. How cool. I read about them last night. I wasn't so sure about it when Muir called them joyous little fellows and the darlings of the mountain streams, but Muir's right. They really are darling." Now that I had seen a water ouzel, I wished I hadn't skipped that chapter. I supposed that's how it was with anything. We are most interested in things we have seen with our own eyes. We all sat down and waited for him to surface again. We watched him surface, shake, dive again, and swim. Even Erika seemed intrigued.

We left the ouzel to his dinner, even though I could have watched him for hours. We finished setting up camp and prepared our own dinner, burritos, with cheesecake for dessert. We watched the light leave the mountaintops. Once the sun disappeared, the temperature dove. We stayed out a little longer, long enough to watch the night sky braid with stars. We looked for the North Star, the big dipper, Cassiopeia. Even though the moon was nearly full, stars glittered like sequins. The Milky Way, a white bridge across the domed sky, stretched from Mt. Lyell to Amelia Earhart Peak. We sat in the shadow of the moon and stars, drinking our hot chocolate, in silence and in wonder.

I would fain to ask my readers to linger awhile in this fertile wilderness to trace its history from its earliest glacial beginnings, and learn what we may of its wild inhabitants and visitors. / JOHN MUIR

Day 25

Topless

Lyell Cirque (10,220) to the Trail Junction with Vogelsang (8,800)   6 MILES

A layer of hoarfrost painted the meadow white. We made oatmeal and ate it with all our layers on. I walked over to the creek, looking for the water ouzel, but he was no longer there. We agreed to hike six miles to the junction of a trail that went to Vogelsang High Sierra Camp. At that point we could have hiked all the way to Tuolumne Meadows, which was only another five or six miles from there. But we had Geoff meeting us three days after that in the Valley, and we all agreed to stay in the high country as long as possible. I also had to admit that part of me still held hopes that Mark would meet us in Tuolumne, and we had told him that we weren't arriving until the next day. I had a suspicion that Erika had thought of this too, because she quickly agreed to another short hiking day.

On our way out we passed Naked Man, though he was now fully clothed, a wise choice, considering the temperature. We waved good-bye to him then crossed the creek again and hiked through scrubby whitebark pines. The trail zigzagged down more steep, rocky switchbacks. We passed the Lyell Fork base camp. Tom said this popular camping area attracted weekend mountaineers, and he was right: a group of middle-aged men with ice axes, crampons, and big plastic boots prepared to conquer the trail. We waved hello to them but didn't stop and make chitchat. Although we had seen a few people camping—Michael and his kids and Naked Man—we hadn't seen many in the last few days, which made us all glad, especially since our trip was coming to its end.

The trail flattened, and I could walk without thinking about every step. We followed the Lyell Fork through forested meadows. Butterflies floated about in the mule's ear and lupine. Before we even felt hungry for lunch, we came to the trail junction with Vogelsang. I couldn't believe how quickly we could now hike six miles. We started to look around for a nice, quiet place to camp.

We quickly found that a quiet place to camp did not exist there. In one spot a man and his wife argued about how to use the bear cables. Because of this area's popularity with campers, the park built cables between the trees to assist people with hanging their food. In another campsite dwelled a family of seven, their quarters set much too close to the river. I imagined them surveying the spot, convincing themselves that it wouldn't make any difference if they camped on the edge of the creek just this once, even though the ranger had explicitly said to camp two hundred feet from water. We managed to find a place to camp far enough away from the rest so that we felt as though we had at least a degree of privacy in this overrun spot.

We set up our camp, washed, ate lunch, and found rocks to sunbathe on near the river. The granite had already warmed in the sun, so the heat soaked into our bodies from both the sun overhead and the rocks beneath us. The creek's sounds made the pleasant park-like setting even more relaxing. Dionne read Muir. She said she was excited to read about Cathedral Peak and Lakes, which was where we were headed next, and the falls, Vernal and Nevada, which we would see on the last day of the trip.

"Listen to this, you guys," Dionne said. "Muir has a great sense of irony. And this reminds me of our fishing days." She read from Muir: "It seems strange that visitors to Yosemite should be so little influenced by its novel grandeur, as if their eyes were bandaged and their ears stopped . . . Yet respectable-looking people were fixing bits of worms on bent pieces of wire to catch trout. Sport they called it. Should church-goers try to pass the time fishing baptismal fonts while dull sermons were being preached, the so-called sport might not be so bad; but to play in the Yosemite temple, seeking pleasure in the pain of fishes struggling for their lives, while God himself is preaching his sublimest water and stone sermons!"

"So, Muir didn't eat meat?" Erika asked. Dionne looked at me for an answer.

"No, he did. But he didn't fish or hunt. That's a great passage, Dionne."

I lay back down, and Erika returned to her maps. The watery sounds of the creek lulled me to sleep. But not for long—the squawk of the woman's voice bellowed among the pines. She sounded like a screaming Steller's jay. I heard her long before I saw her: "I don't care a damn what you say. I have hiked far enough. What do you think? I'm a goddamned pack mule? Jesus Christ." I looked both ways before I saw them coming up the trail from Tuolumne Meadows. They sported matching neon pink-and-green wind suits. The woman had accessorized hers with a leopard print sun visor and huge Jackie O sunglasses, which would have made a fine ensemble at Burning Man, but in Yosemite she looked a bit silly. The man was short, bald, and had big ears. He reminded me of a little monkey.

He told his wife, "For God's sake. You act like we've just hiked to the moon. We've only come five miles. Quit your crying." To that the woman told him that this wasn't her idea of a vacation, and if she had to come to Yosemite in the first place, she would rather be at the Ahwahnee Hotel eating shrimp cocktail. The woman then threw down her backpack, much like I used to drop Big Heiny, right in the middle of our camp and said she wasn't going to go another goddamned step. Erika, Dionne, and I all sat up, staring at this scene of domestic bliss unfold before us.

"Listen, Lily," the man said, "we can camp here, but there's no way I'm not seeing Lyell Glacier. I have been waiting my entire life to see a real-life glacier."

"You can go up ahead and see your stupid mound of ice, Joe. I don't care. I'm just not taking another step." She sat on her backpack.

"You'd better step right out of our camp," Erika said, but not loud enough that they could hear her. Our tent sat in a camp spot that could hold two tents comfortably, maybe three if you were friends, yet we certainly didn't want to share, especially not with Joe and Lily. That was our real estate. These were our rocks. They must have seen us by the river. Hadn't they seen our tent and our packs in our spot?

"Are we going to invite those boys over tonight for another one of those all-night orgies?" I said loud enough so they would hear.

"Should we? I mean, has your herpes infection cleared up?" Dionne called. Why did I always have to be the one with the STD?

"Gross," I whispered and then shouted, "What about your yeast infection?" and we all started laughing.

All the while Joe and Lily were beginning to unpack. If I didn't see it with my own eyes, I would not have believed it. They were smack-dab in the middle of our campsite. Joe began telling Lily how the bear cables work.

"Oh great. Fan-fucking-tastic. Bears, too?" Lily asked. She stood up and threw their blue tarp on the ground. "You said we wouldn't see any. Oh my God. I think I can see bear scratches right here on this tree. How do you expect me to sleep here?" She walked over to get a closer look at the tree behind our tent. I wasn't sure where Lily thought she was. Everyone knew about the bears in Yosemite.

It was clear that no matter how many inappropriate things we said, these two were there to stay. And how could they hear us over their own arguments, anyway? I was depressed by our new neighbors and lay back down. Erika, on the other hand, stood up, unclipped her bikini top, let it drop onto our sunbathing rock, and walked through the clearing in the trees to our tent, where Lily and Joe were assessing the size of the bear responsible for the claw marks on the Jeffrey pine.

"My, my," Joe said, as Erika sauntered topless through our campsite. Lily stood there with her hands on her hips, her mouth open. I imagined my mother asking her if she was trying to catch flies with her mouth. Dionne and I were just as amazed as Lily. Maybe Naked Man was onto something.

Lily said something to Joe in no more than a whisper. She began stuffing the ground tarp back into her pack. Joe had a crooked smile on his face. He just stood there watching Erika.

"I mean it, Joe. If you don't stop staring at that young girl's titties and come with me right now—"

Lily threw her pack over a shoulder and then tugged it onto her back. Joe watched Erika unzip the tent, pull out her floppy hemp hat, and put it on her head. Lily marched off, the tarp falling out of her unzipped pack.

"I mean it, Joe. Let's go, or we're talking divorce city."

She stomped away. Her water bottle fell from her pack. Joe put his pack back on and reluctantly followed, picking up Lily's things and looking back every so often with a grateful smile.

As soon as they disappeared into the forest, Dionne and I got up off our sunbathing rock and gave Erika a standing ovation. She tipped her hemp hat and bowed.

Most people are on the world,
not in it. / JOHN MUIR

Day 26

Fainting and Bears

Tuolumne Meadows (8,580) and
Lower Cathedral Lakes (9,460)   10 MILES

"What's your hurry" Erika asked.

"No hurry." I sat on Big Heiny, waiting. I kept waking up in the night, wondering if Mark really would show. I gave up on something cute to wear, since I didn't even have anything clean. I wore my blue-and-white flower print boxers with a black sports bra. The sports bra was the only thing that didn't have dirt or macaroni and cheese smeared on it, and my stomach felt flat enough to wear the sports bra without a shirt over it, like Erika and Dionne usually did. I had Erika braid my hair again because if I did it myself, a mile down the trail, I would look like a porcupine had fallen from a tree, landed on me, and was clinging to my head. So, I was pretty as I could be, considering the circumstances.

"Aren't you going to eat?" Erika asked.

"Not hungry," I said. Dionne raised her eyebrows. I really wasn't hungry; besides, I didn't want to ruin my flattish stomach with an oatmeal roll. I could tell Dionne wished she could go without break-fast, but if she skipped a meal, she knew Erika and I would both notice.

Finally, they finished eating, and we all started hiking down the trail. On our way out, we saw Lily and Joe. They were arguing about how their stove worked, and she was saying, "At the Tuolumne Lodge I could have had hotcakes and syrup."

"I'm not sure I ever want to get married," I told Erika and Dionne.

"I do," said Erika. "Not all couples are like that. I plan to get married, have two children, a boy and a girl, and I am going to name the girl after me."

"You're going to name her Erika?"

"No, my last name."

"What if your husband doesn't want that name?" Dionne asked.

"That's too bad. I have had it picked out ever since I was little. The only thing that would stop me is if my sister uses it first, which she'd better not because it was my idea in the first place."

"Well, good luck with that," I said.

"What's that supposed to mean?" Erika asked.

"Good luck."

"Not all the married people we've seen have been unhappy. Not the old people we saw doing the whole trail," Dionne said, "or the honeymooners on the ferry."

"Honeymooners don't count. I just wouldn't want to end up like Lily and Joe."

"Then don't act like Lily," Erika said.

"I don't think it's all Lily's fault," I said. "It didn't seem like she wanted to go hiking in the first place. Maybe she's just tired of Joe dragging her around."

We followed the trail through the lodgepole forest and boggy meadow, where the path forked because of mud. I did my best to stay on track without stomping through the meadow.

"Do you want to lead?" Erika asked me.

"Me?" I had not hiked in front once the entire trail.

"Sure, why not?" Erika said.

I took the lead and realized how nice it was not to be watching someone else's boots. The trail meandered slightly downhill. I wasn't sure if it was because of my position in front, but I felt like we flew through the meadow.

We finally reached a creek. "Rafferty Creek," Erika said. "Four miles an hour. Why haven't you been hiking like this the whole trip?"

"Because I haven't been in front."

"Was that it?" Erika laughed. We followed the trail to Tuolumne Meadows and arrived at the camp store, and I looked around. No Mark. I wasn't sure what I'd expected—that he would have driven all the way there from Mammoth to hike with us for two days? That he would have waited around at the store in Tuolumne until we arrived?

"Well, no Mark," Erika said.

"Should we call him?" Dionne asked. Erika looked at me, and we both shook our heads. I thought I had wanted to see him, but now that he wasn't there, I realized I felt relieved. It wouldn't have seemed right, hiking to the end of the trail with him. We needed to do it together, just us three women. I let my stomach out and bought a carton of ice cream to celebrate. We bought a couple of other things for the trail, namely Pop-Tarts. We all used the restroom, mostly to wash our hands and faces, and then we sat down outside at a table. Dionne and Erika chose burgers and fries for lunch. I dug into my Ben & Jerry's.

We looked at the map and guidebook together. Tom's description of how to get back to the trail seemed confusing. No matter how many times I read the directions, I couldn't make heads or tails of them. I pointed out that Tom said that most JMT hikers hitch a ride to Budd Creek Trailhead. A woman overheard me and said, "That book is out-of-date. There's a shuttle bus now." I was delighted: easy and convenient public transportation that delivered us to the trailhead; then we would be just four miles from Cathedral Lakes. We had already hiked almost six miles, and ten miles meant a respectable hiking day, especially since we would have a fifteen-mile day the next day.

"It also says here that JMT purists who want to hike the entire trail will follow these instructions to the Budd Creek trailhead," Erika said.

"How many more miles is that?" Dionne asked.

"It's about four or five more."

"So, that would be fourteen miles today?" I asked.

"We've hiked more than that in one day," Erika said.

"Not after eating a carton of ice cream."

"That's not my fault, is it?" Erika said, not willing to budge.

Dionne looked at the map and asked, "We're going to hike up Half Dome, right?"

"Yep," Erika said. "And I say we sleep on top."

"Round trip, that's an extra four miles added to the trail," Dionne said. "That would make up for today."

To my surprise Erika agreed to take the shuttle. Maybe she had considered how those extra miles would feel after a burger and fries. Maybe she really was letting up. And because Dionne hadn't rushed off to the restroom, I convinced myself she had gotten better, so ironically, I celebrated by going back in the store and buying chocolate chip cookies to go with my ice cream. I didn't stop to think that I was in the middle of my own binge.

When I came back, I asked if we were allowed to sleep on top of Half Dome. Erika told us that while we weren't technically allowed, we had earned it. That seemed like a justification to me. The family who had practically camped in the river in Lyell Canyon thought they had earned the right to riverfront property because they had hiked five miles.

Erika had wanted to sleep on top ever since some guys on the trail bragged to her that they had. She thought that sleeping on top of Half Dome merited boasting, though I didn't see how unless you actually climbed the face. I wasn't about to argue this point, not now that I'd be riding a shuttle bus. I had learned to choose my battles, and this wasn't a mountain, or a dome, worth dying on.

We loaded onto the bus with all the other tourists, and everyone—except us, of course—smelled like shampoo and laundry detergent. Someone even wore a jasmine perfume that made me feel a little sick to my stomach. When the bus took off, I noticed how quickly we moved. Even at four miles an hour, hiking was much slower than driving. I also found my eyes following all the sharp angles and bright colors inside the bus. On a placard above our heads Smokey the Bear warned us about the dangers of campfires; he wore a bright red and electric yellow firefighter hat. Aside from the wildflowers, sunsets, snow algae, and neon wind suits, most of the things we had been looking at were various shades of brown, green, white, and blue. In nature something bright like the red of a snow plant seemed stunning. But here the bright colors were ubiquitous, so they looked garish, ugly. I felt overloaded with all of the colors, angles, and smells. I started to feel dizzy and nauseous. We had been on the trail less than a month; I wondered how it must feel to ride a bus or navigate a shopping mall after six months on the Pacific Crest Trail. Getting used to being on the trail may be an easier adjustment than coming off it.

We arrived at the trailhead, and Erika asked me if I wanted to lead again. I agreed and felt like I had to hike as quickly as I did earlier. The trail climbed straight uphill, gaining almost a thousand feet in three miles. I did my best to set a strong pace. After a short while I started to feel woozy again, like I did on the bus. My ears rang, and my mouth over-salivated like I had just sucked on a lemon. I tried to breathe through my nose and let it pass. My legs felt heavy and my arms numb. My heart's whoosh echoed in my ears. More high-pitched buzzing and spinning. Everything looked fuzzy, like someone had just lowered the curtains on the world. Then everything went black.

Erika, Dionne, and three strange women stood over me, their faces distorted like they were peering at me through a giant magnifying glass. One of the strange women tugged at my hip belt, trying to unclasp my backpack. She said, "I'm a nurse, I'm a nurse." All I wanted was for her to leave me alone. Finally, I managed to sit up, and she pulled the pack off me. She said, "I think you fainted."

"I'm okay." I tried to stand up, but everyone said no. Dionne gave me some of her water, and drinking it helped me feel better. The nurse told me I must hike down to the first aid center immediately. I shook my head.

"She'll be okay," Erika said, and I nodded, grateful that Erika was staying true to her unflappable nature.

"Are you okay?" Dionne asked. She had this concerned look on her face like she thought maybe I would die and she'd be stuck hiking alone with Erika.

"I'm fine," I reassured everyone. The only other time I had fainted like that had been after getting out of a too-hot Jacuzzi too quickly. And it was the same thing: woozy, ringing ears, the dark curtain falling.

The nurse wanted me to hike down to Tuolumne right that very minute to seek medical attention. I told her that we had a plan, that we were going to sleep on Half Dome, that Geoff was coming to get us the day after tomorrow for waterskiing at Bass Lake. She stayed unconvinced, shaking her head like she thought I didn't know what was good for me.

"Maybe you can take a shuttle to Happy Isles and meet your friends later," she suggested.

I started to cry at the thought of the shuttle, at the thought of not completing the trail with Dionne and Erika. There was no way I wasn't finishing the hike because of a little fainting spell. After all that we had been through, I was determined to finish even if I had to crawl.

Erika arrived, once again, to the rescue: "We haven't been eating a lot, and not much sugar. She didn't eat this morning and then just ate a whole pint of ice cream and a package of cookies. That's probably what did it." The nurse asked why I would eat that before hiking and on an empty stomach. It was clear that the nurse went from feeling sorry for me to thinking I was a stupid girl.

The nurse shook her head again and said, "Well, Cathedral Lakes is still an uphill three miles."

"I've already hiked over two hundred miles. And lots of hills. Mountains, really. I can do it." Now the nurse and her friends thought I was both stupid and crazy. I wasn't sensible enough to heed their advice, so they left me to my own stupidity, said their good-byes, and marched down the trail. I sat for a little while longer and then got up. I felt weak but okay to hike. Erika and Dionne thought I should still lead; just in case something happened, they would see me go down. I struggled up the trail, probably only at a rate of one mile an hour, until the trail leveled off and started down through a meadow.

The trail finally turned off to Lower Cathedral Lake. Unicorn Peak and the Cockscomb notched the sky above us. We reached the trail junction to the lakes. I began to feel a little bit more in the world. I hoped Erika had been right, that it had just been all that sugar.

"Tom says a lot of bears hang out at this lake," Dionne said.

"Like the rest of Yosemite," Erika said. "But we saw all those scratches in the trees in Lyell Canyon, and we didn't see any bears there."

"Maybe Lily and Joe scared them off," I said.

"Now that's a possibility," Erika said.

We found a sandy campsite at the southeastern tip of the lake; we walked over for a view of Medlicott Dome, Pywiack Dome, and the spired Cathedral Peak beyond. Behind us Echo Peaks, Tressider Peak, and Tenaya Peak scraped the evening sky. The almost-full moon swung over the shining granite domes to the east; at the same time, the sun set over the lake, the snow-crowned Echo Peaks, and glowing pointed tips of Cathedral Peak, turning the lake purple and the reflected snowy mountains a rosy hue. Cathedral Peak hovered above in all its rugged splendor: spiky granite spines jutting into the sky like the spires of a Gothic cathedral.

A fat marmot scampered by, the first one we had seen since Muir Pass. This one looked considerably better fed, like the one at Trail Camp on Whitney. He waddled back once we opened our food bags. We had to shoo him away all through dinner.

After dinner I passed on the chocolate pudding. I had had enough sugar for one day. Dionne seemed at a loss for what to do. Should she eat the extra? The struggle never ended. Her own heinous load, carried through life, one she might never be able to put down. I wanted to lift it from her back, could not begin to imagine how.

We chose a tall lodgepole for our bear bags and carefully counterbalanced the bags on a thin enough branch that a bear wouldn't be able to climb onto it. Feeding bears in the National Park is against federal law, but worse than that, it's bad for the bears. Not only does it mean bears will eat things like chocolate Pop-Tarts, aluminum wrappers and all, but the bears become accustomed to the easy meal; in turn they can become aggressive, and then they are shot. Soon, bringing a bear canister would be required on the trail, which would be much easier than throwing a stone with a rope tied to it over the right branch and counterbalancing the food bags sixteen feet in the air with a stick.

Exhausted from my ordeal, I said good night to Erika and Dionne and headed off to bed early. First one up, first one to bed—both new for me, but I still wasn't feeling healthy, wealthy, or wise.

Someone shook my shoulder. It was still dark.

Erika whispered, "Wake up."

What did she want? I rolled over and turned the other way.

"No, really," she said. "Wake up. I hear branches cracking and breaking. I think it's a bear trying to get our food."

I sat up and heard the crackling of a tree branch too. Dionne was still asleep. I must have been so tired I didn't even hear them get into the tent. Erika and I grabbed our headlamps, put on our Tevas, and went out to investigate. We ran to our bear tree, and sure enough, a giant bear had climbed the tree and stretched herself across the branch that had our food hanging on it. The branch was too skinny to hold her weight, though, so the bear stretched onto the branch vertically, both back paws wrapped around the trunk for support, shaking the branch. She was a smart bear. The food bags bobbed up and down, and pine needles and cones scattered onto the rocks below.

"Get out of that tree, bear," Erika yelled. "I mean it. That's not your food. That's our food. You thief. You'd better back down out of that tree right this minute."

At first I thought about how ridiculous this was: Erika talking to a bear like she was going to understand what Erika was saying and politely follow the request. But the bear shimmied back to the trunk, slowly turned around, and backed down the tree. Erika could command even a hungry bear. We were so close I could see the black pads of her paws, the curled claws. Erika and I both backed up but kept our headlights shining on her. The bear backed down a few feet, still looking longingly at our food bags above.

"That's not yours," Erika continued. "Come on out of that tree." The bear followed Erika's instructions.

"That's a good bear," I shouted.

Dionne came running up with her camera. The camera flashed bright against the dark night. I feared it would anger the bear, who had now reached the bottom of the tree and stood on the ground, fewer than twenty feet away. The bear stopped again and looked at us, wondering if we were going to leave her alone anytime soon. We all three started screaming like maniacs, "Time to go away now, bear. Go along now." The bear stood there, now on her hind legs, staring at us. I knew running was the last thing I was supposed to do, but it was exactly what I wanted to do. Dionne stopped taking pictures and started backing away. We kept shouting, "Bear, go away. Go away now. Go home, bear." Even in the middle of it, I realized how ridiculous this sounded because the bear, after all, was already home.

We waved our arms above our heads, trying to look tall, like the ranger showed us. The bear probably decided three raving humans were not worth the trouble, so she finally got off her haunches and lumbered away, stopping to look back every couple of steps, which heightened our ranting frenzy, until she disappeared into the forest.

"Did you get any good pictures?" Erika asked Dionne.

"I don't know. It's so dark." We all turned around and walked back to the tent.

"That was a big bear." I turned around to make sure she wasn't hiding in the shadows, ready to make another go at our food once we were back in the tent.

Just as we settled back into our sleeping bags, we heard people camped on the other side of the lake screaming at the bear. Then a few minutes later someone else clanged together pots and pans. The bear made her midnight rounds, in search of an easy meal—probably a nightly occurrence all summer at this lake.

"I'm glad that bear didn't get our Half Dome Pop-Tarts," Dionne said.

Erika and I both agreed. I hoped my sugar hangover would be gone by then and I would be ready for our celebratory Pop-Tarts on the top of Half Dome.

It is easier to feel than to realize, or in any way explain, Yosemite's grandeur. / JOHN MUIR

Day 27

The Three Wise Women

Cathedral Lakes (9,460) to Half Dome (7,015)   15 MILES

I half-expected our food to be gone when we woke up, but it still hung suspended from the tree. Pink cumulous clouds billowed behind Cathedral Peak. I hoped it wasn't a sign of rain. We had almost fifteen miles of hiking in front of us. We conferenced over breakfast about the plan. Erika agreed with the camping rule on Half Dome for the general public; she had said, "Think of all the people using the bathroom up there." But, she said, we could sleep up there in a way that would not cause any problems. If we made dinner below and then left our heavy packs behind, we could climb the cables at dusk, sleep on top without a tent, eat our Pop-Tarts at sunrise, and return by dawn before anyone had to use the restroom.

"What do you mean by cables?" I asked.

"Well, it's steep, so they've put up cables. Don't worry about it. They're like handrails." For Erika the word *steep* was just a fact, holding no particular emotion. It's as if she had said, Why, the sky is blue.

"There are handrails up the mountain?" Dionne asked.

"Like Angels Landing in Zion?" I asked.

"Yes, just like that."

"What if we have to pee?" Dionne asked.

"Pee is fine. Just not the other." That was easy for Erika to say. One of the unfortunate side effects of my being nervous was an unleashing of the bowels. During track meets in high school I would be crouched in the starting blocks, waiting for the gun to fire, and an uncontrollable urge to go to the bathroom would overcome me. A couple of times I told the girl in the lane next to me about my bathroom urges. This would cause her to false start, leading her to believe that my confession was a ploy to disqualify her. Really, I just wanted to know if anyone else felt like I did. I imagined those cables and how they might affect my bowel issues, and I worried that I would be up there, sullying one of Yosemite's treasures with what Erika referred to as "the other."

We hiked to the junction with the JMT and then followed the trail past the smaller, shallow upper Cathedral Lake. We stopped to take a picture with our self-timer of the three of us, sitting on the granite, looking past the forested valley to Cathedral Peak. We crested Cathedral Pass and hiked along the ridgeline past Echo Peaks and Tressider, the peak named for Donald Tressider, who was once fired for taking Mary Curry, daughter of the owners of the Yosemite concessions company and his future wife, rock climbing up Half Dome. In spite of that setback, he later went on to become the president of Stanford University.

Clark Range lay beyond. We traversed under the Columbia Finger and then headed down a sloping valley, scattered with lodgepole pines. We crossed Long Meadows, which really were quite long, and then Sunrise Camp, one of the backcountry camps where tourists can stay. By this point the very idea of a lodge with bathrooms, showers, and a staff in the backcountry seemed out of place to me, as if both realities—the wilderness and the conveniences of the city—clashed against each other, falsifying both.

We started climbing again to the eastern slope of Sunrise Mountain, edged Sunrise Creek, and began another descent of steep switchbacks down the rocky canyon. The light fell like a yellow net on the granite. We crossed a creek and then followed the trail up a boulder-strewn moraine.

"Look, Half Dome," Erika said and pointed. Through the trees we caught our first glimpse. "We'll be on top of that tonight." The white, domed rock gleamed, the vertical face looking like a zealous butcher had taken a knife to it. I liked that its name reflected what it was, rather than honoring an important man.

We stopped for lunch and then continued on between the cliffs of Clouds Rest and the Moraine Domes. The severe cliffs and the bald granite domes made me feel small. We think we are so important, our problems so large, but then a place like this renders us small, our problems nothing more than the echo of birdsong in wind, maybe not even so much as that. Against the immensity of the granite domes I felt a humbling, a sense of being little on a large planet, a tiny part of a larger universe: a speck of dust in the cosmos, a billionth of a second in the time frame of the world. Connected. I realized that if ever I felt smaller than someone else, I could just compare us both to a galaxy or a star or even one of Yosemite's giant granite domes.

I felt grateful that Jesse left when he did and that we didn't end up hiking the rest of the trail with him or even Mark. Without them we had come to rely on each other and on ourselves. Luck and circumstance provided the chance to find our "girl power." We found our connection to each other, our place within wildness. The John Muir Trail was more than a completed goal. We didn't conquer the mountains; instead, we learned to feel safe walking among them, to feel more at home in nature. And with each step we came closer to knowing ourselves.

I hadn't been able to articulate all of the reasons I had come on this trip, but now I knew why. Maybe it's true that you can't know what you're looking for until you find it. This valley wouldn't mean as much to me if I had hiked up for the day. Or even two days. Being out there for a month opened something up that stayed closed in my day-to-day life. It is like when the streetlamps go out and the sky burns with stars. And you realize they had always been there, even if you couldn't see them.

I still wasn't ready to climb into a tree in a windstorm—I may never be—but I now understood the impulse to feel the vibration of a storm, to hear the heartbeat of the world. John Muir got it right when he said the beauty of this place can only be felt, not explained.

The end of our trip was in sight; the next day we would be back in the world of cars and freeways, buildings and beds. Before, I had counted the days until a shower or a chocolate shake. Now I was sad to see the end. I had proven to myself that I could do it, which meant that I would always be able to look back on this trip whenever faced with a difficult thing, no matter what it was. I would remember that if I did it yesterday, I could do it today. I knew that these feelings would fade, that I would slip back into routine, though I hoped it would be a life without Thoreau's "quiet desperation." This trip, being out in the Range of Light, allowed me to be a better version of myself. I finally felt happy in my body, at peace in the world, hitched to the universe. I hoped to always hold a part of it inside me, to etch this moment into memory.

We hiked in silence, and I hoped Erika and Dionne felt the happiness I did. I hoped their hearts were glad. I knew it would be a struggle for us all once we left the trail, especially for Dionne. I hoped Muir was right: I hoped in nature she had found a cure for what ailed her.

Erika stopped up ahead and unfolded the map. "This is the trail to Clouds Rest. We have another half-mile before the trail junction to Half Dome. Then we'll hike to the bottom of the cables and eat dinner."

"I like that name, Clouds Rest," Dionne said. "It's pretty."

"I think that would make a good trail name," Erika said.

"For you?" I asked.

"Why not?"

I couldn't imagine calling Erika "Clouds Rest." Commander, yes. Clouds Rest, no. We continued to the junction with Half Dome and followed the trail through a mixed pine forest. The glacier-polished

Half Dome glowed in the late-afternoon sun. We found a small camp spot near the bottom of the cables to eat dinner and were visited by a pair of marmots, who seemed to be working together like a couple of pickpockets. One chirped to distract us, while the other tried to steal the goods, but we were onto them. Erika offered to carry her giant pack up Half Dome so we could put our stuff in it. I didn't argue with her. I was more than happy to leave Big Heiny behind, and if anyone could climb the side of Half Dome with an ungainly external frame backpack, it was Erika. We brought warm clothes, a tarp, our sleeping bags, our cameras, Pop-Tarts, and our toothbrushes. We hung the rest of our food from a branch and left our backpacks unzipped, just in case mice and marmots wanted to have a look. It was better to give them an accessible way in than have them chew holes through the nylon.

Erika pulled on her pack, and we set off to tackle the cables. A box of leather gloves sat at the bottom to help hikers hold onto the handrails, for which I was grateful. Erika offered to go last. Dionne wanted to go first, and that was fine by me. Wooden slats were bolted into the rock to help with the ascent. I pulled myself up with my gloved hands, gripping the cables. We climbed in the shadows, the yellow light sliding off the forested valley. I found the ascent easier than I could have imagined. It was steep, but between my girlfriends, I felt safe. Most people had already headed down, and no one else was climbing up at that time of night, so we seemingly had the mountain to ourselves.

The flat top surprised me; from a distance the top looked curved. I supposed it was the same way as with the earth—this was just a smaller scale of the world. We headed to the edge of Half Dome for a view. We looked out across to North Dome and Basket Dome, silver and luminous against a pink sky. Two other groups milled around on top—all men. One group consisted of four middle-aged men, who passed a bottle of tequila around. They offered us some, but we shook our heads no.

Another was a group of three Germans about our age and very polite. They introduced themselves as Magnus, Jorg, and Wilhelm.

We told them we were Zsa Zsa, Cassiopeia, and Clouds Rest, which they pronounced "Clausres." The sky turned pink then orange. The mountains sketched a black silhouette, and a mosaic of wispy cirrus clouds drifted overhead. We took turns with the Germans, photographing each other, and they asked us if we were staying on top, which by now, with the sun gone, should have been obvious. They were cheerful fellows with none of the self-consciousness of American boys. When we told them about our trip, one of them clapped his hands together, another one did a happy little jump into the air, and they all smiled and laughed.

Wind blocks, little half-moon rock walls, were built where others had camped before—sleeping up there hardly proved a novel idea. We chose one of these smooth spots with a rock shelter. We went off to brush our teeth and find a secluded place to pee before bed. When we passed the middle-aged men on our way back, they were well into a second bottle of tequila. They whistled and catcalled at us. One said, "Hey baby. I've got something here for you." The other three laughed as if their friend had told the funniest joke ever. Instead of shrinking into our sweatshirts, scurrying away like field mice, we stopped and turned to face them. We could only see the outlines of their bodies in the moonlight. We felt strong and confident because we had hiked over two hundred miles, so we shouted back: "Who do you think you are? Don't bother us. Go back to the sleazy bar where you belong, tourists." And from Erika: "Drink some more tequila and take a long walk toward the edge of the cliff."

"Oooooh," one of them yelled, "tough chicks."

We said: "You've got that right," "You have no idea," and, "That's right, we are." I didn't know if they were stunned into silence or were too drunk to think of a good comeback, but they didn't continue with their repartee.

We got back to our sleeping bags, and Jorg shouted, "Way to let them have it."

Magnus said, "That was very funny, Clausres."

"They are very drunk, I think," Wilhelm said. "Americans seem to like their liquor, no? In Germany we love beer—it's much softer."

The Germans set up their sleeping bags in another wind shelter far enough away to give us our privacy but between us and the tequila men. Erika and Dionne let me sleep in the middle. I felt strong as ever, and we had our Germans to look after us, but with those drunk men there and without a tent, I preferred to sleep in the middle. Some things are slow to change. I wasn't afraid of being out there, yet I was still afraid of who might be out there with me, something I would no doubt have to navigate for many years to come. I supposed all women who want to go out into nature have to work through these fears, feelings that most men, and a few lucky women, never encounter.

Yet I have found that the more time spent in wild places, the more the fear has receded, calmed perhaps by the natural world itself. I've started to learn I can make my own maps rather than follow the lines drawn for me. After twenty-eight days on the John Muir Trail, we felt ready to claim our places in nature, our own unique language for the landscape: one based on intimacy rather than independence, community rather than competition. I realized I had been relying on a male translation of nature rather than listening to my own voice. That night, of all the words I could have used to describe how I felt, the most accurate would have been *connected*.

"Good night," we shouted over to our German friends. "We'll see you at sunrise." We waved to them, casting moon shadows. They waved back. Wrapped up in their sleeping bags, they looked like three cocoons. The full moon glowed in the sky, large enough to pass for a face. The drunk men shouted in the distance, something about the three wise women.

*Here ends my forever memorable first High Sierra
excursion. I have crossed the Range of Light, surely
the brightest and best of all the Lord has built; and
rejoicing in its glory, I gladly, gratefully, hopefully
pray I may see it again.* / JOHN MUIR

Day 28

Yosemite Valley and Beyond

Half Dome (7,015) to Happy Isles (4,035)   7 MILES

At sunrise Erika woke us up as planned. We had two packages of
Pop-Tarts to celebrate the sunrise, the end of our trip. Jorg, Magnus, and Wilhelm were awake too, so we shared the Pop-Tarts with
them. Dionne brought two over to them, and we split the other
two. The sun balanced orange on the granite, the black sky fading.
A full moon set on the other side. We sat between the sun and the
moon, watching one sink, the other rise. We took pictures of the
sun and the moon, of each other, of our new German friends. With
the drunk men finally passed out, everything was quiet, everything
still. The world held its breath as the sun and moon pulleyed across
opposite ends of the sky. I wasn't doing any yoga, and I was eating
a Pop-Tart instead of a protein shake, but I was up at sunrise, glad
to be part of the world. For the moment I was just the sort of person I wanted to be.

We watched the sky shed its dark skin: black to gray, pink to yellow. Then we walked back over to the edge of Half Dome. The valley
still reposed in shadow. Only the tops of the ridges burned with the
first light of day. The sky deepened to Sierra blue, and we lingered,
taking a few more pictures. After some convincing, I agreed to a

picture of our boots dangling off the edge, our feet suspended over the valley thousands of feet below.

Coming down the cables proved considerably more difficult than climbing up. Erika went first, and I walked down with my knees bent, as low to the rock as possible, heading for the forested valley below. I controlled my vertigo by refocusing on the solid rock beneath my boots. Without the cables, the wooden steps along the way, and the handy leather gloves, it would have been a rough descent, if not impossible. We made it down, and the Germans stood at the bottom, waiting for us. "We want to hike with you," they told us. We agreed. Each of the three Germans had square shoulders, brown hair, blue eyes, and a mouthful of big teeth. I couldn't keep them straight. I had no idea which one was Magnus, which one Wilhelm.

The six of us made our way through a forest of incense cedars and sugar and ponderosa pines. I didn't mind that the Germans joined us for the last leg of our trip. We had relied on ourselves, on each other, for long enough that we didn't need them, so I felt like they joined us on our terms, making it different than if we had picked up Mark in Tuolumne. The Germans were like trail ornaments, festive and fun decoration, but they didn't change the essential nature.

I identified the trees and flowers for the Germans, and they seemed impressed. We reached the trail to Happy Isles and turned off the John Muir Trail to follow the more scenic route past Vernal Fall. The Germans were happy to go either way; in fact, they were just happy, and nobody wanted to argue in front of them. By now Erika just said, "It's all fine by me." The Germans smiled each time she said it, completely unaware of the irony.

I was glad we had decided to take the more scenic way down, past both Nevada and Vernal Falls. I hadn't seen those falls since I was a girl. I had visited Yosemite with my friend Jill and her mother and aunt, making it my first "girls' trip." I was thrilled to go on that trip; I thought Jill's mother, Gayle, was the most glamorous woman I had ever seen. She was deeply tanned, and she painted her fingernails, toenails, and lips an icy pink. Her hair, frosted, feathered, and sprayed to perfection, put even Farrah Fawcett's locks to shame. Gayle worked as a hairdresser, which I thought was so fabulous that I announced I myself wanted to pursue a career as a beautician. My father promptly took me to the local beauty school so I could see just what my dream would look like. The beauty school was filled with hair bunnies drifting along the concrete floors, bad fluorescent lighting buzzing overhead, and the smells of acetone and permanents wafting through the dingy place, exactly as my father had guessed. All the students loitered outside on a smoking break. They wore pink polyester uniforms, and some of them had frizzy orange hair from practicing on one another. That took care of that.

Even after I had given up my dreams of styling hair, I still worshipped Gayle, who worked at an upscale salon—nothing like the shabby beauty school. So, when Jill invited me for a whole week in Yosemite on a girls' trip, I was thrilled. It took some work to convince my parents since, as they pointed out, Gayle was just a kid herself. She seemed grown-up to me, but that was relative. She was only seventeen years older than Jill and me, making her twenty-seven then, which to my sixty-three-year-old father was a kid. After weeks of terrible nagging, my parents conceded, and I was off to Yosemite on my first girls' trip. I adored everything about it: the tent cabin, the sounds of the river and waterfall, the tame chipmunks; I even loved listening to Gayle and her sister sneak out of the housekeeping cabins after they thought we were sleeping to drink homemade wine coolers and dance to country music at the neighboring tent cabin.

One day we went for a hike with the wine cooler neighbors and their children. There must have been ten of us. The adults told us we were going to Vernal Fall on something called the Mist Trail. From there we could go on to Nevada Fall or return to the Ahwahnee Hotel for ice cream. It all sounded fantastic to me—hiking, waterfalls, ice cream. I remember being astounded by giant rocks, the pine trees, the swirling blue rivers, the powerful falls. I loved getting soaked on the Mist Trail. At Vernal Fall all the kids were ready to turn back for ice cream. One of the fathers was ready too, so he offered to take all of us kids down. I wanted to stay with Gayle and the other adults. Jill thought I had lost my mind. More walking uphill, hanging out with the adults, and no ice cream? That was crazy talk to a ten-year-old. But I wanted to see what was ahead, what was around the next corner. I wanted to see Nevada Fall. I would have hiked all the way to Half Dome that day if I could have. It had been twelve years since that trip, and I had not been to Yosemite Valley since, always avoiding it because of the crowds, but I couldn't have been happier returning, this time on foot, to see it all again. I was as awestruck as I had been as a girl.

Each German chose one of us to talk to on the hike down, and I couldn't remember the name of mine. My German wore a little straw hat, a sleek jersey, and huge hiking boots that would be well suited for climbing the Matterhorn. "What do you mean, you have never visited Germany? Why not, Zsa Zsa?" My German asked.

"I just haven't had the chance."

"But you could visit the Alps for hiking. These mountains are very nice, you know? We have castles. And you could visit me." He pointed to himself with both hands in a most earnest way.

We came to the white torrent of Nevada Fall. Muir said that this waterfall does not seem under the dominion of ordinary laws but is, rather, a living creature. The white water poured down onto the black-streaked orange rocks. Like the beat of a drum, the rumbling sound of water found its way into my body, joined in a chorus with my own beating heart.

We followed the Merced and reached a wide place in the river called Emerald Pool above Vernal Fall, where children and adults alike were splashing around. Muir's description of Emerald Pool—a period separating two grand sentences—was apt. The aquamarine water pooled briefly before picking up the pace and continuing on to form Vernal Fall. It was a hot day, and Emerald Pool certainly looked inviting, but I couldn't help think of the current, of the water's inevitable slide to Vernal Fall. "You want to swim, Zsa Zsa?" My German asked. I shook my head. Meanwhile, Dionne tried to explain to her German that Cassiopeia had a boyfriend at the end of the trail. Who knows what Clausres was telling Jorg, the only German whose name I could remember. Too bad Jorg wasn't my German, not that he was better than the others. They were all quite nice. I had just somehow remembered red shirt was Jorg.

The mist from Vernal Fall drenched us, and I felt ten years old again. The water folded over the top of the falls, creating a white curtain of water. The misty spray fashioned rainbows in the sun. We followed the river to a bridge, where I remembered having taken a picture of the falls, framing it, and giving it to my father as a gift. He proudly hung it in his den. It hadn't just been the nagging that convinced my father to let me go to Yosemite with Jill's mother. He had visited the park years earlier, when he himself was a boy. He went on a road trip across the West with two of his classmates and their teacher. They had visited many of the national parks, finally ending in Yosemite. Even fifty years later, my father called that trip the greatest of his life. I realized then that in some ways he was there with me. Love for this place connected us.

At the bridge we stopped for more photographs. Each step of the way the trail became more and more crowded. Day hikers smelled like detergent, shampoo, and bubble gum. I thought I had prepared myself, but by the time we reached the paved portion of the trail, full of baby strollers, teenagers in stilettos, motorized wheelchairs, women in saris, men drinking from beer cans, and kids holding boom boxes to their ears, the world really was too much with us. The colors and sounds and smells were too much—culture shock from too much culture. The six of us weaved through the clean-smelling crowd.

The Germans laughed at all the silly Americans, especially a blond surfer dude wearing a T-shirt with daisies on it, sprinting up the trail with a six-pack of Sierra Nevada. "Geoff," we all shouted and hugged him. He gave us each a beer. The Germans were really laughing now. Erika and I exchanged phone numbers with the three Germans, while Dionne kissed Geoff hello. I learned that my German was Magnus when he wrote his telephone number on a pink Post-it note and gave it to me, saying, "Come see Magnus in Germany." And I realized I was no longer obsessed with how I looked to a man, whether he liked me or not. The irony is that it made me more likable, both to others and, more important, to myself.

We let Wilhelm, Jorg, and Magnus introduce themselves to Geoff, and then we said our good-byes.

We walked the last bit of our trail with Geoff, and he took our photograph next to a sign that listed different destinations and the number of miles. The three of us pointed to the line that read, "Mount Whitney, John Muir Trail, 211 miles."

"We hiked farther than that," Erika said. "Even with the four miles we skipped in Tuolumne Meadows. I bet we hiked closer to 235."

On the way out of town we stopped at the Ansel Adams Gallery at Erika's request and then at a pay phone because I wanted to call my parents.

"Can I talk to Daddy?" I asked my mother.

When he came to the phone, he said, "I've got a map and have been trying to figure out where you were every day."

"Really?"

"Sure."

"We're in Yosemite now. Do you remember how pretty it is?" I asked.

"There'd be no way to forget that. I still have your photograph. Do you remember? Yosemite is one of the most beautiful places on earth," he said.

"I remember." I had framed a photo of Vernal Fall and given it to my father as a gift.

"Where are you off to now, kiddo?"

"We're going to Bass Lake, to Geoff's dad's, to go water-skiing."

"Okeydoke. Take good care. Don't forget the buddy system."

"Don't worry, Daddy, I won't. We've been sticking together."

"That's great. Just great."

"I love you, Daddy."

"Love you too, kiddo."

Memory sometimes acts as a corrective lens, allows us to say the things we never said, take back the things we regret, but the truth is I don't remember what I said to my father at the end of that phone conversation. Did I tell him I loved him? It's possible, but in truth I can't remember. Yet the memory that is burned into my imagination is the picture of him bent over the maps, following the trail he had highlighted with a yellow marker. There with us every step of the way.

We then drove up to Glacier Point for the quintessential view of Yosemite Valley. Dionne wanted to see with her own eyes the sight that had convinced Theodore Roosevelt this was a place worthy of federal protection. We stood, looking back at the forested valley, and Erika pointed to Half Dome and said, "We slept right there on top of that curved, white dome. Don't you like being able to say that?"

"I guess we do," Dionne and I both admitted. It didn't feel like we woke up there that morning. It had been one of those days that seemed like it lasted a week, one of those months that felt like a lifetime. So much I had learned about myself that summer in the Sierra, so much that remained a mystery. If nothing else, I would remember joy is not just in the having done but in the doing, not in the arriving somewhere but in the almost somewhere. Years later, when I eventually became the sort of person who practiced yoga, my instructor would tell me that the journey from pose to pose is the feminine, the pose itself, or the destination, represents the masculine, and we must honor both as equally important.

Erika and I rode to Bass Lake in the back of Geoff's truck. It wouldn't be long before we were there—an ending and another beginning. I lay on my back, using Big Heiny for a pillow. I watched the blue sky, clouds, trees, telephone wires, and the ceiling of an occasional tunnel fly past overhead. Erika was already asleep next to me, dreaming of who knows what—probably her next adventure. Who knew, maybe I'd think about hiking the Pacific Crest Trail next. Things looked a lot different from this side of the trip.

Dionne sat up front with Geoff, her head on his shoulder. I thought about what we had done, the ways we had reinvented ourselves, what would be—I wouldn't have been able to predict that, after sharing stories and photographs, the three of us soon would part ways, left to remember reaching all those passes, the last light of day over alpine lakes, the characters we met along the way, on our own. These were the memories we would hold close for a while; eventually, they would scatter in with the rest, and we would return to them only sometimes.

Erika would go on to marry, settle in the Colorado Rockies with her husband, and have her two blond children, a girl and a boy. Dionne followed her own rough path, finally, to recovery. After my own first summer in the Sierra, I prayed, like Muir, that I would see the Sierra again. My father had always said that the wish, a true wish, will always find its way, and eventually, mine would. After dividing my time between graduate school in California and ski instructing in Colorado, I would go on to make my home in the Sierra, hiking daily on paths that connect back to the John Muir Trail.

Afterword

This past July, my husband and I set off to hike the John Muir Trail, nearly thirty years after that first hike with Erika and Dionne. Like that first summer, I wasn't sure I would be able to complete the trail. I've had multiple sports injuries recently, including another bad knee, but I knew that whether or not I finished didn't matter. What mattered was the time I spent outdoors in my beloved Sierra Nevada mountains.

On that first thru-hike, I cried on nearly every pass, struggling with pain or exhaustion or the group dynamics. This time, I cried on every pass for very different reasons. I was grateful that my fifty-one-year-old body could still carry me up and down mountains, bringing me into areas of sublime and rugged beauty. I knew I was exactly where I needed to be, where the mountains made me feel small and large at the same time. The passes were the highlight for me this time, not because I'm more physically fit but because I'm mentally and emotionally stronger. I have buried both my parents, other family members, and dear friends over the past three decades. I took care of my mother when she was dying. I married and divorced and married again. I have done much harder things than hike a couple of hundred miles.

It's also true that backpacking in general is easier than it once was. The equipment is lighter and the technical clothes more functional. Readers have often commented on how unprepared we were, but information about the trail wasn't as easily available as it is now. We couldn't Google it, so we relied on paper maps and guidebooks rather than the ubiquitous websites, blogs, apps, and social media groups that now exist. We had the best equipment available (except maybe Erika, who wore a huge external-frame pack), but nothing was light or convenient. Very few people hiked with cell phones (the iPhone wouldn't be released for another fourteen years), and if something happened to one of us, we had to rely on ourselves.

When we hiked the JMT in August 1993, we often hiked for multiple hours at a time over snow-covered passes, often losing the trail (without GPS to help us). The river crossings back then were dicey, even in late summer. This time, a long drought and warmer temperatures meant we didn't encounter snow at all, and we only had to take our shoes off twice for shallow river crossings. The trail felt tamer with its many directional signs and newly constructed bridges over some of the more dangerous river crossings, but then we were caught in a frightening high-elevation lightning storm, and the trail once again felt like a wild place, one that was indifferent to my survival.

And maybe I'm faster now because I don't have to stop to look up every flower and tree. I have lived in the Sierra long enough that they are now old friends.

My complaints about the crowds on Whitney and in Yosemite during that first journey are laughable compared to now. This summer, we felt like we were competing for campsites. We ended up adding miles to our itinerary, hiking off the JMT to find solitude. At one point I told my husband that the John Muir Trail felt like Disneyland. According to the PCTA, thirty-three people reported completing the PCT in 1993 (The JMT follows the PCT for roughly two hundred miles). In 2022, that number ballooned to over eight hundred. But the good news is that the demographics of the trail are also changing. In 1993, 13 percent of people completing the PCT were women. Now that percentage is nearly 43 percent. Unfortunately, trail users are still 86.5 percent white, proving gains in other kinds of diversity have not been made.

Our changing climate, drought, and years of fire suppression have meant thru-hikers are now facing trail closures and harmful air quality due to wildfires. In 2021, 33 percent of those who did not complete the PCT cited smoke and fire as the reason. This past summer, we hiked through the burn scar from the 2020 Creek Fire, which torched a total of 379,895 acres, and we are now seeing megafires in California of more than a million acres. I used to write about the natural world with a sense of awe and wonder; more and more, I'm writing about nature through a lens of nostalgia and grief.

Almost Somewhere is about a backpacking adventure in the early 1990s, but it's also a coming-of-age story about female friendships, identity, and an interrogation of my complicated feelings about the natural world. I was deeply invested in finding my own feminine vision and language for the landscape. What I hadn't considered is that early European explorers came to their vision and their words for the landscape through a history of land theft and genocide, so it's no surprise the language reflects colonization and conquest. John Muir writes about the Sierra Nevada as an untouched Garden of Eden, which effectively erases the human population who lived here for thousands of years.

The writer Louis Owens calls our notion of wilderness "nothing more than a figment of the European imagination. Before the European invasion, there was no wilderness in North America; there was only the fertile continent where people lived in a hard-earned balance with the natural world." The creation of the National Parks system, to conserve what we have come to know as wilderness, was predicated on an ugly past, one that includes a land grab of Indigenous ancestral homelands, brutal treatment, murder, and erasure. The "early" American nature writers I read in school did not include Native Americans, so the true history of the land did not enter my imagination until many years later. There's still value in reading Muir, but we need more than that single vision to understand the history of our landscape and our place in it.

At one point in this book, I wondered how the early explorers, including Muir, managed to wander through the Sierra before the dynamite-blasted trails existed. I now know the John Muir Trail was built over a footpath used by Native Americans for thousands of years. The original name is Nüümü Poyo, meaning "The People's Road." Until recently, I wasn't aware of the original name. The truth continues to be hidden from schoolchildren. If we care about the land we now call American wilderness, we must acknowledge the full story of the past and work toward both environmental and social justice so wild spaces are safe and welcoming to all.

Despite my injuries, we completed the John Muir Trail this summer. I consulted *Almost Somewhere* every night in the tent to see how each section differed from my memory. I realized I wanted to update some of the language in the book. The changes I have made in this edition are small but important. I had overused words like *lunatic, crazy,* and *maniac* when talking about men on the trail who scared me. My understanding of mental illness has evolved since then. I have left some of this language intact, showing the naivety of my twenty-two-year-old self, but I also acknowledge these words reinforce prejudice and discrimination. While I may cringe at some of my descriptions, I know this book represents not just a moment in my life but a moment in time; hopefully, we continue to evolve, becoming more aware, more sensitive, more kind.

Both Erika and Dionne have graciously agreed to my using their real names and the photographs from the trip we took together. I should also say that Erika has made it clear that our memories of that trip differ in some ways; she believes I made her out to be more athletic and capable than she was, while portraying myself less so. Perhaps it's true that I have always seen myself as weaker and clumsier than I really am.

Since the publication of *Almost Somewhere*, I've published two other books: *Bad Tourist: Misadventures in Love and Travel* and *Animal Bodies: On Death, Desire, and Other Difficulties,* and I'm currently at work on a craft book and a novel. I hike in the Sierra Nevada alone most days and don't feel the fears I once experienced because the landscape feels very much like home. I'm older, and women gain a certain freedom that comes with aging. I no longer see myself through the patriarchal gaze as I once did, and I know that being alone in the outdoors is safer for women than many other places.

When I returned home to Tahoe from my thru-hike this summer, I went to the book's source material: the tiny journal I kept on that first trip. I turned to the back, to the last words: *We made it!* This hard-earned sentence made me smile and brought me back to that triumphant moment of giddy exhilaration and accomplishment. I also found this passage: *I think it [this trip] will make me realize I have a lot of endurance and I can do or be whatever I want.* That thru-hike thirty years ago, my own first summer in the Sierra, taught me I could live the life I had always imagined: writing books, traveling with my husband, and hiking in the mountains I so love. *I made it!*

SUZANNE ROBERTS
October 2022
South Lake Tahoe CA

Book Club and Classroom Discussion Questions for *Almost Somewhere: Twenty-Eight Days on the John Muir Trail*

1. *Almost Somewhere* functions as an anti-guidebook, exploring all the things not to do while backpacking. What are some of the mistakes the hikers make? Can you relate to any of them? Why or why not?

2. In *Almost Somewhere*, the narrator goes on a journey that is as much mental, emotional, and spiritual as it is physical. Have you ever taken a journey or a physical test of your own that also encompassed both literal and symbolic terrain?

3. The struggles the three women face out on the trail are both external and internal. What are some of these struggles, and are they resolved throughout the book? Why or why not?

4. One of the things Suzanne grapples with in this memoir is the tension between desire and shame. Do you think she is able to resolve this conflict? Why or why not?

5. One of the main topics in the book is how female friendships form and evolve. How do the friendships change once Jesse leaves the group? What does the narrator gain from these friendships? How do Erika and Dionne help the narrator discover who she is?

6. The narrator continually grapples with her own identity, sexual subjecthood, imposter syndrome, and body issues. Are these issues resolved? Could you relate to any of these themes?

7. The narrator struggles with how to be supportive of Dionne while she battles bulimia. Have you had an experience of trying to help someone close to you with serious problems?

8. Throughout the book, the author makes use of humor. What are some of the deeper issues she is trying to address through the use of humor? Did this approach work? Why or why not?

9. The narrator is trying to create a uniquely feminine vision of the landscape as a counter to all the male nature writers she has read. Is she able to do this? If so, how is it different than the descriptions of nature she has previously read from John Muir and others?

10. What is each character seeking from the wilderness? Do they attain what they seek, or do they find something else? Have you ever looked to the landscape for something? If so, what was it, and did you get what you were looking for, or did you receive something unexpected?

11. This is a memoir of outdoor adventure in the 1990s. How have things changed since then? Are these changes positive, negative, or something else?

12. From the beginning of the book, the narrator isn't sure she will be able to finish the trail. Have you ever set out to accomplish something you weren't sure you could finish? If so, what happened?

SELECTED BIBLIOGRAPHY

Abbey, Edward. *Desert Solitaire: A Season in the Wilderness*. New York: Ballantine Books, 1968.

Anderson, Lorraine, ed. *Sisters of the Earth: Women's Prose and Poetry about Nature*. New York: Vintage Books, 1991.

Austin, Mary. *The Land of Little Rain*. New York: Modern Library, 2003.

Bird, Isabella. *A Lady's Life in the Rocky Mountains*. Sausalito CA: Comstock Editions, 1960.

Blackwell, Laird R. *Wildflowers of the Sierra*. Redmond WA: Lone Pine Publishing, 1997.

Cohen, Michael P. *The Pathless Way: John Muir and the American Wilderness*. Madison: University of Wisconsin Press, 1984.

Dickinson, Emily. *Selected Poems*. New York: Dover Publications, 1990.

Foreman, Dave. *Confession of an Eco-Warrior*. New York: Crown Trade Paperbacks, 1993.

Lanner, Ronald M. *Made for Each Other: A Symbiosis of Birds and Pines*. New York: Oxford University Press, 1996.

Marlowe, Christopher. "A Passionate Shepherd to His Nymph." In *The Complete Poems*. New York: Dover Publications, 2003.

Millman, Dan. *Way of the Peaceful Warrior: A Book That Changes Lives*. Los Angeles: J. P. Tarcher, 1984.

Muir, John. "Flood-Storm in the Sierra." In *John Muir: Nature Writings*, edited by William Cronon, 607–17. New York: Library of America, 1997.

———. *John of the Mountains*. Edited by Linnie Marsh Wolfe. New York: Houghton Mifflin Harcourt, 1979.

———. "Living Glaciers of California." In *John Muir: Nature Writings*, edited by William Cronon, 618–28. New York: Library of America, 1997.

———. *The Mountains of California*. New York: Dorset Press, 1988.

———. "My First Summer in the Sierra." In *John Muir: Nature Writings*, edited by William Cronon, 147–310. New York: Library of America, 1997.

———. *Our National Parks*. Boston: Houghton Mifflin, 1917.

———. "Snow-Storm on Mount Shasta." In *John Muir: Nature Writings*, edited by William Cronon, 634–48. New York: Library of America, 1997.

———. *Steep Trails*. Edited by William F. Badè. Boston: Houghton Mifflin, 1918.

———. "Stickeen." In *John Muir: Nature Writings*, edited by William Cronon, 549–76. New York: Library of America, 1997.

———. "The Story of My Boyhood and Youth." In *John Muir: Nature Writings*, edited by William Cronon, 1–147. New York: Library of America, 1997.

———. *A Thousand-Mile Walk to the Gulf*. Edited by Robert Enberg and Donald Wesling. Madison: University of Wisconsin Press, 1980.

———. *The Yosemite*. San Francisco: Sierra Club Books, 1988.

Niehaus, Theodore. *Sierra Wildflowers: Mt. Lassen to Kern County*. Berkeley: University of California Press, 1974.

Pasternack, Boris. *Doctor Zhivago*. New York: Pantheon, 1997.

Tennyson, Alfred Lord. "Charge of the Light Brigade." In *Selected Poems*. New York: Penguin Classics, 2008.

Thoreau, Henry David. *Walden; Or Life in the Woods*. New York: Dover Publications, 1995.

———. *Walking*. Boston: Applewood Books, 1987.

Whitman, Walt. *Leaves of Grass: The Complete 1855 and 1891–92 Editions*. Edited by John Hollander. New York: Library of America, 2011.

Winnet, Thomas. *Guide to the John Muir Trail*. Berkeley: Wilderness Press, 1978.

Wordsworth, William. "The World Is Too Much with Us Late and Soon." In *Selected Poetry of William Wordsworth*, edited by Mark Van Doren. New York: Modern Library, 2002.

To order or obtain more information on these or other University of Nebraska Press titles, visit www.nebraskapress.unl.edu.

Animal Bodies: On Death, Desire, and Other Difficulties

Suzanne Roberts explores the link between death and desire and what it means to accept our own animal natures, the parts we most often hide, deny, or consider only with shame—our taboo desires and our grief. With lyricism, insight, honesty, and dark humor, these essays illuminate the sometimes terrible beauty of what it means to be human, deepening the conversation on death and grief, sexuality, and the shame that comes from surviving the world in a female body with all of its complexities.

Bad Tourist: Misadventures in Love and Travel

Both a memoir in travel essays and an anti-guidebook, *Bad Tourist* takes us across four continents to fifteen countries, showing us what *not* to do when traveling. A woman learning to claim her own desires and adventures, Suzanne Roberts encounters lightning and landslides, sharks and piranha-infested waters, a nightclub drugging, burning bodies, and brief affairs as she searches for the love of her life and finally herself. Fearlessly confessional, shamelessly funny, and wholly unapologetic, Roberts offers a refreshingly honest account of the joys and absurdities of confronting new landscapes and cultures, as well as new versions of herself.

Milton Keynes UK
Ingram Content Group UK Ltd.
UKHW011114080923
428134UK00019B/272

9 781496 236920